States' Rights and
American Federalism

Recent Titles in the Series
Primary Documents in American History and Contemporary Issues

The Abortion Controversy: A Documentary History
Eva R. Rubin, editor

Women's Rights in the United States: A Documentary History
Winston E. Langley and Vivian C. Fox, editors

Founding the Republic: A Documentary History
John J. Patrick, editor

Major Crises in Contemporary American Foreign Policy: A Documentary History
Russell D. Buhite, editor

Capital Punishment in the United States: A Documentary History
Bryan Vila and Cynthia Morris, editors

The Gun Control Debate: A Documentary History
Marjolijn Bijlefeld, editor

The AIDS Crisis: A Documentary History
Douglas A. Feldman and Julia Wang Miller, editors

Sexual Harassment in America: A Documentary History
Laura W. Stein

The Role of Police in American Society: A Documentary History
Bryan Vila and Cynthia Morris, editors

Genetic Engineering: A Documentary History
Thomas A. Shannon, editor

The Right to Die Debate: A Documentary History
Marjorie B. Zucker, editor

U.S. Immigration and Naturalization Laws and Issues: A Documentary History
Michael LeMay and Elliott Robert Barkan, editors

STATES' RIGHTS AND AMERICAN FEDERALISM

A Documentary History

Edited by FREDERICK D. DRAKE and LYNN R. NELSON

Primary Documents in American History and Contemporary Issues

GREENWOOD PRESS
Westport, Connecticut • London

Library of Congress Cataloging-in-Publication Data

States' rights and American federalism : a documentary history /
   edited by Frederick D. Drake, Lynn R. Nelson.
       p.   cm.—(Primary documents in American history and
   contemporary issues, ISSN 1069-5605)
     Includes bibliographical references and index.
     ISBN 0-313-30573-0 (alk. paper)
     1. Federal government—United States—History Sources.   2. State
   rights—History Sources.   I. Drake, Frederick D., 1947-   .
   II. Nelson, Lynn R., 1946-   .   III. Series.
   JK311.S73   1999
   320.473—dc21   99-21705

British Library Cataloguing in Publication Data is available.

Library of Congress Catalog Card Number: 99-21705
ISBN: 0-313-30573-0
ISSN: 1069-5605

First published in 1999

Greenwood Press, 88 Post Road West, Westport, CT 06881
An imprint of Greenwood Publishing Group, Inc.
www.greenwood.com

Printed in the United States of America

The paper used in this book complies with the
Permanent Paper Standard issued by the National
Information Standards Organization (Z39.48-1984).

10 9 8 7 6 5 4 3 2 1

Contents

Series Foreword xi

Introduction xiii

Chronology of Key Events in States' Rights and American
Federalism xxvii

**PART I: States' Rights and American Federalism in the
American Founding Era, 1620–1789** 1

Document 1: The Mayflower Compact, 1620 12

Document 2: The Fundamental Orders of Connecticut, 1639 13

Document 3: Organization of the Government of Rhode
Island, March 16–19, 1642 16

Document 4: On Liberty, 1645 17

Document 5: Penn's Plan of Union, 1697 19

Document 6: Albany Plan of Union, 1754 21

Document 7: Declarations of the Stamp Act Congress,
October 2, 1765 23

Document 8: From a Farmer in Pennsylvania to the
Inhabitants of the British Colonies, Letter II,
1767 24

Document 9: Thoughts on Government, Letter of John
Adams, January 1776 26

Document 10: Unanimous Declaration of the Thirteen United
States of America, July 1776 31

Document 11: In Defense of State Sovereignty, Thomas Burke,
              1777   35

Document 12: James Madison's "Vices of the Political
              System," April 1787   37

Document 13: The Virginia Plan Presented to the Federal
              Convention, May 29, 1787   44

Document 14: John Dickinson of Delaware on Federalism at
              the Constitutional Convention, June 7, 1787   46

Document 15: The New Jersey Plan Presented to the Federal
              Convention, June 15, 1787   48

Document 16: James Madison of Virginia Compares the
              Virginia and New Jersey Plans at the
              Constitutional Convention, June 19, 1787   50

Document 17: James Wilson of Pennsylvania on Federalism at
              the Constitutional Convention, June 25, 1787   53

Document 18: The Northwest Ordinance, July 13, 1787   55

Document 19: *Federalist* Number 10, Publius and the
              Extended Republic, November 22, 1787   59

Document 20: Agrippa Writes a Letter to the People in
              Opposition to an Extended Republic and the
              Constitution of the United States, December 3,
              1787   65

PART II: Federalism and the Meaning of the Tenth
          Amendment, 1789–1835   67

Document 21: George Mason's Objections to the Proposed
              Constitution, October 1, 1787   73

Document 22: James Madison's Proposal to Congress for a
              Bill of Rights, June 8, 1789   74

Document 23: The Sedition Act, July 14, 1798   79

Document 24: The Kentucky Resolutions, November 16, 1798   81

Document 25: *United States v. Peters*, 1809   86

Document 26: Report and Resolutions of the Hartford
              Convention, January 1815   89

Document 27: *Barron v. Baltimore* (1833)   91

PART III: **States' Rights in the Antebellum Period and the Civil War, 1828–1865** 95

Document 28: Liberty and Union, Now and Forever, One and Inseparable, January 1830 101

Document 29: John C. Calhoun's Fort Hill Address, 1831 104

Document 30: John C. Calhoun against the Force Bill, February 15, 1833 105

Document 31: Andrew Jackson's Second Inaugural Address, March 4, 1833 107

Document 32: Abraham Lincoln's Address before the Young Men's Lyceum of Springfield, Illinois, January 27, 1838 109

Document 33: The Seventh of March Speech: Daniel Webster and the Compromise of 1850 112

Document 34: John C. Calhoun, the Compromise of 1850, and State Autonomy, First Session of Congress, 1850 114

Document 35: William H. Seward, the Compromise of 1850, and an Appeal to a Higher Law, First Session of Congress, 1850 118

Document 36: William H. Seward and the Declaration of Independence: An Appeal to Higher Law, 1856 121

Document 37: *Dred Scott v. Sandford* (1857): Roger B. Taney and States' Rights 123

Document 38: James Buchanan's Fourth Annual Message: States and Withdrawal from the Union, December 3, 1860 125

Document 39: Resolutions of Secession: Mississippi (January 11, 1861), South Carolina (December 20, 1860), and Virginia (April 17, 1861) 127

Document 40: Abraham Lincoln's First Inaugural Address, March 4, 1861 132

Document 41: The Emancipation Proclamation, January 1, 1863 135

**PART IV: Changes Involving States' Rights and Federalism
            from the Civil War to the New Deal, 1865–1940**   139

Document 42:   Women's Suffrage Petition to Congress,
               December 1871   147

Document 43:   Booker T. Washington, Atlanta Exposition
               Address, 1895   149

Document 44:   An Episcopal Priest Challenges Enforcement of
               the Fourteenth Amendment, 1905   151

Document 45:   Theodore Roosevelt on Lincoln and the Race
               Problem, February 13, 1905   155

Document 46:   Elihu Root Calls for the Preservation of Local
               Self-Government of the States,
               December 12, 1906   157

Document 47:   Wilson Rejects the Old Ideal of Limited
               Government, October 30, 1909   159

Document 48:   Woodrow Wilson's New Freedom Changes the
               Old Order, 1913   160

Document 49:   Kate Gordon's Letter to the Governors of the
               Southern States, 1913   162

Document 50:   Petition from Women Voters, Anti-Suffrage
               Party of New York, 1917   163

Document 51:   State of Tennessee Approves Nineteenth
               Amendment, August 1920   164

Document 52:   President Calvin Coolidge on the
               Responsibilities of the States, May 30, 1925   165

Document 53:   President Calvin Coolidge's Fourth Annual
               State of the Union Message, December 7, 1926   166

Document 54:   Herbert C. Hoover's Fourth Annual State of
               the Union Message, December 6, 1932   167

Document 55:   FDR's First Inaugural Address, March 4, 1933   169

**PART V: States' Rights and American Federalism from the
            New Deal to the Present, 1940–1999**   173

Document 56:   Governor Fielding Wright of Mississippi,
               Statement to Democratic Party Leaders,
               January 1948   181

Document 57: The Civil Rights Message of Harry S Truman
              to the U.S. Congress, February 2, 1948   185

Document 58: Governor J. Strom Thurmond of South
              Carolina Speaks to Southern Governors,
              February 7, 1948   190

Document 59: States' Rights Platform of 1948, Southern
              Democratic Convention, Birmingham,
              Alabama, July 17, 1948   193

Document 60: Eisenhower's First Annual Message to the Congress
              on the State of the Union, February 2, 1953   196

Document 61: President Eisenhower Writes South Carolina
              Governor James F. Byrnes, August 14, 1953   197

Document 62: *Brown v. Board of Education of Topeka* (1954)   199

Document 63: The Southern Manifesto, 1956   203

Document 64: President Johnson Urges Enactment of the
              Voting Rights Act of 1965   205

Document 65: U.S. Commissioner of Education Harold Howe
              II on the Relationship of the Federal
              Government to State and Local Education,
              December 17, 1966   206

Document 66: A Journalist Reports on the Effects of the 1964
              Civil Rights Act, January 12, 1967   207

Document 67: Press Interview with George Wallace, 1968   208

Document 68: Reagan Resurrects States' Rights, January 1981 211

Document 69: Contract with America, 1994   213

Document 70: The Devolution Tortoise and the Centralization
              Hare: The Slow Process in Down-Sizing Big
              Government, 1998   216

Document 71: U.S. Supreme Court Expands States' Rights   218

Document 72: Minority Opinion Challenges State Immunity
              from Law Suit   221

PART VI: Conclusion   223

Index   225

Series Foreword

This series is designed to meet the research needs of students, scholars, and other interested readers by making available in one volume the key primary documents on a given historical event or contemporary issue. Documents include speeches, debates and letters, congressional testimony, Supreme Court and lower court decisions, government reports, biographical accounts, position papers, statutes, and news stories.

The purpose of the series is twofold: (1) to provide substantive and background material on an event or issue through the text of pivotal primary documents that shaped policy or law, raised controversy, or influenced the course of events; and (2) to trace the controversial aspects of the event or issue through documents that represent a variety of viewpoints. Documents for each volume have been selected by a recognized specialist in that subject with the advice of a board of other subject specialists, school librarians, and teachers.

To place the subject in historical perspective, the volume editor has prepared an introductory overview and a chronology of events. Documents are organized either chronologically or topically. The documents are full text or, if unusually long, have been excerpted by the volume editor. To facilitate understanding, each document is accompanied by an explanatory introduction. Suggestions for further reading follow the document or the chapter.

It is the hope of Greenwood Press that this series will enable students and other readers to use primary documents more easily in their research, to exercise critical thinking skills by examining the key documents in American history and public policy, and to critique the variety of viewpoints represented by this selection of documents.

Introduction

THE IMPORTANCE OF FEDERALISM

During the 1830s, nearly forty years after the writing of the U.S. Constitution and in the midst of the crisis of nullification, James Madison reaffirmed the centrality of federalism while writing the preface to what would become his "Notes on the Federal Convention." The Virginian, now in his eighties and approaching the end of his life, knew of federalism's historical importance as he recalled when delegates to the Constitutional Convention had gathered in Philadelphia in 1787 to construct an American plan of government. Now Madison, whose career was exceptional in both its sweep and significance, wrote with vivid recollection about federalism and the Constitution: "It remained for the British Colonies, now United States, of North America, to add to those examples [of ancient and modern confederacies], one of a more interesting character than any of them." James Madison remarked pointedly how the federal system was "founded on popular rights" and combined "the federal form with the forms of individual Republics, as may enable each to supply the defects of the other and obtain the advantages of both."[1] Thus, the sage of Montpelier singled out the Constitution's solution to the issue of federalism as its most central and noteworthy feature.

What was created—federalism—at the Constitutional Convention by James Madison and others was designed to achieve a "happy combination" of the relevant concerns of statesmen who were deeply dedicated to providing new securities for "public good and private rights" in a manner that would "preserve the spirit and form of popular government" (see Document 19).[2] Federalism is deep-seated in our historical experience and broadly based in its effects on daily lives of individuals. The founders believed that governmental powers had to be distributed between state and national governments and that this division would serve as a balancing function of powers, a protection of individual liberties, and a promotion of the common good. Madison emphasized the special relationship that federalism would have to individual rights when he wrote *Federalist* Number 51. He stated:

In a free government, the security for civil rights must be the same as for religious rights. . . . [S]ecurity in both cases will depend on the number of interests and sects; and this may be presumed to depend on the extent of country and number of people comprehended under the same government. This view of the subject must particularly recommend a *proper federal system* [italics added] to all the sincere and considerate friends of republican government.[3]

Precisely what James Madison meant by a *proper federal system* might serve as a guide for Americans today who wish to examine the changing relationship between the states and national governments. The checks and balances system, typically conceived as applying to conditions only within the national branches, might be more fully examined as including the powers of the state and national governments. The shifting balance of power changes over time. American history is marked by an ongoing debate surrounding the rights of the individual and the power of state and national governments.

The federal system certainly was important to James Madison and his contemporaries, and it has been important to succeeding generations of Americans who lived their lives and struggled with collective issues and concerns in the nineteenth and twentieth centuries. Today, the relationship between state and national governments is illustrated in public response to centralization of power. Interest in states' rights and federalism has drawn the public and scholars to documents that contributed to the origin of the relationship between state and national governments. Moreover, recent events in Russia and in nations that have restored their independence in Eastern Europe illustrate the cross-cultural interest in balancing the locus of power.

Numerous ideas on government emanated from European and American colonial writings and were reformulated during the American founding era. It was in this period, as the thirteen colonies gained independence from Great Britain, that Americans wrote state constitutions, the Articles of Confederation, the U.S. Constitution, and the Bill of Rights. As a result of their constitution writing experiences and their deep interest in ideas that expressed the principles of republican government, Americans created a system of government that is both empowered and limited. James Madison defined the problem of having a government that is sufficiently powerful without risking individual rights. He explained in *Federalist* Number 51:

But what is government itself but the greatest of all reflections on human nature? If men were angels, no government would be necessary. If angels were to govern men, neither external nor internal controls on government would be necessary. In framing a government which is to be administered by men over men, the great difficulty lies in this: You must first enable the government to control the governed; and in the next place, oblige it to control itself. A dependence on the people is no doubt the primary control on the government; but experience has taught mankind of the necessity of auxiliary precautions.[4]

At the national level James Madison wanted both a limited government and an empowered government. Rights, we know, are at risk if government has too much power—and, conversely, if government has too little power. The Constitution was written to address the problem of having a national government that is sufficiently powerful and strong enough to secure rights without risking rights. Madison's "dependence on the people" meant that he wanted citizens to participate in government. Yet their participation alone would not guarantee people's rights; rather, Madison's well-constructed Constitution, that is the "auxiliary precautions," would secure rights, even if achieved imperfectly.

While the founders of American constitutional democracy contributed several ideas on political thought, one of the most unique creations was federalism. The founding of an American constitutional republic in the eighteenth century with a federal system of democratic government attracts the attention of thoughtful citizens today not only in the United States but also those who are attempting to establish constitutional democracy in other nations. An analysis of documents that illustrates the American experience in dealing with states' rights and federalism can benefit people who are pursuing the formation of democratic governments. The same type of examination serves American citizens too. The founding documents should be central to the education of all students. Members of the founding generation frequently referred to the importance of an education that perpetuates the "fragile republic." Historian Bernard Bailyn points out the emergence of national power during the American Revolution was not a "sudden break in the ideological history of our national origins." Bailyn writes, "The essential spirit of eighteenth-century reform—its idealism, its determination to free the individual from the power of the state, even a reformed state—lived on, and lives on still."[5]

The American system of federalism has survived over two hundred years. It has changed, to be sure, from the time it was created in the eighteenth century to its present form. This book examines American federalism for the benefit of those who want to understand its evolution and the changing relationship in the locus of power between state and national governments.

DEFINING STATES' RIGHTS

States' rights is a reflection of the American historical experience in the colonial and Revolutionary periods when beliefs were first articulated that states could best solve pressing issues and would best protect the rights of individuals. Historical experience reinforced trust in local government over confidence in a general government. This was so because state communities, it was believed, were more homogeneous and more responsive to popular control than the heterogeneous community and distant general government.

States' rights may be defined as "the prerogative power of a state to exercise its inherent authority."[6] According to states' rights doctrine, sovereignty resides with each state; thus, the final arbiter is the state individually, and not necessarily among the states collectively. States' rights advocates see a constant danger in subverting state authority to a preponderant national power. The call for a guard against a national government too large in power is based on a belief that local government recognizes far better the desires of its citizens and can better reflect their wishes. It is also premised on the fear that a national or general government will eventually dominate the federal system. States' rights calls for a limitation in powers of the general government. States have their own interests and if the general government becomes too dominant, a majority of the states and a majority of the population, respectively, might deny the consent of a minority of states or a minority of the people, respectively, to maintain their interests.

The Articles of Confederation expressed this stronger faith in local government by reserving most powers of government to the thirteen states. The Antifederalists, opponents to ratification of the Constitution of the United States, argued in the 1780s against domination by the general government. They placed greater confidence in state governments. From the Antifederalists' perspective of state government, a strong attachment exists between citizens and their respective local communities (see Document 20). The attachment is so strong that in theory, individual wills combine into a Rousseauean "general will." Through general will, community interests are revealed and dominate to the extent that, according to historian Donald S. Lutz, "community interests were considered superior to those of individuals."[7] The "good of the community" allowed for abridgment of rights for community purposes, and the Antifederalists were compelled to create a plan for national government that would not disrupt state autonomy and collective state decision making.

To achieve their goals, Antifederalists needed to limit the powers of a general government so that the more homogeneous interests of the states would be protected against the more heterogeneous interests of the national community. At the state level the Antifederalists supported republican, or representative, models of government that were based on legislative supremacy. Historian Gordon S. Wood has noted an essential feature of the Antifederalist thinking and its importance to states' rights contentions. He wrote, "The representatives of the people would not act as spokesmen for the private and partial interests, but all would be 'disinterested men, who could have no interest of their own to seek,' and 'would employ their whole time for the public good; then there would be but one interest, the good of the people at large.' "[8]

In essence, state representatives were to be raised to their place of public trust through the consent of the citizens. These representatives would serve as an agent for the political community whom they represented, and, it was assumed, the state community would be unified and harmonious within itself. Antifederalists believed that state government officials would more likely be kept virtuous than general government officials because of popular control through frequent elections at the state level. Majority rule within the state would prevail in the Antifederalist plan for a general government.

The writing of the U.S. Constitution empowered the general, or national, government while limiting its power to encroach on individual liberties. Following the ratification of the Constitution, Antifederalists attempted to alter the structure of the Constitution with proposed amendments, which ranged from state loyalty oaths for federal officials to altering the structure of the Constitution. Antifederalists, for example, attempted to change the structure and reduce the powers of the new regime. Madison proposed a Bill of Rights (see Document 22) that weakened the opponents of the Constitution and lessened the possibility of substantive amendments. Harboring doubts, most Antifederalists nevertheless supported the Constitution. Once it had been ratified, however, the Antifederalists did not create an Anticonstitutional party. They supported the principles of federalism as expressed in the Constitution. Their battle would loom over the intent, or interpretation, of the Constitution.[9] Arguments over the meaning of power and its distribution among the governments echo still in governmental chambers today.

When the Kentucky Resolutions of 1798 (see Document 24) circulated in response to the Alien and Sedition Acts (which were passed by the national government), a key phrase summarized the position of states' rights advocates. Thomas Jefferson, author of the Kentucky Resolutions, stated:

Resolved, that the several States composing the United States of America, are not united on the principles of *unlimited submission to their General Government* [italics added].

Some fifty years later John C. Calhoun of South Carolina would extend Antifederalist and Kentucky Resolution views to the fullest. Calhoun extended the consent of a state to sustain the actions of the general government (see Documents 29, 30, and 34). His call for concurrent majority-states' rights was intended to ensure that the states possessed the nullification power to secure their own interests within a federal framework.

The appeal to states' rights did not end in the mid-nineteenth century. Although the extreme of states' rights—secession from the Union—was defeated with the outcome of the Civil War, states' rights has remained a reference point concerning social movements and matters related to increasing powers of the national government. For example, southern women activists in the late nineteenth and early twentieth centuries appealed to their states rather than the national government concerning voting rights. Generally states' rights suffragists feared that a national amendment would enfranchise African Americans and extend federal power into a domain they believed was reserved for state action. In civil rights for African Americans, there was a call for gradualism and accommodation. Several prominent southern spokespersons, whether right or wrong, felt this policy bought time for African Americans to prove their own worth. Certainly this social issue existed within the context of states' rights and federalism, and its argument resurfaced as part of national discussion during the civil rights movement of the 1940s, 1950s, and 1960s.

Until recent years, the states' rights position was almost exclusively equated with resistance to increasing civil rights protections, opposition to social legislation on a national level, and conservative economic beliefs. The renewed interest in governmental autonomy of the states is in part a response to controlling national power, especially bureaucratic power, in the late twentieth century. The response against a larger and more powerful national government that gained momentum in the New Freedom of President Woodrow Wilson, the New Deal of President Franklin D. Roosevelt, and the Great Society of President Lyndon Baines Johnson led to "New Federalism." The response, initiated in the presidency of Richard M. Nixon, reached a crescendo when President Ronald Reagan reinvigorated the states' rights theory in an antigovernment campaign of New Federalism that proved popular enough to win him the presidency. In his first inaugural address, Reagan proclaimed that "the Federal government did not create the states; the states created the Federal government" (see Document 68).[10]

The renewal is also a reflection of the American historical experience in the colonial and Revolutionary periods when beliefs developed that states would better solve pressing issues and would safeguard more effectively the rights of individuals. The confidence in local government, whether right or wrong, preceded a confidence in national government.

DEFINING FEDERALISM

If we classify the types of democratic systems of government existing worldwide today, we would have a varied list. A number of governments, such as that of Great Britain, are *unitary* systems: power is located in a central authority that may or may not distribute power to its subdivisions. Under a unitary system, the authority of the nation's central government is legally supreme. State or local governments possess little or no powers independent of the national government and are therefore regarded as subsidiaries that carry out local tasks. Other governments, such as the Confederate States of America in the 1860s, typify *confederations*: authority rests largely in local or state governments. Only certain powers are permitted to belong to the national government. In a confederacy, the separate states of a nation govern themselves independently and act together through alliances aimed at achieving mutual military, political, or economic benefit. When the framers drafted the Constitution, they had to make decisions about the balance between the states and the national government they were creating. The framers' decision, for the most part, was a third system of government, *federalism*, although the word does not appear in the Constitution.

The word *federal* comes from the Latin *foedus*, which means "of or pertaining to a covenant, compact, or treaty." *Federal* is used to signify alliances between independent sovereignties.[11] Under a federal system, political authority is divided between regional governments and the central government. A widely used textbook defines federalism "as the mode of political organization that unites separate polities within an overarching political system by distributing power among general and constituent governments in a manner designed to protect the existence and authority of both."[12] Another useful definition of federalism is that several political entities are joined "into a larger political unity while preserving the basic political integrity of each entity."[13]

The power of the central or national government is typically enumerated in a written constitution. Under the U.S. Constitution, any powers not specifically granted to the national government are presumed to be retained by state governments. State and local governments have their own spheres of jurisdiction and have often been extolled as important laboratories for governmental experimentation. There are those who hold a deep conviction that individual states are better able than the national government to perform and provide answers to critical issues.

The federal system has five basic characteristics. First, federalism provides a division of legal authority between state and national governments. Overlap occurs, but two legally distinct spheres of government exist. Second, the states are subordinate to the national government in areas such as taxation and regulation of interstate commerce. Third, federalism has produced cooperation between state and national governments in programs such as education, interstate highway construction, environmental protection, and health, unemployment, and social security concerns. Fourth, the Supreme Court has served as a legal "arbiter of the federal system" when claims and counterclaims of state and national powers conflict. And fifth, under federalism the two levels of government exercise direct authority simultaneously over people within their territory. Dual citizenship exists under federalism, and individuals can claim a wide range of rights and privileges from both state and national governments.[14] This last characteristic is particularly important if we are to understand the relationship between individuals and their state and national governments.

Political scientists distinguish between two types of federalism: *dual* and *cooperative*. From one vantage point, federalism can be viewed as a "layer" cake; from another, it may be pictured as a "rainbow or marble" cake.[15] Proponents of states' rights hold that the Constitution is a *compact*, or agreement, between the states and the federal government. Both the states and the national government are supreme within their own sphere. By no means are state governments subordinate to the national government. Advocates of a dual federalism approach draw on the Tenth Amendment to the Constitution. They argue that the national government cannot "invade" the power that is reserved to the states.

Proponents of the position that the people, not the states, created the federal government advocate a cooperative approach to state-nation relations. Cooperative federalism argues that the supremacy clause and the necessary and proper clause of the Constitution grant power to the national government, even if the actions of the national government touch state functions. Most assuredly, the cooperative federalism approach, which was emphasized during the New Deal of the 1930s and continued its momentum after World War II, views the state and national governments as partners, but the national government sets policy for the nation.

The concept of American federalism as created in the eighteenth century was bold and has affected us throughout our history, and continues today. For example, southern leaders in the 1950s and 1960s opposed the desegregation of public schools on the grounds that public education was reserved to the states and that desegregation was meddling by the federal government in an area where it held no jurisdiction. On the other hand, proponents of desegregation in the 1950s urged the federal government to enforce school desegregation, arguing that segregated schools were both separate and unequal. Thus, advocates of both dual federalism and cooperative federalism refer to the Constitution for their respective approaches to government.

Having rejected both unitary and confederation systems, the framers had to decide how to divide power. Constitutional historian C. Herman Pritchett describes this division of power as an elaborate "pattern of allocation" that was purposefully ambiguous. The distribution of power, based on a creative compromise, subsequently led to some important disagreements and differing interpretations concerning constitutional relationships between the people and their governments.[16]

TWO ISSUES CONCERNING STATES' RIGHTS AND AMERICAN FEDERALISM

Documents provide a record that informs us of the origins and changes in the nature of states' rights and American federalism. In the course of this book, two issues frame the significance of the majority of these documents and their relationship to states' rights and American federalism: citizenship and individual rights. Although these two issues can stand separately, often they intertwine and affect each other. Moreover, their relationship to each other becomes more involved and elaborate when placed in the context of states' rights and American federalism. American ideals were first expressed in documents, such as the Declaration of Independence (see Document 10) and the Preamble to the Constitution of the United States. The struggle between the ideal and the real is an ongoing concern. To paraphrase James Madison, the best government is the one that is the least imperfect. States' rights and American federalism provide a fluid, jurisdictional framework for discussion of the ideal. It is the tension and the interaction between state and national government that defines the ideal and provides the means for its realistic achievement.

The first issue, citizenship, permeates humankind's historical experience. The Greeks and Romans first recognized the importance of being a citizen. Citizenship has cross-cultural importance with the rise of nation-states and certainly permeates debates today as all governments decide who their citizens are (and who they are not). In the twentieth century, constitutional governments have increased in number, and although they vary in their ideas about democracy and in the ways democracy can be carried out, constitutional governments—whether state and national in the United States or governments in Asia, Africa, Europe, and the Americas—must decide who and who will not be citizens.

Citizenship was a central issue among Enlightenment writers, who expressed a strong belief that human beings are rational and therefore can create governments. The importance of citizenship gained more prominence in the history of the United States with the writing of the Declaration of Independence, the Articles of Confederation, and then the U.S. Constitution with its Bill of Rights. Thomas Jefferson's eloquent phrase that "Governments are instituted among Men" emphasized the social contract between governments and people and the importance of popular sovereignty, in which the people rule. The Declaration of Independence and the Preamble to the Constitution argued that the people were the source of authority for governments. Subsequent years following the American Revolution, the American Civil War, and the progressive era provided for the inclusion of more members of society to participate as citizens. However, it was the ideas as expressed in the Age of Reason and the ideas as expressed during the American Revolution and the creation of the U.S. Constitution that postulated the people as the ultimate source of authority for governments.

This expression of belief challenged Aristotle's influence on "mixed government" theory,[17] which fit the postmedieval period when authority of government came from different sources. Under the British system of government, the executive branch, or monarchy, derived power from God. The House of Lords, the upper chamber in Britain's Parliament, derived its source of power from the aristocracy. And the House of Commons found authority in the people. A similar application of the "mixed government" theory could be found in the pre-revolutionary French government and its monarch and legislative assembly, the Estates-General. The U.S. Constitution established a different system with all its branches of the government based on popular sovereignty. That people would have the right to citizenship in order to exercise popular sovereignty is fundamental to the issue of states' rights and federalism.

Both state and national governments in the United States have constitutions that recognize their source of authority as the people. Questions about the relationship of the people to both the state and national governments (as existing in the eighteenth century when federalism was created) have persisted in the American political experience. Who is included and who is excluded among the people as sources of authority? Are both state and national governments effectively close to the people they govern? Can citizens of a state who are at odds with a national policy turn to the state as a way to negate their disagreement? Is it possible for citizens to turn to the national government as a way to negate actions of their state government? How vital is citizenship to individual rights? What fundamental changes have occurred in the relationship between the importance of citizenship and the relationship of state and national governments?

A second important issue is the profound relationship of states' rights and federalism on individual rights. The Bill of Rights comprise the first ten amendments, which became part of the U.S. Constitution in 1791. They were designed primarily to protect the individual from the national or central government. The First, Second, and Third Amendments deal with political issues and enumerate such rights. Amendments Four through Eight proscribe government power to put an individual in jeopardy by limiting the power of government to investigate. The Ninth and Tenth Amendments involve compromise with the people and the states, with the former emphasizing rights and the latter stressing powers. During the American Revolution, states too had their own declarations of rights. They had preceded the Bill of Rights in the U.S. Constitution. Are rights as expressed in state governments similar to the rights as expressed in the U.S. Constitution and the Bill of Rights? Where do rights originate? How does the concept of limited government protect rights? How have popular consent and fundamental or higher law shaped rights? How have the conditions of social change affected rights? How has the Fourteenth Amendment, one of the most important changes in the U.S. Constitution, affected individual rights and the relations of state and national governments?

The documents in this book serve as a source to examine the protean nature of rights and the appeals to state and national governments for protection of rights. Of special emphasis is James Madison's call for a "practicable sphere," which he emphasized in *Federalist* Numbers 10 and 51. Madison's stress on the "middle ground" advocated a reform in 1787 to 1792 that would repair the defects he saw in the Articles of Confederation. Madison's "practicable sphere" and structural system were designed to protect minority rights. The Virginian and architect of the Constitution asserted the need for limited government to restrain majority abuses but without denying the majority its right to rule.

This book has five parts, with each part contributing to our understanding of the continuing debate surrounding states' rights and federalism. Part I is organized around the writing of the Constitution and the legacies of constitutional debates, including the contributions of Federalist and Antifederalist thought. Part II focuses on the writing of the Bill of Rights and the citizen as situated in the federal system. Part III emphasizes the ongoing debate of states' rights and federalism as joined by reference to the Declaration of Independence. Advocates of states' rights, led by John C. Calhoun, referred to Antifederalist arguments and the Constitution itself as a guarantor of states' rights. William H. Seward appealed to the Declaration of Independence as a source of higher law to thwart states' rights arguments. Part IV focuses on the plight of African Americans and women in pursuing their rights as citizens of the United States and the several states. The old theme of establishing responsible citizenship dominated the gradualist strategy of Booker T. Washington, who had a faith that citizenship would come to African Americans as they proved themselves to be responsible individuals. Part V emphasizes that the policy of gradualism gives way to desegregation of American society through federal action. Gunnar Myrdal's *An American Dilemma* points out that gradualism had not proved successful in gaining full participation for all American citizens.

The issue of states' rights and federalism forces us to examine and constantly reexamine governments' relationships to important decisions regarding citizenship and the protection of individual rights. Rightly so, James Madison described the federalism that was created in 1787 at the Constitutional Convention as a "happy combination" that was designed to protect the "public good and private rights" in a system of popular government.

NOTES

1. James Madison, "Preface to Debates in the Convention: A Sketch Never Finished nor Applied," *Notes of Debates in the Federal Convention of 1787 Reported by James Madison*, foreword by Adrienne Koch (Athens: Ohio University Press, 1985), p. 3.

2. *The Federalist*, ed. Jacob E. Cooke (Cleveland: World Publishing, 1961), Federalist Number 10, pp. 63, 61.

3. Federalist Number 51, pp. 351–352.

4. Ibid., p. 349.

5. Bernard Bailyn, *The Ideological Origins of the American Revolution* (Cambridge, Mass.: Belknap Press of Harvard University Press, 1967, 1992), p. viii.

6. Marshall L. DeRosa, *The Confederate Constitution of 1861: An Inquiry into American Constitutionalism* (Columbia: University of Missouri Press, 1991) p. 22.

7. Donald S. Lutz, *Popular Consent and Popular Control* (Baton Rouge: Louisiana State University Press, 1979), p. 224.

8. Gordon S. Wood, *The Creation of the American Republic 1776–1787* (Chapel Hill: University of North Carolina Press, 1969), p. 59.

9. Lance Banning, "Republican Ideology and the Triumph of the Constitution, 1789 to 1793," *William and Mary Quarterly* 31 (April 1974): 167–188.

10. "President Reagan's First Inaugural Address, January 20, 1981," *Binghamton Review*, http://www.netstep.net/review/rrlstia.html.

11. J.G.A. Pocock, "States, Republics, and Empires: The American Founding in Early Modern Perspective," in *Conceptual Change and the Constitution*, ed. J.G.A. Pocock and Terence Ball (Lawrence: University Press of Kansas, 1988), pp. 60–61.

12. Daniel J. Elazar, *American Federalism: A View from the States*, 3rd ed. (New York: Harper & Row, 1984), p. 2.

13. Ralph C. Chandler, Richard A. Enslen, and Peter G. Renstrom, *The Constitutional Law Dictionary* (Santa Barbara, Calif.: ABC-Clio Informations Services, 1987), 2:29.

14. Otis H. Stephens and Gregory J. Rathjen, *The Supreme Court and the Allocation of Constitutional Power* (San Francisco, Cal.: W.H. Freeman, 1980), p. 341.

15. Two essays describing cooperative and dual federalism and their importance are by Daniel J. Elazar and Morton Grodzins. See Daniel J. Elazar, "The Scope of Co-operation," in Laurence J. O'Toole, Jr., ed., *American Intergovernmental Relations* (Washington, D.C.: Congressional Quarterly, 1993), pp. 49–56, and Morton Grodzins, "The Federal System," in O'Toole, *American Intergovernmental Relation*, pp. 57–66. The Grozins-Elazar conception of federalism suggests that

"dual federalism never existed from 1790–1860 and that there was "much sharing" and intergovernmental activity and responsibility during this period, just as there appears to be today. For a critique of the Grodzins-Elazar construct of federalism, see Harry N. Scheiber, "The Condition of American Federalism: An Historian's View," in O'Toole, *American Intergovernmental Relations*, pp. 67–74.

16. C. Herman Pritchett, *Constitutional Law of the Federal System* (Englewood Cliffs, N.J.: Prentice-Hall, 1984), p. 58.

17. The Iroquois Confederation, composed of Mohawk, Seneca, Onondaga, Oneida, and Cayuga, were disposed to an Aristotelian "mixed government" even though they had not read Aristotle. Members attempted to overcome anger, jealousy, greed, and revenge among themselves through the creation of the Iroquois Confederation Council. Bruce E. Johansen argues plausibly that Benjamin Franklin had knowledge of the Iroquois Confederation in *Forgotten Founders: Benjamin Franklin, the Iroquois, and the Rationale for the American Revolution* (Ipswitch, MA: Gambit Publishers, 1982). Johansen claims that the origin of bicameralism in U.S. constitutionalism can be traced to the decision-making processes put into practice by the Confederation Council as Mohawk and Seneca sat on one side and the Oneida and Cayuga on the other, while Onondaga acted as facilitators. Donald S. Lutz points out that the Iroquois League arrangement was more a "tricameralism" than a "bicameralism" since the Onondaga were a third body. Lutz states, "It is difficult to see how we went from Iroquois tricameralism to unicameralism in the Articles of Confederation and then to bicameralism in the U.S. Constitution. If one sees an incipient Supreme Court in the role of the Onondaga, then one has to look for an American practice of making the Supreme Court part of the legislature." See Donald S. Lutz, "The Iroquois Confederation: An Analysis," *Publius* 28 (Spring 1998): 105.

The Great Binding Law of the Iroquois Confederation is an important orally transmitted constitution that has a place in independent study for its consensual-oligarchic method of selecting leaders, which differed from democracies in the western tradition. For further reading on the difficulties in tracing American constitutionalism to the Iroquois Confederation and the little influence of the Iroquois Confederation on the writing of the U.S. Constitution, see Elisabeth Tooker, "The United States Constitution and the Iroquois League," *Ethnohistory* 37 (Summer 1990): 305–336; Donald S. Lutz, *The Origins of American Constitutionalism* (Baton Rouge: Louisiana State University Press, 1988); and Donald S. Lutz, *A Preface to American Political Theory* (Lawrence: University Press of Kansas, 1992), particularly chapters 3–5.

Chronology of Key Events in States' Rights and American Federalism

1776   The thirteen colonies declare their independence.

1781   The thirteen states write the Articles of Confederation.

1787   Delegates meet in Philadelphia to revise the Articles of Confederation.

Philadelphia convention delegates write the Constitution of the United States.

Confederation Congress writes the Northwest Ordinance.

Advocates and opponents of the Constitution publish the *Federalist* and *Antifederalist* essays.

1789   George Washington assumes the presidency and delivers his First Inaugural Address.

James Madison introduces the Bill of Rights in Congress.

1791   States ratify the Bill of Rights.

1798   Congress passes the Alien and Sedition Acts.

James Madison and Thomas Jefferson write the Virginia and Kentucky Resolutions.

1800   James Madison delivers his Report of 1800 to the Virginia legislature, reaffirming the Virginia and Kentucky Resolutions.

1814   Federalists meet in Hartford, Connecticut, in opposition to the War of 1812.

1816   Justice Joseph Story articulates the supremacy of the national government in *Martin v. Hunter's Lessee*.

1819   Chief Justice John Marshall asserts national supremacy in the decision in *McCulloch v. Maryland*.

1820   Congress deliberates slavery in the territories and passes the Missouri Compromise.

1828   The Tariff of Abominations incenses the South. John C. Calhoun writes
        but does not sign the *South Carolina Exposition and Protest*. Georgia, Mis-
        sissippi, and Virginia legislatures follow South Carolina's lead.

1832   The nullification crisis reaches a high point, and Andrew Jackson issues
        the Force Act.

1833   The Supreme Court in *Barron v. Baltimore* announces that the Bill of
        Rights applies only to the national government and not to the states.
        The Court's decision limits the powers of the federal government, not
        the state governments. The rights of individuals are not protected from
        state or local governments.

1850   Congress passes the Compromise of 1850.

1854   Congress debates popular sovereignty and passes the Kansas-Nebraska
        Act.

1857   The Supreme Court announces the *Dred Scott* decision.

1860   Southern states secede from the Union and form the Confederate States
        of America.

1861   Jefferson Davis delivers his First Inaugural Address on February 18,
        1861, as president of the Southern Confederacy.

        Abraham Lincoln delivers his First Inaugural Address on March 4, 1861,
        as president of the United States and asserts the authority of the national
        government over states.

        The Civil War begins on April 12, 1861.

1863   Abraham Lincoln issues the Emancipation Proclamation, which frees the
        slaves in the rebellious states.

1865   General Lee surrenders to General Grant, and the Civil War ends.

1868   States ratify the Fourteenth Amendment, which extends the Bill of
        Rights to the states. The Fourteenth Amendment removes the limitation
        of protecting rights of individuals from state or local governments with-
        out due process of law.

1869   The Supreme Court decides whether southern states had left the Union
        in *Texas v. White*.

1877   Reconstruction ends as the last federal troops are removed from the
        South.

1896   The Supreme Court announces that separate but equal facilities are con-
        stitutional in the decision in *Plessy v. Ferguson*.

1901   Theodore Roosevelt assumes the presidency, ushers in progressive re-
        forms, and emphasizes the leading role of the national government.

1913   President Woodrow Wilson's New Freedom increases the authority of
        the national government in federal-state relations.

1933   President Franklin Roosevelt's New Deal expands the responsibility of
        the national government and the impact the federal government has on
        the lives of citizens.

1946   The Supreme Court determines in *Colegrove v. Green* that justices should not interfere in state legislative apportionment issues.

1948   President Harry S. Truman's Fair Deal measures increase the role of the national government, especially in civil rights.

        Southern Democrats reassert states' rights through the creation of the States' Rights (Dixiecrat) party.

1954   The Supreme Court overturns the doctrine of separate but equal in *Brown v. Board of Education of Topeka, Kansas.*

1955   The Supreme Court under Chief Justice Earl Warren directs states to implement the *Brown* decision "with all deliberate speed."

1956   Southern legislators respond to the *Brown* decision with the Southern Manifesto.

1957   First Civil Rights Act since Reconstruction is passed.

        President Dwight Eisenhower sends federal troops to Little Rock, Arkansas, to protect students at the newly integrated Central High School and places the National Guard on federal service.

1962   The Supreme Court announces in *Baker v. Carr* that state legislative apportionment, particularly unequal representation on voting power, is a concern of federal justices.

1964   The Supreme Court in *Reynolds v. Sims* involves itself in the right of states to decide state legislative apportionment.

1965   President Lyndon Johnson launches the Great Society and increases the role of the national government in health, housing, education, and employment for all Americans.

1969   President Richard Nixon's New Federalism attempts to return resources and power to the people.

1976   The Supreme Court announces its ruling In *National League of Cities v. Usery*, making states more secure in federal-state relations.

1978   The Supreme Court countermands the policy of the University of California at Davis, which considered race and other minority status as factors in the admission of medical students to state universities. The *Bakke* decision does not negate the *Brown* decision of 1954. It challenges the use of racial and ethnic origins in offering preferential treatment to individuals.

1981   President Ronald Reagan begins his administration with strong, emphatic support for a New Federalism directed toward shifting substantial power to the states.

1985   The Supreme Court rules in *Garcia v. San Antonio Metropolitan Transit Authority* that the structure of the federal system itself protected state sovereignty. This decision increases anxiety among states' rights advocates.

1994   Republican members of the House of Representatives declare the Contract with America to reassert the authority of state governments.

1995   The Supreme Court emphasizes balance between state and national power in *United States v. Lopez*. This decision moves in the direction of states' rights by limiting the extension of the commerce clause in the creation of "gun-free zones."

1996   The Supreme Court decides in the case, *Seminole Tribe of Florida v. Florida*, that Congress had no authority to pass a law permitting states to be sued in federal court. Under the Eleventh Amendment all states are regarded as sovereign entities. This decision struck down the Indian Gaming Regulatory Act, which permitted Native Americans to sue states to force negotiations over tribal casinos.

1997   In *Printz v. United States*, the Supreme Court ruled that a provision in the Brady Handgun Violence Prevention Act violated state sovereignty. The court based its decision on the Tenth Amendment, and the court declared that the necessary and proper clause does not compel state law enforcement officers to carry out federal tasks.

1999   The Supreme Court brought balance to the issue of federalism and the role of the states in *Alden v. Maine*.

Part I

States' Rights and American Federalism in the American Founding Era, 1620–1789

In the fall of 1786, in the midst of a rebellion led by Daniel Shays in Massachusetts, concern that the republican experiment might fail pressed hard on reformers such as James Madison. When Thomas Jefferson, who was in France during most of the 1780s, read the U.S. Constitution, he concluded that the new plan of government was a conservative reaction sparked by Shays's Rebellion. Jefferson said as much when he wrote that British aides had produced repeated "lies" after the American Revolution about radical American circumstances until Americans themselves were beginning to believe them. Delegates to the 1787 Constitutional Convention had overreacted, Jefferson assessed, to the Shaysite rebellion, and "in the spur of the moment" the delegates had set up "a kite to keep the henyard in order."[1] Jefferson's fear, in fact, was that the Constitution would jeopardize the Union by giving too much power to the new national government. Was the Constitution written out of false haste and undue reaction to a mid-1780s crisis? Did it provide the national government with too much power? At this stage Jefferson feared a strong central government.

Americans had been confident in their revolt against Great Britain, a revolution inspired for the most part to establish a republican experiment in government. In 1776, the thirteen states had announced their independence from the British empire. Thomas Jefferson, principal author of the Declaration of Independence, contended nearly fifty years after writing this important document that the Declaration of Independence (see Document 10) was "the fundamental act of union of these States."[2] The American states would not collapse into a condition of anarchy, he said, because as they left the British empire, their independence led them into a new and unparalleled "act of union."

The Declaration of Independence strongly asserted a national identity of Americans who were unified in the cause of republican government. It called for a national unity based on powerful bonds, particularly a shared suspicion of distant and despotic governments that brought American patriots together. While Americans had a strong national identity, the Declaration of Independence established a weak national government. The thirteen states gave constitutional form to the "union" or federal alliance described by Jefferson's Declaration. The Articles of Confederation, the first written national constitution, confirmed that the national government should be weak.

Americans also had an extreme dislike for mercantilism (a European trading practice, whereby monarchies protected business interests) because as colonists they were barred from trading with their neighbors and confined to the markets of a mother country three thousand miles away. The Articles of Confederation established a loose alliance for diplomatic purposes, with each state maintaining its sovereignty, freedom, and independence. Following the Revolution, the British government of Lord Shelburne gave Americans generous terms with a mutually advantageous trade treaty that flew in the face of Britain's mercantilist policy. When Shelburne's government fell, however, the liberal trade arrangement vanished. Within a few years of independence, Americans of the 1780s experienced a deep economic depression.

By the end of 1786 some of the states were coming out of the economic depression and returning to economic prosperity. This occurred because European wars demanded American foodstuffs. Due to the timing of the Constitution's writing, it was assumed that the delegates to the Constitutional Convention had brought about prosperity by founding a new nation. Certainly the Philadelphia Convention of 1787 had granted the central government three crucial powers that it had been denied under the Articles of Confederation: the power to tax, to raise an army, and to control commerce. Possibly the return to economic prosperity would have occurred anyway under the old Articles of Confederation, but the new plan of government also offered a proper federal system, a solution James Madison felt that was most noteworthy. Madison hoped the U.S. Constitution would remedy the crisis of the 1780s and preserve the experiment in republican government.

James Madison of Virginia hoped the solution would create a large, compound republic. The Virginian had a primary commitment, which was to sustain a "federal balance" that would preserve his state's rights, identity, and interests while providing the means for the government of the Union to function effectively on the international stage. Madison held a cosmopolitan view and saw the Constitution as a "more perfect union." Thinking internationally, Madison envisioned the law of nations as being more operative in the world when linked to strong nationhood. He believed the new system of government would secure peace in a way that had been discussed by the most enlightened minds of Europe.[3]

Madison thought America had much potential, but its promise was endangered by the feeble union or weak federal alliance as conceived under the Declaration of Independence. The "union" under the Declaration constantly threatened to fly apart. Madison meant to shore up the union by strengthening national powers in a practicable manner. He also envisioned the establishment of governing mechanisms that would place restraints on passions. Madison wanted national policies that would rectify the economic problems, which were at the heart of political and social debility. Frivolous importation of foreign luxuries, coupled with the restriction of foreign markets for American goods, endangered the economic preconditions of a healthy participation in the public life.[4] Without the economic conditions necessary for a decent living standard, citizens were incapable, he felt, of looking beyond their own immediate burdens and requirements. If, however, the constitutional and economic maladies could be corrected and stabilized, then the people's virtues could be reestablished and the republican experiment could be successful.

Virtue for James Madison and others of the eighteenth century was not a remote and abstract quality known only by tradition, nor did it imply a superhuman dedication to disinterested participation in political affairs. It was not a self-effacing quality that few could ever possess. Virtue required citizens to be vigilant in their commitment to public life. They were to believe in majority rule without a coerced submission to its decisions; to participate in a politics that allowed only limited responsibilities to public officials, and even then, with a watching for any signs or appearances of interests separate from those of the people. This eternal vigilance had come out of the British Whig tradition and the writings of eighteenth-century critics who strongly condemned corruption in the British governmental system and its public administration. Their strident criticism of the Tory system of administration and finance and their suspicions about government and its leaders strongly influenced Madison and other Americans whose faith in the republican experiment was steadfast. The British financial structure did make it possible for Britain to conduct four great wars for empire with France from 1689 to 1763. The financial system also helped Britain compete commercially with France and other European nations. Defenders of the new financial system accepted the firm commitment of specific revenues for steady payment of the interest on the national debt and a close relationship with the Bank of England to purchase vast amounts of government certificates in exchange for monopolies on trade.

Critics of the new British financial system were less opposed to the commerce, manufacturing, and liquid forms of wealth than the dispari- ties that resulted when power followed wealth. They feared that ex- tremes of wealth and poverty meant loss of freedom. What constituted a good citizen who possessed the qualities for citizenship was of fun- damental importance to Whig opposition beliefs and the thinking of James Madison. Critics of the British financial system held that only when citizens owe nothing to others for livelihood can they be masters of themselves and capable of virtuous participation in a healthy public life.[5] The critics who worried about the disparities in wealth and the undermining of a virtuous citizenry by unvirtuous leaders influenced James Madison and others. Their thoughts on citizenship were impor- tant in the eighteenth century and are no less important today.

British thinking, as explained and understood by country Whig op- position (seventeenth and eighteenth-century English defenders of indi- vidual liberty who feared centralized government and its corrupting influence on officeholders), flowed to Americans such as Madison. Brit- ain was viewed as a monster devouring American freedom. British eco- nomic policies kept freemen in poverty. Eighteenth-century Britain, Madison and other Americans believed, was bent on conspiring against American freedoms. If continued, these policies would lead to corrup- tion rather than virtue, decay rather than vigor. In the eighteenth- century American mind, the success of American independence meant that virtue and vigor would flourish. But in the 1780s, economic col- lapse, disenchantment, and abuses of power had resulted. A new constitutional system, Madison believed, would invigorate the revolu- tionary principles, refurbish virtue and vigor, prevent abuses of power, and protect rights.

The Constitution of 1787 created a system that counterbalanced in- terests, powers, and ambitions. Majority injustices and popular distur- bances disturbed James Madison. While concerned by the 1780s turmoil in Massachusetts, as well as the commotion taking place in his own state of Virginia, Madison blamed the majority abuses less on a fear of popular government than the weaknesses of the Confederation. Madison was not antidemocratic. He believed in majority rule coupled with the protection of minority rights. Madison's chief concern was to strengthen the structure of government to preserve the spirit of republicanism. English traditions and American experiences in the British empire merged to influence the emergence of federalism at the Constitutional Convention of 1787.

THE PROPER SPHERE OF GOVERNMENT AND REPUBLICAN PRINCIPLES

The founding fathers reflected thoughtfully on the relationship between the individual and government and on the very nature of republicanism. Historian Gordon Wood has noted how the American Revolution stimulated the republican tendencies inherent in American life. By adopting republicanism, Americans took advantage of the opportunity to abolish the remnants of their feudal and monarchical society and to create a "new, enlightened republican relationships among people."[6] Republicanism took on various meanings. Most historians today believe that republicanism meant more than representative government. It also stressed the importance of a virtuous citizenry who cherished the public good as well as their own self-interests. Private virtues such as frugality and industriousness were important; however, public virtue, which involved placing the interests of the community above self-interest, were paramount in republican thought. The best leaders were those who possessed a "disinterested" perspective, that is, the willingness to elevate the public good above their individual self-interests. The quality of "disinterestedness" transcended governmental leaders to include all citizens. Whereas most historians stressed the influence of Lockean liberalism, with its emphasis on individual rights, Wood has postulated that the belief in republicanism also supported the social leveling that occurred during the Revolution.[7] Thus, a belief in both individual rights and the common good were requisite conditions for a republican government. For many, individual rights and the common good would best be achieved within the smaller geographic entities of the states; for others, a larger national government best guaranteed both the rights of individuals and the common good.

Serious deliberation took place during both the American Revolution and in the debates at the Constitutional Convention of 1787. Certainly, few in 1776 envisioned a strong national government. The best minds at the time when the Declaration of Independence was written argued that a republic had to be small and that state legislatures, which were close to the people, could do little harm. State legislatures, it was believed, would best represent their constituents. Between 1776 and 1787, however, serious deficiencies in the Articles of Confederation, the nation's first written constitution, became apparent. Many in 1787 agreed that the Union had to be strengthened but that the states had to remain. Although the Annapolis Convention in September 1786 issued a report calling only for a revision of the Articles of Confederation, the Constitutional Convention far exceeded its charge. Most of the delegates agreed to go beyond "revision" of the Articles of Confederation because they were concerned over the haphazard and uncooperative behavior of the various states during the Revolutionary War and its aftermath. They also worried about the abuses perpetrated by some state legislatures. The conventional wisdom was that a legislature could not itself tyrannize. Certain legislatures, however, confiscated property and devised schemes through the force of state laws that seemed arbitrary and capricious. The inefficiency, corruption, and quarrels among the states forced a rethinking about the need to strengthen the sovereignty of the national government.

As delegates to the convention came to Philadelphia, they were aware of the abuse of law, not the absence of law, that had created local legislative tyranny. James Madison, who no doubt came to the convention as the most prepared delegate, expressed apprehension regarding the structure of government under the Articles of Confederation with its propensity for misgoverning (see Document 12). Madison considered the relationship between states and the central government. He was most concerned about was what was happening within the states. Their appalling condition did contribute to his decision to turn more toward an energetic central government within an "extended republic" to correct what he perceived were inherent weaknesses in the confederation system.

Madison and many of the delegates to the Constitutional Convention were worried about "the oppressive behavior of the state legislatures."[8] Madison wished to empower the central government with veto power over state laws, especially those that might be deemed injurious to protection of liberties.[9] As James Madison wrote the memorandum "Vices of the Political System" (see Document 12), he had in mind the need to save "the fundamental principle of republican Government." He believed, as did many others, that the "majority who rule in such [both state and national] Governments are the safest Guardians of both public Good and private rights."[10] It is important to note the plurality of "Governments" and "Guardians" in this protection of public good and private rights. Madison was meticulous in his selection of words when he wrote speeches and memoranda. The use of the plural in "Governments" and "Guardians" was not an accident. Madison did not preclude state governments from his plan as conceived on the eve of the federal convention.

An understanding of what Madison sought—an extended republic that would allow for majority rule while protecting minority rights— can be understood only within the context of Madison's proper sphere of government. Madison believed that the Articles of Confederation as a "federal constitution" was an alliance of "independent and Sovereign States" that could not preserve the Union.

VARIATIONS OF FEDERALISM AT THE CONSTITUTIONAL CONVENTION

Political scientist Michael P. Zuckert informs us that as Constitutional Convention delegates entered into the debate over revising the Articles of Confederation, they had no fewer than "six rather distinct versions of federalism" before them (see Documents 13–17). These versions varied from "most federal in nature to most unitary."[11] Traditional federalism was embodied in the Articles of Confederation, while the New Jersey Plan (see Document 15) reformed federalism and moved away from a system that lacked enforcement powers. The Connecticut Compromise inserted state agency into the general government by way of equal representation in the Senate. In this sense, the Connecticut Compromise was the opposite of the Virginia Plan (see Document 13), which had called for a bicameral legislature, with each legislative chamber based on proportional representation. While James Madison had authored most of the Virginia Plan, which was read by Edmund Randolph, he had an even more national perspective of his own at the convention by including a federal negative, that is, the power of the national legislature to veto state legislative actions. Madison relied on an "extended republic" to protect individual rights. His national compound was less a national consolidation than the proposal of Alexander Hamilton, whose economic nationalism and reliance on an active government to promote the "general interests" of the people pushed to the extreme the concept of a strong, national government. Most of the delegates to the convention regarded this as too radical.

ANTIFEDERALIST VIEWS

American thinking about state and national government relations in the 1780s reached a crucial crescendo when Federalists and Antifederalists debated the ratification of the Constitution. Federalists in their support for ratification of the Constitution and antifederalists in their opposition engaged in a heated public discussion of all aspects of federalism. Its legacy beckons each generation to reconsider the authority of state and national governments in relation to each other and the citizenry, and to do this through serious deliberation.

Following the Constitutional Convention of 1787, both Federalists and Antifederalists wanted some form of federalism—that is, a system of government in which powers were divided between state and national governments. Also, both insisted on republicanism, that is, a government based on the will of the people and accountable to the people but mediated by the discussions in legislatures. Both stressed the importance of a virtuous citizenry who would put the public good ahead of their own selfishness. Where the Federalists and Antifederalists differed was in their meticulous examination of the meaning of good government and the relationship that would be established between governments and the people.

The Antifederalists held the more traditional view that sovereign states created a general government that possessed certain limited purposes, particularly protection from external threats and the conduct of American foreign relations. They also viewed the general government as directly accountable to the states that created it, not the people. The states, as sovereign units of republican government, would be directly responsible to the people. Moreover, Antifederalists believed it was unwise to experiment with republicanism in a territory as large as the United States. They held fast to the ideas of Charles Baron de Montesquieu of France that only in smaller areas such as states could the people be properly represented and involved in their government.

Antifederalists feared despotism would result under a government ruling over an extended territory. Antifederalist James Winthrop of Massachusetts, writing under the pseudonym Agrippa (see Document 20), represented the views of many Antifederalists who shared Montesquieu's admonition that republican principles would operate effectively only in small, confined territories. Effective representation occurs in state and local governments.

In essence, Antifederalists perceived a true republic to possess six characteristics. First, they believed it could exist only in a small territory with few people. Second, they felt representatives in government should mirror the ideas and traits of their constituents. The latter should be homogeneous in their traditions, beliefs, and customs and be virtuous citizens who think in terms of the public good. Legislative action should reflect the interests of the social groups operating within this territorial sphere. Third, they firmly believed that majority rule should prevail. Within a small republican territory, people should have sufficient opportunity and the desire to participate in their government. Fourth, a government is limited and tyranny is to be prevented by majority rule, which is expressed through popular participation in government. Fifth, the government has little need to exert strong, coercive powers because the people are likely to be content with their government and prepared to conform to its legislation since it reflects their desires. And sixth, the government is accountable to the people. The accountability is direct since officials are elected regularly and have short terms of office.[12]

FEDERALISTS' VIEWS

In contrast, the Federalists viewed both levels of government to be responsible directly to the people, as creators of both their state and national governments. Moreover, Federalists believed that a large "extended republic" was the prescription necessary to save the republican experiment that had been fought for during the American Revolution and nearly lost during the critical period of the 1780s under the Articles of Confederation. They believed it could be preserved only with the plan of government proposed under the Constitution. Immediately after the Constitutional Convention, Alexander Hamilton, James Madison, and John Jay produced a series of eighty-five essays, known collectively as *The Federalist*, that appeared in the New York press between October 1787 and May 1788. Writing under the pseudonym "Publius," the three authors articulated the construction of a just and viable republican Constitution for the nation.[13] *The Federalist* constituted a distinguished and original American contribution to political thought. "Good government," argued Publius, came from "capable" people who make governments "from reflection and choice."[14] *The Federalist* established the standards for republicanism, natural rights, and a government operating under a written constitution. At the forefront *The Federalist* explained key concepts of a constitutional democracy such as the rule of law, distribution of power, limited government, representative government, individual rights, popular sovereignty, political participation, and civil society. These essays described, moreover, how complex problems of constitutional democracies, such as the blending of liberty with order, majority rule with minority rights, and private rights with public good, could best be guaranteed in an extended republic.

MADISON'S EXTENDED REPUBLIC AND PRACTICABLE SPHERE: IMPLICATIONS FOR STATES' RIGHTS AND FEDERALISM

Throughout the *Federalist* essays, both Hamilton and Madison reiterated the theme of the "extended republic." Today, the Tenth *Federalist* essay is considered one of the most important statements concerning federalist principles. That was not always the case. In 1787, the Tenth *Federalist* had no more important status than any of the other *Federalist* essays. Nor was its particular importance noticed in the nineteenth century. Then, in 1913, historian Charles Beard elevated its importance.

Beard viewed the Tenth *Federalist* as supporting an economic interpretation of the writing of the Constitution. He drew the conclusion that the Constitution was a reform intended as counterrevolution, with differing classes struggling for power. Beard's interpretation dominated the first half of the twentieth century and still has supporters today. In the 1930s, Irving Brant, a major biographer of James Madison, gave a second meaning to the Tenth *Federalist*. Brant saw Madison as shifting from a strong nationalist perspective in the 1780s to a states' rights position in the 1790s. Brant believed that the Tenth *Federalist* confirmed his view of Madison's "nationalism" in the 1780s. A third interpretation has come from Martin Diamond and Robert Dahl, who in the 1950s and 1960s challenged Beard's economic interpretation. Diamond and Dahl emphasized Madison's reference to factions in the essay. Their pluralist interpretation stressed the struggle of interests, not classes as Beard had said. The Diamond-Dahl interpretation pointed out that such collisions of special interests would produce public good. Diamond brought to bear the powerful idea that Madison's solution to the problems of a liberal democracy rested in the idea of multiplying interests that operated in an extended commercial republic. Diamond also built into his interpretation a conviction that Madison pursued a wholly national plan at the Constitutional Convention, that is, that Madison shared with Hamilton a vision for a unitary national government. A fourth interpretation, that of Gordon Wood, has noted a disingenuous commitment to democratic radicalism. Wood has noted that the tone of the Tenth *Federalist* stressed "enlightened statesmen." The call for a better type of people to lead the nation muddied the language of democracy.

Recently historian Lance Banning has challenged prior interpretations of the Tenth *Federalist*. Banning noted convincingly that the Tenth *Federalist* was not the culmination of James Madison's thoughts, a mistake all others have made in constructing their ideas about James Madison, and calls the Tenth *Federalist* to be read with other writings of Madison in mind. He has mentioned, in particular, the importance of the Fifty-first *Federalist* and its emphasis on a "practicable sphere." To Banning, the Tenth *Federalist* in combination with the Fifty-first *Federalist* provides a fuller explanation of Madison's vision of state and national governments. Madison, says Banning, wanted core values set in republican principles to guide American practices in government.[15] Madison's appeal to a "practicable sphere" or "middle ground" between localism and distant leaders establishes the importance of both state and national governments in the federal system. Both governments, in combination, act to provide the framework for our laws and public actions.

In the last two decades of the twentieth century, the ideas of government expressed in both Antifederalist collections and *The Federalist* have gained new prominence publicly. The 1987 bicentennial commemoration of the Constitution, and the interest of people who want to invigorate democracy in newly formed nations, have found the essays to be seminal documents. Perhaps James Madison's call for a "practicable sphere" or "middle ground" is still a worthy goal in balancing out the interests of the national and the interests of the particular.

NOTES

1. Letter of Thomas Jefferson, *The Papers of Thomas Jefferson*, ed. Julian P. Boyd et al. (Princeton: Princeton University Press, 1950–), 12:356.

2. Minutes of the Board of Visitors, University of Virginia, March 4, 1825, in *Writings of Thomas Jefferson*, ed. Merrill Peterson (New York: Viking Press, 1984), p. 479.

3. Peter S. Onuf, *Origins of the Federal Republic: Jurisdictional Controversies in the United States, 1775–1787* (Philadelphia: University of Pennsylvania Press, 1983), p. 205.

4. Drew R. McCoy, *The Elusive Republic: Political Economy in Jeffersonian America* (Chapel Hill: University of North Carolina Press, 1980), chap. 3.

5. J.G.A. Pocock, "Machiavelli, Harrington, and English Political Ideologies in the Eighteenth Century," *William and Mary Quarterly* 3rd ser., 22, no. 4 (October 1965): 549–583.

6. Gordon Wood, *The Radicalism of the American Revolution* (New York: Alfred A. Knopf, 1991), p. 106.

7. Ibid., pp. 95–225.

8. Gordon Wood, "The Political Ideology of the Founders," in Nell L. York, ed., *Toward a More Perfect Union: Six Essays on the Constitution* (Provo, Utah: Brigham Young University, 1988), p. 10, as cited in Lance Banning, *The Sacred Fire of Liberty: James Madison and the Founding of the Federal Republic* (Ithaca, N.Y.: Cornell University Press, 1995), p. 441.

9. James Madison, "Vices of the Political System of the United States," April 1787, in Robert A. Rutland, ed., *The Papers of James Madison* (Chicago: University of Chicago Press, 1975), 9:354.

10. Ibid., pp. 361–369.

11. Michael P. Zuckert, "Federalism and the Founding: Toward a Reinterpretation of the Constitutional Convention," *Review of Politics* 48 (1986): 166–210.

12. Murray Dry, "The Case against Ratification: Anti-Federalist Constitutional Thought," in Leonard W. Levy and Dennis J. Mahoney, eds., *The Framing and Ratification of the Constitution* (New York: Macmillan Publishing, 1987), pp. 271–291; Richard E. Ellis, "The Persistence of Antifederalism after 1789," in Richard Beeman, Stephen Botein, and Edward C. Carter II, eds., *Beyond Confederation: Origins of the Constitution and American National Identity* (Chapel Hill: University of North Carolina Press, 1987), pp. 295–314; Gordon Wood, *The Creation of the Americana Republic, 1776–1787* (Chapel Hill: University of North Carolina Press, 1969), 513–516; and John J. Patrick, *Liberty and Order in Constitutional Government:*

Ideas and Issues in the Federalist Papers (Richmond: The Virginia Jefferson Association, 1989), ED 313 315.

13. *The Federalist*, ed. Jacob E. Cooke (Cleveland: World Publishing, 1961). Hamilton wrote fifty-one of the essays, Madison twenty-nine essays, and Jay five essays. Several essays discussed national sovereignty with states' rights, including the Ninth, Fourteenth, and Thirty-ninth *Federalist* with the Thirty-ninth being the most prominent in blending national and federal elements. The insufficiency and defects of the confederation system, or older federal system, are discussed in the Fifteenth through the Twenty-second essays. Hamilton, as author of the Fifteenth *Federalist*, emphasized the "sacred knot" binding the public together.

14. *Federalist* Number 1, in ibid., p. 3.

15. Lance Banning's chapter 7, "The Practicable Sphere of a Republic," provides an excellent analysis of scholarship on the Tenth *Federalist* and its importance. See Lance Banning, *The Sacred Fire of Liberty: James Madison and the Founding of the Federal Republic* (Ithaca: Cornell University Press, 1995), pp. 195–223.

DOCUMENT 1: The Mayflower Compact, 1620

Originally the document we call the Mayflower Compact was known as "The Plymouth Combination" or simply "The Combination." No matter what its name, the document meant that people had agreed to combine themselves into a "civil body politick." In 1793, the Mayflower Compact written by the Pilgrims was published for the first time for the public to read. The choice of the word *compact* was significant. A compact was more lasting than a "contract," which implied a temporary relationship between the people and the agreement. The religious people who wrote the "Mayflower Compact" were Pilgrims, a radical Puritan group desiring to create a new city of God run by the prescriptions of the Bible.

The Mayflower Compact was modeled after the language of church covenant. God witnessed the consent of each member of the community. The Pilgrims formed an indivisible group, yet one that provided liberty. In Latin the word for covenant is *foedus*, from which "federalism" is derived. Historian Donald Lutz points out that it is clear from the beginning of the English experience in America, federalism was an important principle of government. Initially the idea of federalism combined individuals. Later, federalism would combine communities rather than individuals.

In the Mayflower Compact, the larger entity was the "civil body politick." The smaller units were those individuals who signed the covenant. The signees both created the government by their own consent and agreed to run the government by consenting to its laws and leaders.

The Mayflower Compact had three important effects. First, it created a new people since not all aboard the *Mayflower* were Pilgrims. Second, it created a government when it combined into a "civil body politick." And third, it established fundamental values, which would be changed into bills of rights, as well as the commitment of a people. Later, communities would replace individuals in the belief in federalism.

* * *

In The Name of God, Amen. We, whose names are underwritten, the Loyal Subjects of our dread Sovereign Lord King *James*, by the Grace of God, of *Great Britain, France*, and *Ireland*, King, *Defender of the Faith*, &c. Having undertaken for the Glory of god, and Advancement of the Christian Faith, and the Honour of our King and Country, a Voyage to plant the first colony in the northern Parts of Virginia; Do by these Presents, solemnly and mutually in the Presence of God and one another, covenant and combine ourselves together into a civil Body Politick, for our better Ordering and Preservation, and Furtherance of the Ends aforesaid; And by Virtue hereof do enact, constitute, and frame, such just and equal Laws, Ordinances, Acts, Constitutions, and Offices, from time to time, as shall be thought most meet and convenient for the general Good of the Colony; unto which we promise all due Submission and Obedience. In WITNESS whereof we have hereunto subscribed our names at *Cape Cod* the eleventh of *November* in the Reign of our Sovereign Lord King *James* of *England, France*, and *Ireland*, the eighteenth and of *Scotland*, the fifty-fourth. *Anno domini*, 1620.

Source: Henry Steele Commager, ed., *Documents of American History*, 7th ed. (New York: Appleton-Century-Crofts, 1963), 15–16.

DOCUMENT 2: The Fundamental Orders of Connecticut, 1639

The Fundamental Orders of Connecticut was the first constitution in America. It created the first federal political system, extending the principles of the Mayflower Compact. Connecticut started as two colonies—the Colony of Connecticut and the Colony of New Haven. Each colony had a cluster of towns, with each town having its own government. In 1639, the towns decided to establish a common government while preserving their own governments. The common government had certain powers that were binding on all of them. The towns retained some of their powers. This relationship of a general government working with local governments was based on the principle of federalism.

The Fundamental Orders of Connecticut instituted two important ideas of federalism. First, it allowed other towns to join the common government. And second, newer towns or parts could join as equal partners the older towns under the general government. These two ideas—joining a common government and entering as equal partners— were important contributions of federalism. These two ideas continued throughout the writing of the Constitution of the United States in 1787 and the writing of the Northwest Ordinance that same year. The Constitution and the Northwest Ordinance, particularly the latter, emphasized that newer states would be equal partners with the older, or original, states.

Like the Mayflower Compact, the Fundamental Orders of Connecticut created a new people (in this case the people of Connecticut), created a new government (the Commonwealth of Connecticut), and identified commonly held values that the people of Connecticut shared: order, peace, religion, equality, liberty, and majority rule.

The Fundamental Orders listed powers of the general government in Article 10 and included a supremacy clause. Similarly, a list of powers and a supremacy clause became part of the Constitution of the United States nearly 140 years later. Towns were linked by the common general government. Towns, it should be noted, kept certain powers in the federal system of the Fundamental Orders of Connecticut.

* * *

1. It is Ordered . . . that there shall be yerely two generall Assemblies or Courts, the one the second thursday in Aprill, the other the second thursday in September, following; the first shall be called the Courte of Election, wherein shall be yerely Chosen . . . soe many Magestrats and other publike Officers as shall be found requisitte: Whereof one to be chosen Governour for the yeare ensueing and untill another be chosen, and noe other Magestrate to be chosen for more than one yeare; provided allwayes there be six chosen besids the Governour; which being chosen and sworne according to an Oath recorded for that purpose shall have power to administer justice according to the Lawes here established, and for want thereof according to the rule of the word of God; which choise shall be made by all that are admitted freemen and have taken the Oath of Fidellity, and doe cohabitte within this Jurisdiction, (having beene admitted Inhabitants by the major part of the Towne wherein they live,) or the major parte of such as shall be then present.

4. It is Ordered . . . that noe person be chosen Governour above once in two yeares, and that the Governour be alwayes a member of some ap-

proved congregation, and formerly of the Magestracy within this Jurisdiction; and all the Magestrats Freemen of this Commonwelth: . . .

5. It is Ordered . . . that to the aforesaid Courte of Election the severall Townes shall send their deputyes, and when the Elections are ended they may proceed in any publike searvice as at other Courts. Also the other Generall Courte in September shall be for makeing of lawes, and any other publike occation, which conserns the good of the Commonwelth.

7. It is Ordered . . . that after there are warrants given out for any of the said Generall Courts, the Constable . . . of ech Towne shall forthwith give notice distinctly to the inhabitants of the same . . . that at a place and tyme by him or them lymited and sett, they meet and assemble them selves togather to elect and chuse certen deputyes to be att the Generall Courte then following to agitate the afayres of the commonwelth; which said Deputyes shall be chosen by all that are admitted Inhabitants in the severall Townes and have taken the oath of fidellity; provided that non be chosen a Deputy for any Gencrall Courte which is not a Freeman of this Commonwelth. . . .

8. It is Ordered . . . that Wyndsor, Hartford and Wethersfield shall have power, ech Towne, to send fower of their freemen as their deputyes to every Generall Courte; and whatsoever other Townes shall be hereafter added to this Jurisdiction, they shall send so many deputyes as the Courte shall judge mecte, a resonable proportion to the number of Freemen that are in the said Townes being to be attended therein; which deputyes shall have the power of the whole Towne to give their voats and alowance to all such lawes and orders as may be for the publike good, and unto which the said Townes are to be bownd.

9. It is ordered . . . that the deputyes thus chosen shall have power and liberty to appoynt a tyme and a place of meeting togather before any Generall Courte to advise and consult of all such things as may conceme the good of the publike, as also to examine their owne Elections. . . .

10. It is Ordered . . . that every Generall Courte . . . shall consist of the Governor, or some one chosen to moderate the Court, and 4 other Magestrats at lest, with the major parte of the deputyes of the severafl Townes legally chosen; and in case the Freemen or major parte of them, through neglect or refusall of the Governor and major parte of the magestrats, shall call a Courte, it shall consist of the major parte of Freemen that are present or their deputyes, with a Moderator chosen by them: In which said Generall Courts shall consist of the supreme power of the Commonwelth, and they only shall have power to make lawes or repeale them, to graunt levyes, to admitt of Freemen, dispose of lands undisposed of, to severall Townes or persons, and also shall have power to call ether Courte or Magestrate or any other person whatsoever into question for any misdemeanour, and may for just causes displace or deale otherwise according to the nature of the offence; and also may

deale in any other matter that concerns the good of this commonwelth, excepte election of Magestrats, which shall be done by the whole boddy of Freemen.

In which Courte the Governour or Moderator shall have power to order the Courte to give liberty of spech, and silence unceasonable and disorderly speakeings, to put all things to voate, and in case the vote be equall to have the casting voice. But non of these Courts shall be adjorned or dissolved without the consent of the major parte of the Court.

11. It is ordered . . . that when any Generall Courte uppon the occations of the Commonwelth have agreed uppon any summe or sommes of mony to be levyed uppon the severall Townes within this Jurisdiction, that a Committee be chosen to sett out and appoynt what shall be the proportion of every Towne to pay of the said levy, provided the Committees be made up of an equall number out of each Towne.

Source: Kermit L. Hall, *Major Problems in American Constitutional History*, Vol. 1: *The Colonial Era Through the Civil War* (Lexington, Mass.: D.C. Heath, 1992), pp. 36–38.

DOCUMENT 3: Organization of the Government of Rhode Island, March 16–19, 1642

The colony of Rhode Island grew up in Narragansett Bay. The colonists of Rhode Island were dissenters of Massachusetts Bay and were disputatious on nearly all matters. On one belief they were in agreement: the state had no right to coerce belief. This conviction was combined with a suspicion of centralized power of government.

Eventually Rhode Island created a colony-wide government out of many towns. It was similar, in this sense, to the Fundamental Orders of Connecticut (1639) (see Document 2). The Organization of the Government of Rhode Island framed a general government with towns retaining jurisdiction as well. Articles 3, 14, and 17 of the Organization of the Government of Rhode Island illustrate this belief in federalism. Note also the reference to democracy as a body of freemen and the belief in the importance of just laws.

* * *

. . .

3. It is ordered and unanimously agreed upon, that the Government which this Bodie Politick doth attend unto in this Island, and the Jursdiction thereof, in favour of our Prince is a DEMOCRACIE, or Popular Gov-

ernment; that is to say, It is in the Power of the Body of Freemen orderly assembled, or the major part of them, to make or constitute Just Lawes, by which they will be regulated, and to depute [trust] from among themselves such Ministers as shall see them faithfully executed between Man and Man.

. . .

14. It is ordered, that a Booke shall be provided, wherein the Secretary shall write all such Lawes and Acts, as are made and constituted by the Body, to be left always in that Towne where the said Secretary is not resident; and also that coppies of such Acts as shall be made now or hereafter, at the General Courts concerning necessary uses and ordinances to be observed, shall be fixed upon some public place where all men may see and take notice of them; or that copies thereof be given to the Clerks of the Bank, who shall read them at the head of the Companie.

. . .

17. It is ordered, that a Line be drawn and a way be cleared between the Townes of Nuport and Portsmouth, by removing of the wood and mowing it; that drift Cattle may sufficiently pass; and for the performance thereof, Capt. Morris, of the on Towne, and Mr. Jeoffreys of the other, are appointed to draw the Line, and to be paid thereof, and the Townes to perform the rest.

Source: Donald S. Lutz, ed., *Documents of Political Foundation Written by Colonial Americans: From Covenant to Constitution* (Philadelphia: Institute for the Study of Human Issues, 1986), pp. 189–193.

DOCUMENT 4: On Liberty, 1645

Governor John Winthrop was a Puritan lawyer who led the Massachusetts Bay colony from its inception. In 1629, as Puritans were on their way to the Americas, Winthrop had given a stirring sermon, "A Model of Christian Charity," on board the *Arabella*, carrying them to the New World. He called on his fellow Puritans to establish a society that would be "a city upon a hill," an example for all people and a beacon for the rest of the world to emulate. The persecuted Puritans were to build a "wilderness Zion" in America. In "A Model of Christian Charity," Winthrop recognized social hierarchy. He called on all Puritans to contribute to the community to be established. He asserted that it was God's will that "in all times some must be rich, some poor, some high and eminent in power and dignitie, others meane and in subjection." The Puritans would establish a community and a representative government.

John Winthrop was the governor of Massachusetts Bay colony twelve times between 1630 and 1649. In 1643, he helped to organize the New England Confederation and served as its first president. In 1645, he was acquitted of grievances against him that had come before the General Court of Massachusetts Bay colony. His speech "On Liberty" espoused principles of liberty within a framework of moral authority, and every year after he was chosen as governor of Massachusetts Bay. Winthrop raised a long-lasting issue within the federal debate. There needs to be an authority that guides freedom. He distinguished two types of liberty, natural and federal (or government within moral prescriptions). Would the liberty be constrained by local authority or by a general authority? Authority located in local government possessed the benefit of closeness to the people governed. General authority provided a uniform regulation of such activities as commerce. Winthrop did not confuse liberty with license. His speech to the General Court laid a foundation for debates over local and general governments and their relationship to individual liberties.

* * *

... The great questions that have troubled the country are about the authority of the magistrates and the liberty of the people. ...

For the other point concerning liberty, I observe a great mistake in the country about that. There is a twofold liberty, natural (I mean as our nature is now corrupt) and civil or federal. The first is common to man with beasts and other creatures. By this, man as he stands in relation to man simply, hath liberty to do what he lists: it is a liberty to evil as well as to good. This liberty is incompatible and inconsistent with authority, and cannot endure the least restraint of the most just authority. The exercise and maintaining of this liberty makes men grow more evil, and in time to be worse than brute beasts: omnes sumus licentia deteriores. This is that great enemy of truth and peace, that wild beast, which all the ordinances of God are bent against, to restrain and subdue it. The other kind of liberty I call civil or federal; it may also be termed moral, in reference to the covenant between God and man, in the moral law, and the politic covenants and constitutions, amongst men themselves. This liberty is the proper end and object of authority, and cannot subsist without it; and it is a liberty to that only which is good, just, and honest. This liberty you are to stand for, with the hazard (not only of your goods, but) of your lives, if need be. Whatsoever crosseth this is not authority, but a distemper thereof. This liberty is maintained and exercised in a way of subjection to authority; it is of the same kind of liberty wherewith Christ hath made us free. The woman's own choice makes such a man her husband; yet, being so chosen, he is her lord, and she is to be subject to him, yet in a way of liberty, not of bondage; and a true wife accounts her subjection her honor and freedom, and would not think her condition safe and free but in her subjection to her husband's authority. Such is the liberty of the church under the authority of Christ, her king and husband; his yoke is so easy and sweet to her as a bride's ornaments; and if through frowardness [disobedience] or wantonness, etc., she shake it off, at any time, she is at no rest in her spirit until she take it up again; and whether her lord smiles upon her, and embraceth her in his arms, or whether he frowns, or rebukes, or smites her, she apprehends the sweetness of his love in all, and is refreshed, supported, and instructed by every such dispensation of his authority over her. On the other side, ye know who they are that complain of this yoke and say, let us break their bands, etc., we will not have this man to rule over us. Even so, brethren, it will be between you and your magistrates. If you stand for your natural corrupt liberties, and will do what is good in your own eyes, you will not endure the least weight of authority, but will murmur, and oppose, and be always striving to shake off that yoke; but if you will be satisfied to enjoy such civil and lawful liberties, such as Christ allows you, then will you quietly and cheerfully submit unto that authority which is set over you, in all the administrations of it, for your good.

Wherein, if we fail at any time, we hope we shall be willing (by God's assistance) to hearken to good advice from any of you, or in any other way of God; so shall your liberties be preserved, in upholding the honor and power of authority amongst you.

Source: James R. Andrew and David Zarefsky, *American Voices: Significant Speeches in American History* (White Plains, N.Y.: Longman, 1989), pp. 5–6, and Douglass Project, 1996, http://douglass.speech.nwu.edu/wint_a54.htm.

DOCUMENT 5: Penn's Plan of Union, 1697

William Penn, a follower of George Fox and the Society of Friends established Pennsylvania as a Quaker colony in 1681. In 1697, he offered a Plan of Union, designed to unite the English colonies in order to promote security, peace, and safety without sacrificing the independent nature of each colony as established in its charter. Over fifty years later, in 1754, Pennsylvanians led by Benjamin Franklin would propose the Albany Plan of Union (see Document 6) to unite the En-

glish colonies during the French and Indian Wars. Neither plan—
Penn's Plan of Union and the Albany Plan of Union—was accepted.

* * *

A brief and plain scheme how the English colonies in the North parts
of America,—viz., Boston, Connecticut, Rhode Island, New York, New
Jerseys, Pennsylvania, Maryland, Virginia, and Carolina,—may be made
more useful to the crown and one another's peace and safety with an
universal concurrence.

1. That the several colonies before mentioned do meet once a year, and
oftener if need be during the war, and at least once in two years in times
of peace, by their stated and appointed deputies, to debate and resolve
of such measures as are most advisable for their better understanding
and the public tranquility and safety.

2. That, in order to it, two persons, well qualified for sense, sobriety,
and substance, be appointed by each province as their representatives or
deputies, which in the whole make the congress to consist of twenty
persons.

3. That the king's commissioner, for that purpose specially appointed,
shall have the chair and preside in the said congress.

4. That they shall meet as near as conveniently may be to the most
central colony for ease of the deputies.

5. Since that may in all probability be New York, both because it is
near the center of the colonies and for that it is a frontier and in the
king's nomination, the governor of that colony may therefore also be the
king's high commissioner during the session, after the manner of Scotland.

6. That their business shall be to hear and adjust all matters of com-
plaint or difference between province and province. As, 1st, where persons quit their own province and go to another, that they may avoid
their just debts, though they be able to pay them; 2nd, where offenders
fly justice, or justice cannot well be had upon such offenders in the provinces that entertain them; 3rd, to prevent or cure injuries in point of
commerce; 4th, to consider the ways and means to support the union
and safety of these provinces against the public enemies. In which congress the quotas of men and charges will be much easier and more
equally set than it is possible for any establishment made here to do; for
the provinces, knowing their own condition and one another's, can debate that matter with more freedom and satisfaction, and better adjust
and balance their affairs in all respects for their common safety.

7. That, in times of war, the king's high commissioner shall be general
or chief commander of the several quotas upon service against the common enemy, as he shall be advised, for the good and benefit of the whole.

Source: Henry Steele Commager, ed., *Documents of American History*, 7th ed. (New York: Appleton-Century-Crofts, 1963), 1:39–40.

DOCUMENT 6: Albany Plan of Union, 1754

The Albany Congress met from June 19 to July 10, 1754 in Albany, New York. The meeting was called in response to a directive from the British government that the American colonists should make a treaty with the Iroquois who were wavering in their support of the British on the eve of the French and Indian War. Benjamin Franklin and Thomas Hutchinson wrote the Albany Plan of Union, which was approved by the Albany Congress on July 10. The plan called for a union of all colonies with the exception of Georgia and Nova Scotia. The Albany Plan of Union was sent to the colonies and the British crown for approval. Both rejected it. The colonial assemblies believed the plan gave too much power to the crown, and the British government believed the plan gave too much power to the colonies. The difficulty in governments' giving up a measure of their authority, even in order to obtain a greater measure of security, was apparent. In this case, the threat of security was the French who occupied areas adjacent to the English colonies.

* * *

It is proposed that humble application be made for an act of Parliament of Great Britain, by virtue of which one general government may be formed in America, including all the said colonies, within and under which government each colony may retain its present constitution, except in the particulars wherein a change may be directed by the said act, as hereafter follows.

1. That the said general government be administered by a President-General, to be appointed and supported by the crown; and a Grand Council, to be chosen by the representatives of the people of the several Colonies met in their respective assemblies.

2. That within _____ months after the passing such act, the House of Representatives that happen to be sitting within that time, or that shall be especially for that purpose convened, may and shall choose members for the Grand Council, in the following proportion, that is to say,

Massachusetts Bay	7
New Hampshire	2
Connecticut	5

Rhode Island	2
New York	4
New Jersey	3
Pennsylvania	6
Maryland	4
Virginia	7
North Carolina	4
South Carolina	4
	48

3. ____ who shall meet for the first time at the city of Philadelphia, being called by the President-General as soon as conveniently may be after his appointment.

4. That there shall be a new election of the members of the Grand Council every three years; and, on the death or resignation of any member, his place should be supplied by a new choice at the next sitting of the Assembly of the Colony he represented.

5. That after the first three years, when the proportion of money arising out of each Colony to the general treasury can be known, the number of members to be chosen for each Colony shall, from time to time, in all ensuing elections, be regulated by that proportion, yet so as that the number to be chosen by any one Province be not more than seven, nor less than two.

6. That the Grand Council shall meet once in every year, and oftener if occasion require, at such time and place as they shall adjourn to at the last preceding meeting, or as they shall be called to meet at by the President-General on any emergency; he having first obtained in writing the consent of seven of the members to such call, and sent duly and timely notice to the whole.

7. That the Grand Council have power to choose their speaker; and shall neither be dissolved, prorogued, nor continued sitting longer than six weeks at one time, without their own consent or the special command of the crown.

8. That the members of the Grand Council shall be allowed for their service ten shillings sterling per diem, during their session and journey to and from the place of meeting; twenty miles to be reckoned a day's journey.

9. That the assent of the President-General be requisite to all acts of the Grand Council, and that it be his office and duty to cause them to be carried into execution.

10. That the President-General, with the advice of the Grand Council,

hold or direct all Indian treaties, in which the general interest of the Colonies may be concerned; and make peace or declare war with Indian nations.

11. That they make such laws as they judge necessary for regulating all Indian trade. . . .

Source: Henry Steele Commager, ed., *Documents of American History*, 7th ed. (New York: Appleton-Century-Crofts, 1963), 1:43–45.

DOCUMENT 7: Declarations of the Stamp Act Congress, October 2, 1765

In 1765 the British Parliament passed the Stamp Act as a way to collect money for payment of the French and Indian War and to offset the cost of protecting the colonies in the British empire. The tax was placed on legal documents, insurance policies, newspapers, and other documents and was easy to enforce. Violators were to be tried in Vice Admiralty courts, or military courts without colonists as jurors, rather than colonial common law courts. Colonial response eventually caused the English merchants to call for Parliament to rescind the stamp tax. What is important in federalism is the argument made in this declaration concerning representation in local and general governments. Articles IV and V address this concern. In addition, the trial by jury and the jurisdiction of such trials is expressed in this document.

* * *

THE members of this Congress, sincerely devoted with the warmest sentiments of affection and duty to His Majesty's person and Government . . . esteem it our indispensible duty to make the following declarations of our humble opinion respecting the most essential rights and liberties of the colonists, and of the grievances under which they labour, by reason of several late Acts of Parliament.

. . .

IV. That the people of these colonies are not, and from their local circumstances cannot be, represented in the House of Commons in Great Britain.

V. That the only representatives of the people of these colonies are persons chosen therein by themselves, and that no taxes ever have been, or can be constitutionally imposed on them, but by their respective legislatures.

. . .

VII. That trial by jury is the inherent and invaluable right of every British subject in these colonies.

. . .

XII. That the increase, prosperity, and happiness of these colonies depend on the full and free enjoyments of their rights and liberties, and an intercourse with Great Britain mutually affectionate and advantageous.

XIII. That it is the right of the British subjects in these colonies to petition the King or either House of Parliament. . . .

Source: Marion Mills Miller, Great Debates in American History (New York: Current Literature Publishing, 1913), 1:32–34, and Douglass Project, 1996 http://douglass.speech.nwu.edu/stam__a53.htm.

DOCUMENT 8: From a Farmer in Pennsylvania to the Inhabitants of the British Colonies, Letter II, 1767

John Dickinson practiced law in Philadelphia. When Parliament imposed the Townshend Acts in 1767 on the American colonies, Dickinson formulated arguments in opposition to the duties. His arguments were published as Letters from a Farmer in Pennsylvania. Dickinson's concern was that the general government could impose taxes on people who were not represented in that government. American liberty and economic well-being would be jeopardized if the British were allowed to impose taxes on their exports to the colonies. Dickinson represented Delaware during the Constitutional Convention in Philadelphia and under the pseudonym "Fabius" argued for the adoption of the Constitution.

* * *

MY DEAR COUNTRYMEN,

There is another late Act of Parliament, which appears to me to be unconstitutional and as destructive to the liberty of these colonies, as that mentioned in my last letter; that is, the Act for granting the duties on paper, glass, etc. [the Townshend duties].

The Parliament unquestionably possesses a legal authority to regulate the trade of Great Britain and all her colonies. Such an authority is essential to the relation between a mother country and her colonies; and necessary for the common good of all. He, who considers these provinces as States distinct from the British Empire, has very slender notions of justice, or of their interests. We are but parts of a whole, and therefore there must exist a power somewhere to preside, and preserve the connexion due order. This power is lodged in the Parliament; and we are as much dependent on Great Britain as a perfectly free people can be on another.

. . .

Our great advocate Mr. Pitt, in his speeches on the debate concerning the repeal of the Stamp Act, acknowledged that Great Britain could restrain our manufactures. His words are these: "This kingdom, the supreme governing and legislative power, has always bound the colonies by her regulations and restrictions in trade, in navigation, in manufactures—in everything, except that of taking their money out of their pockets, without their consent." Again he says: "We may bind their trade, confine their manufactures, and exercise every power whatever, except that of taking their money out of their pockets, without their consent."

Here then, my dear countrymen, ROUSE yourselves, and behold the ruin hanging over your heads. If you ONCE admit that Great Britain may lay duties upon her exportations to us, *for the purpose of levying money on us only*, she then will have nothing to do but to lay those duties on the articles which she prohibits us to manufacture—and the tragedy of American liberty is finished. We have been prohibited from procuring manufactures, in all cases, anywhere but from Great Britain (excepting linens, which we are permitted to import directly from Ireland). We have been prohibited in some cases from manufacturing for ourselves, and may be prohibited in others. We are therefore exactly in the situation of a city besieged, which is surrounded by the works of the besiegers in every part but one. If that is closed up, no step can be taken, but to surrender at discretion. If Great Britain can order us to come to her for necessaries we want, and can order us to pay what taxes she pleases before we take them away, or when we land them here, we are as abject slaves as France and Poland can show in wooden shoes and with uncombed hair.

Perhaps the nature of the necessities of dependent states, caused by the policy of a governing one, for her own benefit, may be elucidated by a fact mentioned in history. When the Carthaginians were possessed of the island of Sardinia, they made a decree, that the Sardinians should not raise corn, nor get it any other way than from the Carthaginians. Then, by imposing any duties they would upon it, they drained from the miserable Sardinians any sums they pleased; and whenever that oppressed people made the least movement to assert their liberty, their tyrants starved them to death or submission. This may be called the most perfect kind of political necessity.

A FARMER

Source: Marion Mills Miller, *Great Debates in American History* (New York: Current Literature Publishing, 1918), 1:38–42, and http://douglass.speech.nwu.edu/stam _a53.htm.

DOCUMENT 9: Thoughts on Government, Letter of John Adams, January 1776

In January, John Adams put on paper his *Thoughts on Government*, which became one of the most influential documents in American history. One of Adams's important maxims was the idea of representation. He challenged the Whig thinking of virtual representation in the British House of Commons—that the people as a whole were somehow represented in Parliament. Adams in *Thoughts on Government* expressed the belief that a representative assembly "should be in miniature an exact portrait of the people at large." He continued, "It should think, feel, reason, and act like them." His description of a "continental constitution" pointed the way to federalism, with a general government assuming responsibilities of an inclusive nature and states maintaining jurisdiction over affairs within their respective borders. His Massachusetts model for state constitutions laid a foundation for the U.S. Constitution.

* * *

MY DEAR SIR,—If I was equal to the task of forming a plan for the government of a colony, I should be flattered with your request, and very happy to comply with it; because, as the divine science of politics is the science of social happiness, and the blessings of society depend entirely on the constitutions of government, which are generally institutions that last for many generations, there can be no employment more agreeable to a benevolent mind than a research after the best.

. . .

We ought to consider what is the end of government, before we determine which is the best form. Upon this point all speculative politicians will agree, that the happiness of society is the end of government, as all divines and moral philosophers will agree that the happiness of the individual is the end of man. From this principle it will follow, that the form of government which communicates ease, comfort, security, or, in one word, happiness, to the greatest number of persons, and in the greatest degree, is the best.

. . .

If there is a form of government, then, whose principle and foundation is virtue, will not every sober man acknowledge it better calculated to promote the general happiness than any other form?

Fear is the foundation of most governments; but it is so sordid and brutal a passion, and renders men in whose breasts it predominates so stupid and miserable, that Americans will not be likely to approve of any political institution which is founded on it.

Honor is truly sacred, but holds a lower rank in the scale of moral excellence than virtue. Indeed, the former is but a part of the latter, and consequently has not equal pretensions to support a frame of government productive of human happiness.

The foundation of every government is some principle or passion in the minds of the people. The noblest principles and most generous affections in our nature, then, have the fairest chance to support the noblest and most generous models of government.

A man must be indifferent to the sneers of modern English men, to mention in their company the names of Sidney, Harrington, Locke, Milton, Nedham, Neville, Burnet, and Hoadly. No small fortitude is necessary to confess that one has read them. The wretched condition of this country, however, for ten or fifteen years past, has frequently reminded me of their principles and reasonings. They will convince any candid mind, that there is no good government but what is republican. That the only valuable part of the British constitution is so; because the very definition of a republic is "an empire of laws, and not of men." That, as a republic is the best of governments, so that particular arrangement of the powers of society, or, in other words, that form of government which is best contrived to secure an impartial and exact execution of the laws, is the best of republics.

Of republics there is an inexhaustible variety, because the possible combinations of the powers of society are capable of innumerable variations.

As good government is an empire of laws, how shall your laws be made? In a large society, inhabiting an extensive country, it is impossible that the whole should assemble to make laws. The first necessary step, then, is to depute power from the many to a few of the most wise and good. But by what rules shall you choose your representatives? Agree upon the number and qualifications of persons who shall have the benefit of choosing, or annex this privilege to the inhabitants of a certain extent of ground.

The principal difficulty lies, and the greatest care should be employed, in constituting this representative assembly. It should be in miniature an exact portrait of the people at large. It should think, feel, reason, and act like them. That it may be the interest of this assembly to do strict justice at all times, it should be an equal representation, or, in other words, equal interests among the people should have equal interests in it. Great care should be taken to effect this, and to prevent unfair, partial, and corrupt elections. Such regulations, however, may be better made in times of greater tranquillity than the present; and they will spring up themselves naturally, when all the powers of government come to be in the hands of the people's friends. At present, it will be safest to proceed in all established modes, to which the people have been familiarized by habit.

A representation of the people in one assembly being obtained, a question arises, whether all the powers of government, legislative, executive, and judicial, shall be left in this body? I think a people cannot be long free, nor ever happy, whose government is in one assembly. My reasons for this opinion are as follow:—

1. A single assembly is liable to all the vices, follies, and frailties of an individual; subject to fits of humor, starts of passion, flights of enthusiasm, partialities, or prejudice, and consequently productive of hasty results and absurd judgments. And all these errors ought to be corrected and defects supplied by some controlling power.

2. A single assembly is apt to be avaricious, and in time will not scruple to exempt itself from burdens, which it will lay, without compunction, on its constituents.

3. A single assembly is apt to grow ambitious, and after a time will not hesitate to vote itself perpetual. This was one fault of the Long Parliament; but more remarkably of Holland, whose assembly first voted themselves from annual to septennial, then for life, and after a course of years, that all vacancies happening by death or otherwise, should be filled by themselves, without any application to constituents at all.

4. A representative assembly, although extremely well qualified, and absolutely necessary, as a branch of the legislative, is unfit to exercise the executive power, for want of two essential properties, secrecy and dispatch.

5. A representative assembly is still less qualified for the judicial power, because it is too numerous, too slow, and too little skilled in the laws.

6. Because a single assembly, possessed of all the powers of government, would make arbitrary laws for their own interest, execute all laws arbitrarily for their own interest, and adjudge all controversies in their own favor.

But shall the whole power of legislation rest in one assembly? Most of the foregoing reasons apply equally to prove that the legislative power ought to be more complex; to which we may add, that if the legislative power is wholly in one assembly, and the executive in another, or in a single person, these two powers will oppose and encroach upon each other, until the contest shall end in war, and the whole power, legislative and executive, be usurped by the strongest.

The judicial power, in such case, could not mediate, or hold the balance between the two contending powers, because the legislative would undermine it. And this shows the necessity, too, of giving the executive power a negative upon the legislative, otherwise this will be continually encroaching upon that.

To avoid these dangers, let a distinct assembly be constituted, as a mediator between the two extreme branches of the legislature, that which represents the people, and that which is vested with the executive power.

Let the representative assembly then elect by ballot, from among themselves or their constituents, or both, a distinct assembly, which, for the sake of perspicuity, we will call a council. It may consist of any number you please, say twenty or thirty, and should have a free and independent exercise of its Judgment, and consequently a negative voice in the legislature.

These two bodies, thus constituted, and made integral parts of the legislature, let them unite, and by joint ballot choose a governor, who, after being stripped of most of those badges of domination, called prerogatives, should have a free and independent exercise of his judgment, and be made also an integral part of the legislature. This, I know, is liable to objections; and, if you please, you may make him only president of the council, as in Connecticut. But as the governor is to be invested with the executive power, with consent of council, I think he ought to have a negative upon the legislative. If he is annually elective, as he ought to be, he will always have so much reverence and affection for the people, their representatives and counsellors, that, although you give him an independent exercise of his judgment, he will seldom use it in opposition to the two houses, except in cases the public utility of which would be conspicuous; and some such cases would happen.

In the present exigency of American affairs, when, by an act of Parliament, we are put out of the royal protection, and consequently discharged from our allegiance, and it has become necessary to assume government for our immediate security, the governor, lieutenant-governor, secretary, treasurer, commissary, attorney-general, should be chosen by joint ballot of both houses. And these and all other elections, especially of representatives and counsellors, should be annual, there not being in the whole circle of the sciences a maxim more infallible than this, "where annual elections end, there slavery begins."

. . .

This will teach them the great political virtues of humility, patience, and moderation, without which every man in power becomes a ravenous beast of prey.

This mode of constituting the great offices of state will answer very well for the present; but if by experiment it should be found inconvenient, the legislature may, at its leisure, devise other methods of creating them, by elections of the people at large, as in Connecticut, or it may enlarge the term for which they shall be chosen to seven years, or three years, or for life, or make any other alterations which the society shall find productive of its ease, its safety, its freedom, or, in one word, its happiness.

A rotation of all offices, as well as of representatives and counsellors, has many advocates, and is contended for with many plausible arguments. It would be attended, no doubt, with many advantages; and if the society has a sufficient number of suitable characters to supply the great number of vacancies which would be made by such a rotation, I can see no objection to it. These persons may be allowed to serve for three years, and then be excluded three years, or for any longer or shorter term.

. . .

The dignity and stability of government in all its branches, the morals of the people, and every blessing of society depend so much upon an upright and skillful administration of justice, that the judicial power ought to be distinct from both the legislative and executive, and independent upon both, that so it may be a check upon both, as both should be checks upon that. The judges, therefore, should be always men of learning and experience in the laws, of exemplary morals, great patience, calmness, coolness, and attention. Their minds should not be distracted with jarring interests; they should not be dependent upon any man, or body of men. To these ends, they should hold estates for life in their offices; or, in other words, their commissions should be during good behavior, and their salaries ascertained and established by law. For misbehavior, the grand inquest of the colony, the house of representatives, should impeach them before the governor and council, where they should have time and opportunity to make their defense; but, if convicted, should be removed from their offices, and subjected to such other punishment as shall be thought proper.

. . .

A constitution founded on these principles introduces knowledge among the people, and inspires them with a conscious dignity becoming freemen; a general emulation takes place, which causes good humor, sociability, good manners, and good morals to be general. That elevation of sentiment inspired by such a government, makes the common people brave and enterprising. That ambition which is inspired by it makes them sober, industrious, and frugal. You will find among them some elegance, perhaps, but more solidity; a little pleasure, but a great deal of business; some politeness, but more civility. If you compare such a country with the regions of domination, whether monarchical or aristocratical, you will fancy yourself in Arcadia or Elysium.

If the colonies should assume governments separately, they should be left entirely to their own choice of the forms; and if a continental constitution should be formed, it should be a congress, containing a fair and adequate representation of the colonies, and its authority should sacredly be confined to these cases, namely, war, trade, disputes between colony and colony, the post office, and the unappropriated lands of the crown, as they used to be called.

These colonies, under such forms of government, and in such a union, would be unconquerable by all the monarchies of Europe.

Source: John Adams, "Thoughts on Government," in Charles S. Hyneman and Donald S. Lutz, eds., *American Political Writing During the Founding Era* (Indianapolis: Liberty Fund, 1983), 1:402–409.

DOCUMENT 10: Unanimous Declaration of the Thirteen United States of America, July 1776

The Declaration of Independence was not written in a vacuum. According to Thomas Jefferson, the principal author, the document was "an expression of the American Mind." The first paragraph of the Declaration referred to the creation of a new people who were dissolving the ties that had connected them to the English people. From the very beginning of the Declaration, a question is raised: Is the Declaration an agreement among the states or an agreement among one united people at a national level? If the former, the Declaration implied an agreement among thirteen different peoples. Dual citizenship was implied in the Declaration as Jefferson made reference to both state and national peoples. The last paragraph of the Declaration refers to "Free and Independent States." On the other hand, this document refers to "one people" and uses the singular "People" regarding "the good People of these Colonies."

The relationship between state and national peoples remained to be worked out in the Articles of Confederation and the U.S. Constitution. In addition, the Declaration of Independence would become a "higher law" in subsequent debates over important social issues. For example, during the 1850s, William H. Seward (Document 36) would appeal to the Declaration of Independence phrase "all men are created equal" when he challenged John C. Calhoun's (Document 34) interpretation of states' rights.

* * *

When in the Course of human events, it becomes necessary for one people to dissolve the political binds which have connected them with another, and to assume among the Powers of the earth, the separate and equal station to which the Laws of Nature and of Nature's God entitle them, a decent respect to the opinions of mankind requires that they should declare the causes which impel them to the separation.

We hold these truths to be self-evident, that all men are created equal, that they are endowed by their Creator with certain unalienable Rights, that among these are Life, Liberty and the pursuit of Happiness. That to secure these rights, Governments are instituted among Men, deriving their just powers from the consent of the governed, That whenever any Form of Government becomes destructive of these ends, it is the Right of the People to alter or to abolish it, and to institute new Government, laying its foundation on such principles and organizing its powers in such form, as to them shall seem most likely to effect their Safety and Happiness. Prudence, indeed, will dictate that Governments long established should not be changed for light and transient causes; and accordingly all experience hath shown, that mankind are more disposed to suffer, while evils are sufferable, than to right themselves by abolishing the forms to which they are accustomed. But when a long train of abuses and usurpations, pursuing invariably the same Object evinces a design to reduce them under absolute Despotism, it is their right, it is their duty, to throw off such Government, and to provide new Guards for their future security. Such has been the patient sufferance of these Colonies; and such is now the necessity which constrains them to alter their former Systems of Government. The history of the present King of Great Britain is a history of repeated injuries and usurpations, all having in direct object the establishment of an absolute Tyranny over these States. To prove this, let Facts be submitted to a candid world.

He has refused his Assent to Laws, the most wholesome and necessary for the public good.

He has forbidden his Governors to pass Laws of immediate and pressing importance, unless suspended in their operation till his Assent should be obtained; and when so suspended, he has utterly neglected to attend to them.

He has refused to pass other Laws for the accommodation of large districts of people, unless those people would relinquish the right of Representation in the Legislature, a right inestimable to them and formidable to tyrants only.

He has called together legislative bodies at places unusual, uncomfortable, and distant from the depository of their Public Records, for the sole purpose of fatiguing them into compliance with his measures.

He has dissolved Representative Houses repeatedly, for opposing with manly firmness his invasions on the rights of the people.

He has refused for a long time, after such dissolutions, to cause others to be elected; whereby the Legislative Bowers, incapable of Annihilation, have returned to the People at large for their exercise; the State remaining in the mean time exposed to all the dangers of invasion from without, and convulsions within.

He has endeavored to prevent the population of these States; for that purpose obstructing the Laws of Naturalization of Foreigners; refusing to pass others to encourage their migration hither, and raising the conditions of new Appropriations of Lands.

He has obstructed the Administration of Justice, by refusing his Assent to Laws for establishing Judiciary Powers.

He has made Judges dependent on his Will alone, for the tenure of their offices, and the amount and payment of their salaries.

He has erected a multitude of New Offices, and sent hither swarms of Officers to harass our People, and eat out their substance.

He has kept among us, in times of peace, Standing Armies without the Consent of our legislature.

He has affected to render the Military independent of and superior to the Civil Power.

He has combined with others to subject us to a jurisdiction foreign to our constitution, and unacknowledged by our laws; giving his Assent to their acts of pretended legislation:

For quartering large bodies of armed troops among us:

For protecting them, by a mock Trial, from Punishment for any Murders which they should commit on the Inhabitants of these States:

For cutting off our Trade with all parts of the world:

For imposing taxes on us without our Consent:

For depriving us in many cases, of the benefits of Trial by jury:

For transporting us beyond Seas to be tried for pretended offenses:

For abolishing the free System of English Laws in a neighboring Province, establishing therein an Arbitrary government, and enlarging its Boundaries so as to render it at once an example and fit instrument for introducing the same absolute rule into these Colonies:

For taking away our Charters, abolishing our most valuable Laws, and altering fundamentally the Forms of our Governments:

For suspending our own Legislature, and declaring themselves invested with Power to legislate for us in all cases whatsoever.

He has abdicated Government here, by declaring us out of his Protection and waging War against us.

He has plundered our seas, ravaged our Coasts, burnt our towns, and destroyed the lives of our people.

He is at this time transporting large armies of foreign mercenaries to complete the works of death, desolation and tyranny, already begun with circumstances of Cruelty & perfidy scarcely paralleled in the most barbarous ages, and totally unworthy the Head of a civilized nation.

He has constrained our fellow Citizens taken Captive on the high Seas to bear Arms against their Country, to become the executioners of their friends and Brethren, or to fall themselves by their Hands.

He has excited domestic insurrections amongst us, and has endeavored to bring on the inhabitants of our frontiers, the merciless Indian Savages, whose known rule of warfare, is an undistinguished destruction of all ages, sexes and conditions.

In every stage of these Oppressions We have Petitioned for Redress in the most humble terms: Our repeated Petitions have been answered only by repeated injury. A Prince, whole character is thus marked by every act which may define a Tyrant, is unfit to be the ruler of a free People.

Nor have We been wanting in attention to our British brethren. We have warned them from time to time of attempts by their legislature to extend an unwarrantable jurisdiction over us. We have reminded them of the circumstances of our emigration and settlement here. We have appealed to their native justice and magnanimity, and we have conjured them by the ties of our common kindred to disavow these usurpations, which, would inevitably interrupt our connections and correspondence. They too have been deaf to the voice of justice and of consanguinity. We must, therefore, acquiesce in the necessity, which denounces our Separation, and hold them, as we hold the rest of mankind, Enemies in War, in Peace Friends.

We, therefore, the Representatives of the United States of America, in General Congress Assembled, appealing to the Supreme Judge of the world for the rectitude of our intentions, do, in the Name, and by Authority of the good People of these Colonies, solemnly publish and declare, That these United Colonies are, and of Right ought to be Free and Independent States; that they are Absolved from all Allegiance to the British Crown, and that all political connection between them and the State of Great Britain, is and ought to be totally dissolved; and that as Free and Independent States, they have full Power to levy War, conclude Peace, contract Alliances, establish Commerce, and to do all other Acts and Things which Independent States may of right do. And for the support of this Declaration, with a firm reliance on the Protection of Divine Providence, we mutually pledge to each other our Lives, our Fortunes and our sacred Honor.

JOHN HANCOCK

Source: Henry Steele Commager, ed., *Documents of American History*, 7th ed. (New York: Appleton-Century-Crofts, 1963), 1:100–102.

DOCUMENT 11: In Defense of State Sovereignty, Thomas Burke, 1777

During meetings of the Continental Congress, representatives created the Articles of Confederation. Some representatives proposed a strong general government; others wanted power to remain in state governments. John Dickinson called for a strong central government. Thomas Burke of North Carolina responded with a states' rights position. His response preceded Antifederalist arguments that would emerge after the writing of the U.S. Constitution a decade later. Burke's ideas lasted through the eighteenth and nineteenth centuries and have persisted to the present day.

In this document Burke referred to provisions established in the Articles of Confederation. The reference to state sovereignty and the retention of states to powers "not expressly delegated" for the general government found their way into the Articles of Confederation as Article II. Burke's writing expressed the sentiments of many founders who advocated states' rights and a weaker central government.

* * *

The more experience I acquire, the stronger is my conviction that *unlimited power can not be safely trusted* to any man or set of men on earth. No men have undertake to exercise authority with intentions more generous and disinterested than the Congress and none seem to have fewer or more feeble motives for increasing the power of their body politic. What could induce individuals blest with peaceable domestic affluence to forego all the enjoyment of a pleasing home, to neglect their private affairs, and at the expense of all their time and some part of their private fortunes, to attend public business under many insurmountable difficulties and inconveniences? What but a generous zeal for the public? And what can induce such men to endeavor at increasing the power with which they are invested, when their tenure of it must be exceedingly dangerous and precarious and can bring them individually neither pleasure or profit? This is a question I believe cannot be answered but by a plain declaration that power of all kinds has an irresistible propensity to increase a desire for itself. It gives the passion of ambition a velocity which increases in its progress, and this is a passion which grow in proportion as it is gratified. . . . Great part of our time is consumed in debates, whose object on one side is to increase the power of Congress, and on the other to restrain it. The advocates do not always keep the same side of the contest. The same persons who on one day endeavor to carry through some resolutions, whose tendency is to increase the power of Congress, are often on another day very strenuous advocates to restrain it. From this I infer that no one has entertained a concerted design to increase the power; and the attempts to do it proceed from ignorance of what such a being ought to be, and from the delusive intoxication which power naturally imposes on the human mind. . . .

These and many other considerations make me earnestly wish that the power of Congress was accurately defined and that there were adequate checks provided to prevent any excess. . . .

I enclose you an abstract of the debates in Congress on every question of any consequence that has been determined in Congress since my last. . . . The last matter in the abstract will show you that even thus early, men so eminent as members of Congress are willing to explain away any power that stands in the way of their particular purposes. What may we not expect sometime hence when the seat of power shall become firm by habit and men will be accustomed to obedience, and perhaps forgetful of the original principles which gave rise thereto. I believe Sir the root of the evil is deep in human nature. Its growth may be kept down but it cannot be entirely extirpated [destroyed completely]. Power will sometime or other be abused unless men are well watched, and checked by something they cannot remove when they please. At present, nothing but executive business is done, except the Confederation, and on mere executive business there are seldom any debates; (and still more seldom any worth remembering). We have agreed to three articles; one containing the name; the second a declaration of the sovereignty of the States; and an express provision that they be considered as retaining every power not expressly delegated; and the third an agreement mutually to assist each other against every enemy. The first and latter passed without opposition or dissent, the second occasioned two days debate. It stood originally the third article; and expressed only a reservation of the power of regulating the internal police, and consequently resigned every other power. It appeared to me that this was not what the States expected, and, I thought, it left it in the power of the future Congress or General Council to explain away every right belonging to the States and to make their own power as unlimited as they please. I proposed, therefore an amendment which held up the principle that all sovereign power was in the States separately, and that particular acts of it, which should be expressly enumerated, would be exercised in conjunction, and not otherwise; but that in all things else each state would exercise all the rights and power of sovereignty, uncontrolled. This was at first so little under-stood that it was some time before it was seconded, and South Carolina first took it up. The opposition was made by Mr. Wilson of Pennsylvania, and Mr. R.H. Lee of Virginia. In the end, however, the question was carried for my proposition, eleven ayes, one no, and one divided. The no was Virginia; the divided, New Hampshire. I was much pleased to find the opinion of accumulating powers to Congress so little supported, and I promised myself, in the whole business I shall find my ideas rel-ative thereto nearly similar to those of most of the States. In a word, Sir, I am of opinion the Congress should have power enough to call out and apply the common strength for the common defence, but not for the partial purposes of ambition. . . .

Source: Letters of Thomas Burke to the Governor of North Carolina, March 11, April 29, 1777, in *Letters of Members of the Continental Congress*, ed. Edmund Cody Burnett (Washington, D.C. Government Printing Office, 1921–1936), 2:294–296, 345–346, as quoted in Alpheus Thomas Mason, ed., *The States Rights Debate: Anti-federalism and the Constitution*, 2nd ed. (New York: Oxford University Press, 1972), pp. 23–24.

DOCUMENT 12: James Madison's "Vices of the Political System," April 1787

One month before the Constitutional Convention, James Madison wrote a memorandum he called "Vices of the Political System." This memorandum became the cornerstone of his belief that the Constitu-tion, once finished, promised a republican solution to the shortcomings and defects that exist in republics. Subsequently, his ideas in "Vices of the Political System" would reappear in speeches when he proposed his plan of government at the Constitutional Convention, letters he would write to friends and colleagues, and writings that were published in the *Federalist* essays.

Madison's thinking about the need for a more energetic government based on republican principles had been developing for some time, and he probably worked on this memorandum intermittently for several months before he circulated it. As the time for the Constitutional Con-vention drew near, Madison finished the memorandum in April, in time so others could read it. He hoped that his ideas about government would shape their thinking. Madison wanted to save "the fundamental principle of republican Government."

Madison identified several vices of the American political system.

One was the impotence of the government under the Articles of Confederation. He also spent a great deal of time on the "injustices" of state laws. His chief worry was that unrestricted majorities in state legislatures passed laws that violated the rights of individuals and minorities. The great endeavor then was to provide justice for individuals. In a long section of this document, Madison discussed "Injustices of the laws of the States." This section provides a partial foundation for his ideas to provide a republican remedy for the problems existing in a republican government.

Madison believed in the will of the majority, yet he realized the tendency of majorities to tyrannize minorities. How best to retain majority rule while protecting the rights of individuals and minorities is articulated here. Madison made three important points in his memorandum. First, he called for an "extensive republic" or "enlargement of the sphere" as a way to prevent factions, which he considered dangerous to private rights. Second, he wanted an improvement in the quality of representatives as a way to improve representation in the Republic. And third, he called for a federal veto of state legislation, which was meant as a defensive power to protect the general government from state encroachments. Although a reader might list these three points as equally important, as you read this document decide the importance Madison gave to them. Which of the three proposals does Madison believe is most important? Which of the three are maintained in his other writings? And, most important, how do these three proposals fit in to his overall belief in the "proper sphere" between states and national governments?

* * *

1. Failure of the States to comply with the Constitutional requisitions.

1. This evil has been so fully experienced both during the war and since the peace, results so naturally from the number and independent authority of the States and has been so uniformly examplified in every similar Confederacy, that it may be considered as not less radically and permanently inherent in, than it is fatal to the object of, the present System.

2. Encroachments by the Sates on the federal authority.

2. Examples of this are numerous and repetitions may be foreseen in almost every case where any favorite object of a State shall present a temptation. Among these examples are the wars and Treaties of Georgia with the Indians—The unlicensed compacts between Virginia and Maryland, and between Pena. & N. Jersey—the troops raised and to be kept up by Massts.

3. Violations of the law of nations and of treaties.

3. From the number of Legislatures, the sphere of life from which most of their members are taken, and the circumstances under which their legislative business is carried on, irregularities of this kind must frequently happen. . . .

   As yet foreign powers have not been rigorous in animadverting on us. This moderation however cannot be mistaken for a permanent partiality to our faults, or a permanent security agst. those disputes with other nations, which being among the greatest of public calamities, it ought to be least in the power of any part of the Community to bring on the whole.

4. Trespasses of the States on the rights of each other.

4. These are alarming symptoms, and may be daily apprehended as we are admonished by daily experience. . . .

   The practice of many States in restricting the commercial intercourse with other States, and putting their productions and manufactures on the same footing with those of foreign nations, thought not contrary to the federal articles, is certainly adverse to the spirit of the Union. . . .

5. Want of concert in matters where common interest requires it.

5. This defect is strongly illustrated in the state of our commercial affairs. How much has the national dignity, interest, and revenue suffered from this cause? Instances of inferior moment are the want of uniformity in the laws concerning naturalization & literary property; of provision for national seminaries, for grants of incorporation for national purposes, for canals and other works of general utility, wch. may at present be defeated by the perverseness of particular States whose concurrence is necessary.

6. Want of Guaranty to the States of their Constitutions & laws against internal violence.

6. The confederation is silent on this point and therefore by the second article the hands of the federal authority are tied. . . . According to Republican Theory, Right and power being both vested in the majority, are held to be synonimous. According to fact and experience a minority may in an appeal to force, be an overmatch for the majority. 1. If the minority happen to include all such as possess the skill and habits of military life, & such as possess the great pecuniary resources, one third only may conquer the remaining two thirds. 2. One third of those who participate in the choice of the rulers, may be rendered a majority by the accession of those whose poverty excludes them from a

right of suffrage, and who for obvious reasons will be more likely to join the standard of sedition than that of the established Government. 3. Where slavery exists the republican Theory becomes still more fallacious.

7. Want of sanction to the laws, and of coercion in the Government of the Confederacy.

7. A sanction is essential to the idea of law, as coercion is to that of Government. The federal system being destitute of both, wants the great vital principles of a Political Cons[ti]tution.... The time which has since elapsed has had the double effect, of increasing the light and tempering the warmth, with which the arduous work may be revised. It is no longer doubted that a unanimous and punctual obedience of 13 independent bodies, to the acts of the federal Government, ought not be calculated on....

8. Want of ratification by the people of the articles of Confederation.

8. In some of the States the Confederation is recognized by, and forms a part of the constitution. In others however it has received no other sanction than that of the Legislative authority. From this defect two evils result: 1. Whenever a law of a State happens to be repugnant to an act of Congress, particularly when the latter is of posterior date to the former, it will be at least questionable whether the latter must not prevail; and as the question must be decided by the Tribunals of the State, they will be most likely to lean on the side of the State.
2. As far as the Union of the States is to be regarded as a league of sovereign powers, and not as a political Constitution by virtue of which they are become one sovereign power, so far it seems to follow from the doctrine of compacts, that a breach of any of the articles of the confederation by any of the parties to it, absolves the other parties from their respective obligations, and gives them a right if they chuse to exert it, of dissolving the Union altogether.

9. Multiplicity of laws in the several States.

9. In developing the evils which viciate the political system of the U.S. it is proper to include those which are found within the States individually, as well as those which directly affect the States collectively.... Among the evils then of our situation may well be ranked the multiplicity of laws from which no State is exempt. As far as laws are necessary, to mark with precision the duties of those who are to obey them, and

to take from those who are to administer them a discretion, which might be abused, their number is the price of liberty. As far as the laws exceed this limit, they are a nusance: a nusance of the most pestilent kind. . . .

10. Mutability of the laws of the States.

10. This evil is intimately connected with the former yet deserves a distinct notice as is emphatically denotes a vicious legislation. . . .

11. Injustice of the laws of States.

11. If the multiplicity and mutability of laws prove a want of wisdom, their injustice betrays a defect still more alarming: more alarming not merely because it is a greater evil in itself, but because it brings more into question the fundamental principle of republican Government, that the majority who rule in such Governments, are the safest Guardians both of public Good and of private rights. To what causes is this evil to be ascribed?

These causes lie 1. in the Representative bodies.

2. in the people themselves.

1. Representative appointments are sought from 3 motives. 1. ambition 2. personal interest. 3. public good. Unhappily the two first are proved by experience to be most prevalent. Hence the candidates who feel them, particularly, the second, are most industrious, and most successful in pursuing their object: and forming often a majority in the legislative Councils, with interested views, contrary to the interest, and views, of their Constituents, join in a perfidious sacrifice of the latter to the former. . . .

How frequently too will the honest but unenligh[t]ened representative be the dupe of a favorite leader, veiling his selfish views under the professions of public good, and varnishing his sophistical arguments with the glowing colours of popular eloquence?

2. A still more fatal if not more frequent cause lies among the people themselves. All civilized societies are divided into different interests and factions, as they happen to be creditors or debtors—Rich or poor—husbandmen, merchants or manufacturers—members of different religious sects—followers of different political leaders—inhabitants of different districts—

owners of different kinds of property &c &c In republican Government the majority however composed, ultimately give the law. Whenever therefore an apparent interest or common passion unites a majority what is to restrain them from unjust violations of the rights and interest of the minority, or of individuals? Place three individuals in a situation wherein the interest of each depends on the voice of the others, and give to two of them an interest opposed to the rights of the third? Will the latter be secure? The prudence of every man would shun the danger. The rules & forms of justice suppose & guard against it. Will two thousand in a like situation be less likely to encroach on the rights of one thousand? The contrary is witnessed by the notorious factions & oppressions which take place in corporate towns limited as the opportunities are, and in little republics when uncontrouled by apprehensions of external danger. If an enlargement of the sphere is found to lessen the insecurity of private rights, it is not because the impulse of a common interest or pasion is less predominant in this case with the majority; but because a common interest or passion is less apt to be felt and the requisite combination less easy to be formed by a great than by a small number. The Society becomes broken into a greater variety of interests, of pursuits, of passions, which check each other, whilst those who may feel a common sentiment have less opportunity of communication and concert. . . .

The great desideratum in Government is such a modification of the Sovereignty as will render it sufficiently neutral between the different interests and factions, to control one part of the Society from invading the rights of another, and at the same time sufficiently controuled itself, from setting up an interest adverse to that of the whole Society. In absolute Monarchies, the prince is sufficiently, neutral towards his subjects, but frequently sacrifices their happiness to his ambition or his avarice. In small Republics, the sovereign will is sufficiently controuled from such a Sacrifice of the entire Society, but is not sufficiently neutral towards the parts composing it. As a limited Monarchy tempers the evils of an absolute one; so an extensive Republic meliorates the administration of a small Republic. . . .

Source: James Madison, "Vices of the Political System," in *The Papers of James Madison*, ed. Robert A. Rutland et al. (Chicago: University of Chicago Press, 1975), 9:345–358.

DOCUMENT 13: The Virginia Plan Presented to the Federal Convention, May 29, 1787

Fifteen resolutions constituted the Virginia Plan, which was written largely by James Madison and presented by Edmund Randolph to the delegates attending the Constitutional Convention in Philadelphia. The Virginia Plan served as a starting point for deliberations during the summer of 1787. Madison correctly sensed that delegates did not want patchwork efforts to repair the Articles of Confederation. An effective central government needed an independent source of income and sovereignty. Madison hoped to secure both. Most important, Madison believed the fundamental flaw of the Articles of Confederation was its defective structure. Madison was less concerned with shifting responsibilities to the central government than with ensuring that the central government could properly conduct business in its sphere. Both state and national governments would be empowered to operate in their proper spheres. Madison's call for a federal negative (or veto) was designed to help the central government become "sovereign."

According to the plan, the first chamber in the legislature, the House of Representatives, would elect its members who had been nominated by the "individual legislatures." States would maintain a role in the selection of Senate members. However, this proposal for election of Senate members was altered by the work of John Dickinson of Delaware and Roger Sherman of Connecticut, who proposed that state legislatures should elect members of the U.S. Senate (see Document 14).

* * *

1. Resolved that the Articles of Confederation ought to be so corrected and enlarged as to accomplish the objects proposed by their institution; namely "common defense, security of liberty and general welfare."

2. Resolved therefore that the rights of suffrage in the National Legislature ought to be proportioned to the Quotas of contribution, or to the

number of free inhabitants, as the one or the other rule may seem best in different cases.

3. Resolved that the National Legislature ought to consist of two branches.

4. Resolved that the members of the first branch of the National Legislature ought to be elected by the people of the several States every ____ for the terms of ____; to be of the age of years at least ____, to receive liberal stipends by which they may be compensated for the devotion of their time to public service, to be ineligible to any office established by a particular State, or under the authority of the United States, except those peculiarly belonging to the functions of the first branch, during the term of service, and for the space of after its expiration; to be incapable of re-election for the space of ____ after the expiration of their term of service, and to be subject to recall.

5. Resolved that the members of the second branch of the National Legislature ought to be elected by those of the first, out of a proper number of persons nominated by the individual Legislatures, to be of the age of ____ years at least; to hold their offices for a term sufficient to ensure their independence; to receive liberal stipends, by which they may be compensated for the devotion of their time to public service; and to be ineligible to any office established by a particular State, or under the authority of the United States, except those peculiarly belonging to the functions of the second branch, during the term of service, and for the space of after the expiration thereof.

6. Resolved that each branch ought to possess the right of originating Acts; that the National Legislature ought to be empowered to enjoy the Legislative Rights vested in Congress by the Confederation and moreover to legislate in all cases to which the separate States are incompetent, or in which the harmony of the United States may be interrupted by the exercise of individual Legislation; to negative all laws passed by the several States, contravening in the opinion of the National Legislature the articles of Union; and to call forth the force of the Union against any member of the Union failing in its duty under the articles thereof.

7. Resolved that a National Executive be instituted; to be chosen by the National Legislature for the term of ____ years; to receive punctually, at stated times, a fixed compensation for the services rendered, in which no increase or diminution shall be made so as to affect the Magistracy, existing at the time of the increase or diminution, and to be ineligible a second time; and that besides a general authority to execute the National laws, it ought to enjoy the Executive rights vested in Congress by the Confederation.

8. Resolved that the Executive and a convenient number of the National Judiciary, ought to compose a Council or revision with authority to examine every act of the National Legislature before it shall operate,

and every act of a particular Legislature before a Negative thereon shall be final; and that the dissent of the said Council shall amount to a rejection, unless the Act of the National Legislature be passed again, or that of a particular Legislature be again negatived by ____ of the members of each branch.

9. Resolved that a National Judiciary be established to consist of one or more supreme tribunals, and of inferior tribunals to be chosen by the National Legislature, to hold their offices during good behavior; and to receive punctually at stated times fixed compensation for their services, in which no increase or diminution shall be made so as to affect the persons actually in office at the time of such increase or diminution. That the jurisdiction of the inferior tribunals shall be to hear and determine in the first instance, and of the supreme tribunal to hear and determine in the dernier [the newest fashion] resort, all piracies and felonies on the high seas, captures from an enemy; cases in which foreigners or citizens of other States applying to such jurisdictions may be interested, or which respect the collection of the National revenue; impeachments of any National officers, and questions which may involve the national peace and harmony.

10. Resolved that provision ought to be made for the admission of States lawfully arising within the limits of the United States, whether from a voluntary junction of Government and Territory or otherwise, with the consent of a number of voices in the National legislature less than the whole.

11. Resolved that a Republican Government and the territory of each State, except in the instance of a voluntary junction of Government and territory, ought to be guaranteed by the United States to each State.

12. Resolved that provision ought to be made for the continuance of Congress and their authorities and privileges, until a given day after the reform of the articles of Union shall be adopted, and for the completion of all their engagements.

13. Resolved that provision ought to be made for the amendment of the Articles of Union whensoever it shall seem necessary, and that the assent of the National Legislature ought not to be required thereto.

14. Resolved that the Legislative, Executive, and Judiciary powers within the several States ought to be bound by oath to support the articles of Union.

15. Resolved that the amendments which shall be offered to the Confederation, by the Convention ought at a proper time, or times, after the approbation [approval] of Congress to be submitted to an assembly or assemblies of Representatives, recommended by the several Legislatures to be expressly chosen by the people, to consider and decide thereon.

Source: Henry Steele Commager, ed., *Documents of American History*, 7th ed. (New York: Appleton-Century-Crofts, 1963), 1:134–135.

DOCUMENT 14: John Dickinson of Delaware on Federalism at the Constitutional Convention, June 7, 1787

John Dickinson of Delaware believed in a federal compound, or division of authority. His analysis of the condition of the government mirrored many of James Madison's beliefs. Dickinson felt, however, that just as Madison's "extended republic" should be applied to "meliorate the evils of a small one [republic]," so too he felt the states should have an important role in the federal system. Historian of the Constitutional Convention Max Farrand reported that Dickinson informed Madison that some of the smaller states were warm to the idea of a "good national government." Smaller states, Dickinson was suggesting, wanted a more vigorous national government. Their concern was not how much power the national government was to have. What small states wanted was to avoid the domination of the larger states. Dickinson felt the Virginia Plan's proportional representation in both chambers of the Congress had the potential to destroy the smaller states. Dickinson called for states to be given an agency in the general government.

According to the Virginia Plan, the Senate would be selected by members of the House of Representatives. Dickinson countered this idea, insisting that selection of the Senate should be made by local legislatures. This state involvement would ensure the regular expression of the states as states in the federal system. Their participation, Dickinson argued, would provide stability in the republican experiment.

As a result of Dickinson's efforts, as well as the work of Roger Sherman of Connecticut, it was decided that state legislatures would select members of the Senate in the national legislature. The process of state legislatures' selecting U.S. senators continued until passage of the Seventeenth Amendment in 1913. Since then, U.S. senators have been elected directly by the people of each state.

* * *

The preservation of the States in a certain degree of agency is indispensable. It will produce that collision between the different authorities which should be wished for in order to check each other. To attempt to abolish the States altogether, would degrade the Councils of our Country, would be impracticable, would be ruinous. He compared the proposed National System to the Solar System, in which the States were the planets, and ought to be left to move freely in their proper orbits. The Gentleman from Pennsylvania (Mr. Wilson) wished he said to extinguish these planets. If the State Governments were excluded from all agency in the national one, and all power drawn from the people at large, the consequence would be that the national Government would move in the same direction as the State Governments now do, and would run into all the same mischiefs. The reform would only unite the 13 small streams into one great current pursuing the same course without any opposition whatever. He adhered to the opinion that the Senate ought to be composed of a large number, and that their influence from family weight & other causes would be increased thereby. He did not admit that the Tribunes lost their weight in proportion as their number was augmented and gave a historical sketch of this institution. If the reasoning of [Mr. Madison] was good it would prove that the number of the Senate ought to be reduced below ten, the highest number of the Tribunitial corps.

Source: Notes of Debates in the Federal Convention Reported by James Madison, with a foreword by Adrienne Koch (Athens: Ohio University Press, 1985), pp. 84–85.

DOCUMENT 15: The New Jersey Plan Presented to the Federal Convention, June 15, 1787

William Paterson's New Jersey Plan proposed that the general government would have power to impose taxes and to regulate interstate and foreign commerce. Known as the small state plan, this proposal called for a unicameral legislature with state equality to force concessions from the large state advocates. The New Jersey Plan has been called a "purely federal" plan. The states were to play a major role by administering federal law in the United States. The judicial and executive branches of the general government would supervise the states. Thus, the general government would have relied and operated on the member states. The difference between the New Jersey Plan and the Articles of Confederation was that the general government had powers to act.

* * *

1. Resolved that the Articles of Confederation ought to be so revised, corrected, and enlarged as to render the federal Constitution adequate to the exigencies of Government, and the preservation of the Union.

2. Resolved that in addition to the powers vested in the United States in Congress, by the present existing articles of Confederation, they be authorized to pass acts for raising a revenue, by levying a duty or duties

on all goods or merchandises of foreign growth or manufacture, imported into any part of the United States, by Stamps on paper, vellum or parchment, and by a postage on all letters or packages passing through the general post office, to be applied to such federal purposes as they shall deem proper and expedient; to make rules and regulations for the collection thereof; and the same from time to time, to alter and amend in such manner as they shall think proper: to pass Acts for the regulation of trade and commerce as well with foreign nations as with each other; provided that all punishments, fines, forfeitures and penalties to be incurred for contravening such acts rules and regulations shall be adjudged by the Common law Judiciaries of the State in which any offence contrary to the true intent and meaning of such Acts rules and regulations shall have been committed or perpetrated, with liberty of commencing in the first instance all suits and prosecutions for that purpose, in the superior common law Judiciary in such state, subject nevertheless, for the correction of errors, both in law and fact in rendering Judgment, to an appeal to the Judiciary of the United States.

3. Resolved that whenever requisitions shall be necessary, instead of the rule for making requisitions mentioned in the articles of Confederation, the United States in Congress be authorized to make such requisitions in proportion to the whole number of white and other free citizens and inhabitants of every age sex and condition including those bound to servitude for a term of years and three fifths of all other persons not comprehended in the foregoing description, except Indians not paying taxes; that if such requisitions be not complied with, in the time specified therein, to direct the collection thereof in the non-complying States and for that purpose to devise and pass acts directing and authorizing the same; provided that none of the powers hereby vested in the United States in Congress shall be exercised without the consent of at least States, and in that proportion if the number of Confederated States should hereafter be increased or diminished.

4. Resolved that the United States in Congress be authorized to elect a federal Executive to consist of ＿＿ persons, to continue in office for the term of ＿＿ years, to receive punctually at stated times a fixed compensation for their services, in which no increase or diminution shall be made so as to affect the persons composing the Executive at the time of such increase or diminution, to be paid out of the federal treasury; to be incapable of holding any other office or appointment during their time of service and for ＿＿ years thereafter; to be ineligible a second time, and removable by Congress on application by a majority of the Executives of the several States; that the Executives besides their general authority to execute the federal acts ought to appoint all federal officers not otherwise provided for, and to direct all military operations; provided that none of the persons composing the federal Executive shall on

any occasion take command of any troops so as personally to conduct any enterprise as General or in other capacity.

5. Resolved that a federal Judiciary be established to consist of a supreme tribunal the Judges of which to be appointed by the Executive, and to hold their offices during good behavior, to receive punctually at stated times a fixed compensation for their services in which no increase or diminution shall be made so as to affect persons actually in office at the time of such increase or diminution; that the Judiciary so established shall have authority to hear and determine in the first instance on all impeachments of federal officers, and by way of appeal in the dernier resort in all cases touching the rights of Ambassadors, in all cases of captures from an enemy, in all cases of piracies and felonies on the high Seas, in all cases in which foreigners may be interested, in the construction of any treaty or treaties, or which may arise on any of the Acts for regulation of trade, or the collection of the federal Revenue: that none of the Judiciary shall during the time they remain in office be capable of receiving or holding any other office or appointment during the time of service, or for thereafter.

6. Resolved that all Acts of the United States in Congress made by virtue and in pursuance of the powers hereby and by the articles of Confederation vested in them, and all Treaties made and ratified under the authority of the United States, shall be the supreme law of the respective States so far forth as those Acts or Treaties shall relate to the said States or their Citizens, and that the Judiciary of the several States shall be bound thereby in their decisions, any thing in the respective laws of the Individual States to the contrary notwithstanding; and that if any State, or any body of men in any State shall oppose or prevent carrying into execution such acts or treaties, the federal Executive shall be authorized to call forth the power of the Confederated States, or so much thereof as may be necessary to enforce and compel an obedience to such Acts or an observance of such Treaties.

7. Resolved that provision be made for the admission of new States into the Union.

8. Resolved the rule for naturalization ought to be the same in every State.

9. Resolved that a Citizen of one State committing an offence in another State of the Union, shall be deemed guilty of the same offence as if it had been committed by a Citizen of the State in which the offence was committed.

Source: Notes of Debates in the Federal Convention Reported by James Madison, with a foreword by Adrienne Koch (Athens: Ohio University Press, 1985), pp. 118–121.

DOCUMENT 16: James Madison of Virginia Compares the Virginia and New Jersey Plans at the Constitutional Convention, June 19, 1787

James Madison wanted the national government to be capable of acting directly on the people individually. He had been the major author of the Virginia Plan, which Edmund Randolph read to the delegates who were in attendance in Philadelphia. After William Paterson proposed the New Jersey Plan to the delegates in mid-June, Madison felt it was necessary to respond. He was concerned that the New Jersey Plan would prevent the national government from establishing a direct bond with the people. States, he felt, already had a relationship with their citizens. Madison wanted to affirm an attachment to the national government. Moreover, he was worried that the New Jersey Plan would permit states to encroach on national authority. Madison's call for a federal negative—the power of the national government to veto state laws that violated national powers—was meant to be a defensive measure. Madison did not intend for the national government to use the federal negative in an aggressive and offensive manner. Rather, the national veto would protect the national government from state actions. Madison was fearful that tyranny of the majority operated more easily in local and state frameworks. He thought that protection of the rights of the minority to express their opinions would be most clearly carried out within the larger framework of a national government. Furthermore, Madison was concerned that equal representation of states would lead to unfair representation by overrepresenting less populous states and underrepresenting individuals who lived in states with larger populations.

While reading this document refer to Madison's "Vices of the Political System" (Document 12) to note the similarities in the thinking of the Father of the Constitution.

* * *

Proceeding to the consideration of Mr. Paterson's plan, he stated the object of a proper plan to be twofold. 1. to preserve the Union. 2. to provide a Government that will remedy the evils felt by the States both in their united and individual capacities. Examine Mr. Paterson's plan, & say whether it promises satisfaction in these respects.

1. Will it prevent those violations of the law of nations & Of Treaties

which if not prevented must involve us in the calamities of foreign wars? The tendency of the States to these violations has been manifested in sundry instances. . . . It [The New Jersey Plan of Mr. Paterson] leaves the will of the States as uncontrolled as ever.

2. Will it prevent encroachments on the federal authority? A tendency to such encroachments has been sufficiently exemplified among ourselves, as well in every other confederated republic ancient and Modern. . . . He observed that the plan of Mr. Paterson besides omitting a control over the States as a general defense of the federal prerogatives was particularly defective in two of its provisions. 1. Its ratification was not to be by the people at large, but by the Legislatures. It could not therefore render the acts of Congress in pursuance of their powers even legally paramount to the Acts of the States. 2. It gave to the federal tribunal an appellate jurisdiction only—even in the criminal cases enumerated. . . .

3. Will it prevent trespasses of the States on each other? Of these enough has been already seen. He instanced Acts of Virginia. & Maryland which give a preference to their own citizens in cases where the Citizens of other states are entitled to equality of privileges by the Articles of Confederation. He considered the emissions of paper money & other kindred measures as also aggressions. The States relatively to one an other being each of them either Debtor or Creditor; The Creditor States must suffer unjustly from every emission by the debtor States. We have seen retaliating acts on this subject which threatened danger not to the harmony only, but the tranquillity of the Union. The plan of Mr. Paterson, not giving even a negative on the Acts of the States, left them as much at liberty as ever to execute their unrighteous projects against each other.

4. Will it secure the internal tranquillity of the States themselves? The insurrections in Massachusetts admonished all the States of the danger to which they were exposed. Yet the plan of Mr. P. contained no provisions for supplying the defect of the Confederation on this point. According to the Republican theory indeed, Right & power being both vested in the majority, are held to be synonymous. According to fact & experience, a minority may in an appeal to force be an overmatch for the majority. 1. If the minority happen to include all such as possess the skill & habits of military life, with such as possess the great pecuniary resources, one third may conquer the remaining two thirds. 2. One third of those who participate in the choice of rulers may be rendered a majority by the accession of those whose poverty disqualifies them from a suffrage, & who for obvious reasons may be more ready to join the standard of sedition than that of the established Government. 3. Where slavery exists, the Republican Theory becomes still more fallacious.

5. Will it secure a good internal legislation & administration to the

particular States? In developing the evils which vitiate the political system of the U.S. it is proper to take into view those which prevail within
the States individually as well as those which affect them collectively:
Since the former indirectly affect the whole; and there is great reason to
believe that the pressure of them had a full share in the motives which
produced the present Convention. Under this head he enumerated and
animadverted on 1. the multiplicity of the laws passed by the several
States. 2. the mutability of their laws. 3. the injustice of them. 4. the
impotence of them: observing that Mr. Paterson's plan contained no remedy for this dreadful class of evils, and could not therefore be received
as an adequate provision for the exigencies of the Community.

6. Will it secure the Union against the influence of foreign powers over
its members? He pretended not to say that any such influence had yet
been tried: but it naturally to be expected that occasions would produce
it. . . . The plan of Mr. Paterson, not giving to the general Councils any
negative on the will of the particular States, left the door open for . . .
pernicious machinations among ourselves.

7. He begged the smaller States which were most attached to Mr. Paterson's plan to consider the situation in which it would leave them. In
the first place they would continue to bear the whole expense of maintaining their Delegates in Congress. It ought not to be said that if they
were willing to bear this burden, no others had a right to complain. As
far as it led the small States to forbear keeping up a representation, by
which the public business was delayed, it was evidently a matter of
common concern. . . .

8. He begged them to consider the situation in which they would remain in case their pertinacious adherence to an inadmissible plan, should
prevent the adoption of any plan. The contemplation of such an event
was painful; but it would be prudent to submit to the task of examining
it at a distance, that the means of escaping it might be the more readily
embraced. Let the union of the States be dissolved and one of two consequences must happen. Either the States must remain individually independent & sovereign; or two or more Confederacies must be formed
among them. In the first event would the small States be more secure
against the ambition & power of their larger neighbors, than they would
be under a general Government pervading with equal energy every part
of the Empire, and having an equal interest in protecting every part
against every other part? In the second, can the smaller expect that their
larger neighbors would confederate with them on the principle of the
present confederacy, which gives to each member, an equal suffrage; or
that they would exact less severe concessions from the smaller States,
than are proposed in the scheme of Mr. Randolph?

The great difficulty lies in the affair of Representation; and if this could
be adjusted, all others would be surmountable. . . .

Source: Notes of Debates in the Federal Convention Reported by James Madison, with a foreword by Adrienne Koch (Athens: Ohio University Press, 1985), pp. 140–148.

DOCUMENT 17: James Wilson of Pennsylvania on Federalism at the Constitutional Convention, June 25, 1787

James Wilson shared a belief with James Madison that there was an urgent need to reconstruct the federal system under the Articles of Confederation. Among his contributions to the Constitutional Convention, including the electoral system for electing the president of the United States, Wilson wanted the general government, like the state governments, to be attached to citizens. He played a prominent role in developing the concept that the general government could act consistently on the people.

This speech illustrated the argument surrounding selection of members of the U.S. Senate, the second chamber of the general government's legislature. Wilson mentioned the dual citizenship of the people. He also stressed the attachment the general government should have to the people, not to the states.

* * *

The question is shall the members of the 2d. branch be chosen by the Legislatures of the States? When he considered the amazing extent of country—the immense population which is to fill it, the influence which the Government we are to form will have, not only on the present generation of our people & their multiplied posterity, but on the whole Globe, he was lost in the magnitude of the object. The project of Henry the 4th. & his Statesmen was but the picture in miniature of the great portrait to be exhibited. He was opposed to an election by the State Legislatures. In explaining his reasons it was necessary to observe the twofold relation in which the people would stand. 1. as Citizens of the General Government. 2. as Citizens of their particular State. The General Government was meant for them in the first capacity; the State Governments in the second. Both Governments were derived from the people— both meant for the people—both therefore ought to be regulated on the same principles. The same train of ideas which belonged to the relation of the Citizens to their State Governments were applicable to their relations to the General Government and in forming the latter, we ought to proceed, by abstracting as much as possible from the idea of State

Governments. With respect to the province & objects of the General Government they should be considered as having no existence. The election of the 2d. branch by the Legislatures, will introduce & cherish local interests & local prejudices. The General Government is not an assemblage of States, but of individuals for certain political purposes—it is not meant for the States, but for the individuals composing them; the *individuals* therefore not the *States*, ought to be represented in it: A proportion in this representation can be preserved in the 2d. as well as in the 1st. branch; and the election can be made by electors chosen by the people for that purpose. He moved an amendment to that effect, which was not seconded.

Source: Notes of Debates in the Federal Convention Reported by James Madison, with a foreword by Adrienne Koch (Athens: Ohio University Press, 1985), pp. 188–189.

DOCUMENT 18: The Northwest Ordinance, July 13, 1787

The Northwest Ordinance, written during the summer of 1787, established the equality of future states. It provided a plan of government in the territory north of the Ohio River and east of the Mississippi River. No more than five and no fewer than three states were to be carved out of the territory, which became the states of Ohio, Indiana, Illinois, Michigan, and Wisconsin. The ordinance established a blueprint for admission as a state in the Old Northwest Territory and subsequent additions to the nation.

The Northwest Ordinance was written while the Constitutional Convention was in session in Philadelphia. The Confederation Congress, meeting in New York City, approved the Northwest Ordinance. According to the ordinance, new states were to be equal to the original thirteen states in every (sense). It also provided that citizens of the new states would possess equal rights with citizens of the established states. Because new states were able to enter as equal partners, they would participate in debates of major importance, such as slavery. The very nature of the Old Northwest's population, their interest in agriculture and industry, and the restrictions of the ordinance concerning slavery contributed to the outcomes of public policy issues in the nineteenth century and beyond. The new states with their equal status played an equal role in the federal system.

* * *

Be it ordained by the United States in Congress assembled, That the said territory, for the purposes of temporary government be one district, subject. However, to be divided into two districts, as future circumstances may, in the opinion of Congress make it expedient.

. . .

For the prevention of crimes and injuries, the laws to be adopted or made shall have force in all parts of the district, and for the execution of process, criminal and civil, the governor shall make proper divisions thereof; and he shall proceed from time to time as circumstances may require, to lay out the parts of the district in which the Indian titles shall have been extinguished, into counties and townships, subject however to such alterations as may there-after be made by the legislature.

So soon as there shall be five thousand free male inhabitants of full age in the district, upon giving proof thereof to the governor, they shall receive authority, with time and place, to elect representatives from their counties or townships to represent them in the general assembly: *Provided*, That, for every five hundred free male inhabitants, there shall be one representative, and so on progressively with the number of free male inhabitants shall the right of representation increase until the number of representatives shall amount to twenty-five; after which, the number and proportion of representatives shall be regulated by the legislature: *Provided*, That no person be eligible or qualified to act as a representative unless he shall have been a citizen of one of the United States three years, and be a resident in the district, or unless he shall have resided in the district three years; and, in either case, shall likewise hold in his own right, in fee simple, two hundred acres of land within the same: *Provided, also*, That a freehold in fifty acres of land in the district, having been a citizen of one of the states, and being resident in the district, or the like freehold and two years residence in the district, shall be necessary to qualify a man as an elector of a representative.

The representatives thus elected, shall serve for the term of two years; and, in case of the death of a representative, or removal from office, the governor shall issue a writ to the county or township for which he was a member, to elect another in his stead, to serve for the residue of the term.

The general assembly or legislature shall consist of the governor, legislative council, and a house of representatives. The Legislative Council shall consist of five members, to continue in office five years, unless sooner removed by Congress; any three of whom to be a quorum: and the members of the Council shall be nominated and appointed in the following manner, to wit: As soon as representatives shall be elected, the Governor shall appoint a time and place for them to meet together; and, when met, they shall nominate ten persons, residents in the district, and each possessed of a freehold in five hundred acres of land, and return their names to Congress; five of whom Congress shall appoint and commission to serve as aforesaid: and, whenever a vacancy shall happen in the council by death or removal from office, the house of representatives shall nominate two persons, qualified as aforesaid, for each vacancy, and return their names to Congress; one of whom Congress shall appoint and commission for the residue of the term. And every five years, four months at least before the expiration of the time of service of the members of council, the said house shall nominate ten persons, qualified as aforesaid, and return their names to Congress; five of whom Congress shall appoint and commission to serve as members of the council five years, unless sooner removed. And the governor, legislative council, and house of representatives, shall have authority to make laws in all cases, for the good government of the district, not repugnant to the principles and articles in this ordinance established and declared. And all bills, having passed by a majority in the house, and by a majority in the council, shall be referred to the governor for his assent; but no bill, or legislative act whatever, shall be of any force without his assent. The governor shall have power to convene, prorogue, and dissolve the general assembly, when in his opinion, it shall be expedient.

The governor, judges, legislative council, secretary, and such other officers as Congress shall appoint in the district, shall take an oath or affirmation of fidelity and of office; the governor before the president of congress, and all other offices before the Governor. As soon as a legislature shall be formed in the district, the council and house assembled in one room, shall have authority, by joint ballot, to elect a delegate to Congress, who shall have a seat in Congress, with a right of debating but not of voting during this temporary government.

And, for extending the fundamental principles of civil and religious liberty, which form the basis whereon these republics, their laws and constitutions are erected: to fix and establish those principles as the basis of all laws, constitutions and governments, which forever hereafter shall be formed in the said territory: to provide also for the establishment of States, and permanent government therein, and for their admission to a share in the federal councils on an equal footing with the original States, at as early periods as may be consistent with the general interest:

It is hereby ordained and declared by the authority aforesaid, That the following articles shall be considered as articles of compact between the original States and the people and States in the said territory and forever remain unalterable, unless by common consent, to wit:

ART. 1. No person, demeaning himself in a peaceable and orderly manner, shall ever be molested on account of his mode of worship or religious sentiments in the said territory.

ART. 2. The inhabitants of the said territory shall always be entitled to the benefits of the writ of *habeas corpus,* and or the trial by jury; of a proportionate representation of the people in the legislature; and of judicial proceedings according to the course of the common law. All persons shall be bailable, unless for capital offences, where the proof shall be evident or the presumption great. All fines shall be moderate; and no cruel or unusual punishments shall be inflicted. No man shall be deprived of his liberty or property, but by the judgment of his peers or the law of the land; and, should the public exigencies make it necessary, for the common preservation, to take any person's property, or to demand his particular services, full compensation shall be made for the same. And, in the just preservation of rights and property, it is understood and declared, that no law ought ever to be made, or have force in the said territory, that shall, in any manner whatever, interfere with or affect private contracts or engagements, *bona fide,* and without fraud, previously formed.

ART. 3. Religion, morality, and knowledge, being necessary to good government and the happiness of mankind, schools and the means of education shall forever be encouraged. . . .

ART. 4. The said territory, and the States which may be formed therein shall forever remain a part of this Confederacy of the United States of America, subject to the Articles of Confederation, and to such alterations therein as shall be constitutionally made; and to all the acts and ordinances of the United States in Congress assembled, conformable thereto. The inhabitants and settlers in the said territory shall be subject to pay a part of the federal debts contracted or to be contracted, and a proportional part of the expenses of government, to be apportioned on them by Congress according to the same common rule and measure by which apportionments thereof shall be made on the other States; and the taxes for paying their proportion shall be laid and levied by the authority and direction of the legislatures of the district or districts, or new States, as in the original States, within the time agreed upon by the United States in Congress assembled. . . .

ART. 5. There shall be formed in the said territory, not less than three nor more than five States; and the boundaries of the States. . . . The eastern State shall be bounded by the last mentioned direct line, the Ohio Pennsylvania, and the said territorial line: *Provided, however,* and it is further understood and declared, that the boundaries of these three States shall be subject so far to be altered, that, if Congress shall hereafter find it expedient, they shall have authority to form one or two States in that part of the said territory which lies north of an east and west line drawn through the southerly bend or extreme of lake Michigan. And whenever any of the said States, shall have sixty thousand free inhabitants therein, such State shall be admitted, by its delegates, into the Congress of the United States, *on an equal footing with the original States in all respects whatever*, [italics added] and shall be at liberty to form a permanent constitution and State government: *Provided*, the constitution and government so to be formed, shall be republican, and in conformity to the principles contained in these articles; and, so far as it can be consistent with the general interest of the confederacy, such admission shall be allowed at an earlier period, and when there may be a less number of free inhabitants in the State than sixty thousand.

ART. 6. There shall be neither slavery nor involuntary servitude in the said territory, otherwise than in the punishment of crimes whereof the party shall have been duly convicted: *Provided, always*, That any person escaping into the same, from whom labor or service is lawfully claimed in any one of the original States, such fugitive may be lawfully reclaimed and conveyed to the person claiming his or her labor or service as aforesaid. . . .

Source: Henry Steele Commager, ed., *Documents of American History*, 7th ed. (New York: Appleton-Century-Crofts, 1963), pp. 128–132.

DOCUMENT 19: *Federalist* Number 10, Publius and the Extended Republic, November 22, 1787

James Madison's *Federalist* Number 10 has become one of the most important documents concerning states' rights and American federalism. Written in November 1787, it was Madison's first of twenty-nine contributions to the eighty-five *Federalist* essays. At the time of its writing and throughout the nineteenth century as well, the Tenth *Federalist* was considered no more important than any other of the other *Federalist* essays. In 1913 the Tenth *Federalist* gained recognition as the most important essay. Historian Charles Beard was the first to elevate the importance of the Tenth *Federalist*. He viewed it as supporting an economic interpretation of the writing of the Constitution. Beard drew the conclusion that the Constitution was a reform intended as a counter-revolution with differing classes struggling for power. This interpretation dominated the first half of the twentieth century and still has supporters. The Tenth *Federalist*'s status has persisted throughout the twentieth century, with no fewer than four additional scholarly interpretations contributing to its higher importance among the eighty-five *Federalist* essays (refer to the Part I essay).

James Madison did not believe the Tenth *Federalist* should stand alone. In reading *Federalist* Number 10, it may be appropriate to add the following passage taken from *Federalist* Number 51:

In the extended republic of the United States, and among the great variety of interests, parties and sects which it embraces, a coalition of a majority of the whole society could seldom take place on any other principles than those of justice and the general good; and there being thus less danger to a minor from the will of the major party, there must be less pretext also, to provide for the security of the former, by introducing into the government a will not dependent on the latter; or in other words, a will independent of the society itself. It is no less certain than it is important, notwithstanding the contrary opinions which have been entertained, that the larger the society, *provided it lie within a practicable sphere* [italics added], the more duly capable it will be of self government. And happily for the *republican cause*, the practicable sphere may be carried to a very great extent, by a judicious modification and mixture of the *federal principle*.

By reading this passage in conjunction with *Federalist* Number 10 we have a clearer understanding of Madison's intent to "extend the sphere." Madison sought a practicable sphere that included a "middle ground" where both state and national governments could secure rights of the individual. He sought to repair the defects of government, which had plagued the nation and its citizens under the Articles of Confederation, with a "middle ground" of the federalism principle.

* * *

AMONG the numerous advantages promised by a well-constructed Union, none deserves to be more accurately developed than its tendency to break and control the violence of faction. The friend of popular governments never finds himself so much alarmed for their character and fate, as when he contemplates their propensity to the dangerous vice. He will not fail, therefore, to set a due value on any plan which, without violating the principles to which he is attached, provides a proper cure for it. The instability, injustice, and confusion introduced into the public councils, have, in truth, been the mortal diseases under which popular governments have everywhere perished; as they continue to be the favorite and fruitful topics from which the adversaries to liberty derive their most specious declamations. The valuable improvements made by the American constitutions on the popular models, both ancient and modern, cannot certainly be too much admired; but it would be an unwarrantable partiality, to contend that they have as effectually obviated the danger on this side, as was wished and expected. Complaints are everywhere heard from our most considerate and virtuous citizens, equally the friends of public and private faith, and of public and personal liberty, that our governments are too unstable, that the public good is disregarded in the conflicts of rival parties, and that measures are too often decided, not according to the rules of justice and the rights of the minor party, but by the superior force of an interested and overbearing majority. However anxiously we may wish that these complaints had no foundation, the evidence of known facts will not permit us to deny that they are in some degree true. It will be found, indeed, on a candid review of our situation, that some of the distresses under which we labor have been erroneously charged on the operation of our governments; but it will be found, at the same time, that other causes will not alone account for many of our heaviest misfortunes; and, particularly, for that prevailing and increasing distrust of public engagements, and alarm for private rights, which are echoed from one end of the continent to the other. These must be chiefly, if not wholly, effects of the unsteadiness and injustice with which a factious spirit has tainted our public administrations.

By a faction, I understand a number of citizens, whether amounting to a majority or minority of the whole, who are united and actuated by some common impulse of passion, or of interest, adverse to the rights of other citizens, or to the permanent and aggregate interests of the community.

There are two methods of curing the mischiefs of faction: the one, by removing its causes; the other, by controlling its effects.

There are again two methods of removing the causes of faction: the one, by destroying the liberty which is essential to its existence; the other, by giving to every citizen the same opinions, the same passions, and the same interests.

It could never be more truly said than of the first remedy, that it was worse than the disease. Liberty is to faction what air is to fire, an aliment without which it instantly expires. But it could not be less folly to abolish liberty, which is essential to political life, because it nourishes faction, than it would be to wish the annihilation of air, which is essential to animal life, because it imparts to fire its destructive agency.

The second expedient is as impracticable as the first would be unwise. As long as the reason of man continues fallible, and he is at liberty to exercise it, different opinions will be formed. As long as the connection subsists between his reason and his self-love, his opinions and his passions will have a reciprocal influence on each other; and the former will be objects to which the latter will attach themselves.

The diversity in the faculties of men, from which the rights or property originate, is not less an insuperable obstacle to a uniformity of interests. The protection of these faculties is the first object of government. From the protection of different and unequal faculties of acquiring property, the possession of different degrees and kinds of property immediately results; and from the influence of these on the sentiments and views of the respective proprietors, ensues a division of the society into different interests and parties.

The latent causes of faction are thus sown in the nature of man; and we see them everywhere brought into different degrees of activity, according to the different circumstances of civil society. . . .

But the most common and durable source of factions has been the various and unequal distribution of property. Those who hold and those who are without property have ever formed distinct interests in society. Those who are creditors, and those who are debtors, fall under a like discrimination. A landed interest, a manufacturing interest, a mercantile interest, a moneyed interest, with many lesser interests, grow up of necessity in civilized nations, and divide them into different classes, actuated by different sentiments and views.

The regulation of these various and interfering interests forms the principal task of modern legislation, and involves the spirit of party and faction in the necessary and ordinary operations of the government.

No man is allowed to be a judge in his own cause, because his interest would certainly bias his judgment, and, not improbably, corrupt his integrity. . . .

It is vain to say that enlightened statesmen will be able to adjust these clashing interests, and render them all subservient to the public good. Enlightened statesmen will not always be at the helm. Nor, in many cases, can such an adjustment be made at all without taking into view indirect and remote considerations, which will rarely prevail over the immediate interest which one party may find in disregarding the rights of another or the good of the whole.

The inference to which we are brought is, that the *causes* of faction cannot be removed, and that relief is only to be sought in the means of controlling its *effects*.

. . . When a majority is included in a faction, the form of popular government, on the other hand, enables it to sacrifice to its ruling passion or interest both the public good and the rights of other citizens. *To secure the public good and private rights against the danger of such a faction, and at the same time to preserve the spirit and the form of popular government, is then the great object to which our inquiries are directed* [italics added]: Let me add that it is the great desideratum by which this form of government can be rescued from the opprobrium [disgrace] under which it has so long labored, and be recommended to the esteem and adoption of mankind.

By what means is this object attainable? Evidently by one of two only. Either the existence of the same passion or interest in a majority at the same time must be prevented, or the majority, having such coexistent passion or interest, must be rendered, by their number and local situation, unable to concert and carry into effect schemes of oppression. If the impulse and the opportunity be suffered to coincide, we well know that neither moral nor religious motives can be relied on as an adequate con-

trol. They are not found to be such on the injustice and violence of individuals, and lose their efficacy in proportion to the number combined
together, that is, in proportion as their efficacy becomes needful.

From this view of the subject it may be concluded that a pure democracy, by which I mean a society consisting of a small number of citizens,
who assemble and administer the government in person, can admit of
no cure for the mischiefs of faction. A common passion or interest will,
in almost every case, be felt by a majority of the whole; a communication
and concert result from the form of government itself; and there is nothing to check the inducements to sacrifice the weaker party or an obnoxious individual. Hence it is that such democracies have ever been
spectacles of turbulence and contention; have ever been found incompatible with personal security or the rights of property; and have in
general been as short in their lives as they have been violent in their
deaths. Theoretic politicians, who have patronized this species of government, have erroneously supposed that by reducing mankind to a perfect equality in their political rights, they would, at the same time, be
perfectly equalized and assimilated in their possessions, their opinions,
and their passions.

A Republic, by which I mean a Government in which the scheme of
representation takes place, opens a different prospect, and promises the
cure for which we are seeking. Let us examine the points in which it
varies from pure democracy, and we shall comprehend both the nature
of the cure and the efficacy which it must derive from the Union.

The two great points of difference between a democracy and a republic
are: first, the delegation of the government, in the latter, to a small number of citizens elected by the rest; secondly, the greater number of citizens, and greater sphere of country, over which the latter may be
extended.

The effect of the first difference is, on the one hand, to refine and
enlarge the public views, by passing them through the medium of a
chosen body of citizens, whose wisdom may best discern the true interest
of their country, and whose patriotism and love of justice will be least
likely to sacrifice it to temporary or partial considerations. Under such
a regulation, it may well happen that the public voice, pronounced by
the representatives of the people, will be more consonant to the public
good than if pronounced by the people themselves, convened for the
purpose. On the other hand, the effect may be inverted. Men of factious
tempers, of local prejudices, or of sinister designs, may, by intrigue, by
corruption, or by other means, first obtain the suffrages, and then betray
the interests, of the people. The question resulting is, whether small or
extensive republics are more favorable to the election of proper guardians of the public weal; and it is clearly decided in favor of the latter by
two obvious considerations.

. . .

It must be confessed that in this, as in most other cases, there is a mean, on both sides of which inconveniences will be found to lie. By enlarging too much the number of electors, you render the representative too little acquainted with all their local circumstances and lesser interests; as by reducing it too much, you render him unduly attached to these, and too little fit to comprehend and pursue great and national objects. The federal Constitution forms a *happy combination* [italics added] in this respect; the great and aggregate interests being referred to the national, the local and particular to the State legislatures.

The other point of difference is, the greater number of citizens and extent of territory which may be brought within the compass of republican than of democratic government; and it is this circumstance principally which renders factious combinations less to be dreaded in the former than in the latter. The smaller the society, the fewer probably will be the distinct parties and interests composing it; the fewer the distinct parties and interests, the more frequently will a majority be found of the same party; and the smaller the number of individuals composing a majority, and the smaller the compass within which they are placed, the more easily will they concert and execute their plans of oppression. *Extend the sphere, and you take in a greater variety of parties and interests; you make it less probable that a majority of the whole will have a common motive to invade the rights of other citizens; or if such a common motive exists, it will be more difficult for all who feel it to discover their own strength, and to act in unison with each other* [italics added]. Besides other impediments, it may be remarked that, where there is a consciousness of unjust or dishonorable purposes, communication is always checked by distrust in proportion to the number whose concurrence is necessary.

Hence, it clearly appears, that the same advantage which a republic has over a democracy, in controlling the effects of faction, is enjoyed by a large over a small republic—is enjoyed by the Union over the States composing it. Does the advantage consist in the substitution of representatives whose enlightened views and virtuous sentiments render them superior to local prejudices and to schemes of injustice? It will not be denied that the representation of the Union will be most likely to possess these requisite endowments. Does it consist in the greater security afforded by a greater variety of parties, against the event of any one party being able to outnumber and oppress the rest? In an equal degree does the increased variety of parties comprised within the Union, increase this security. Does it, in fine, consist in the greater obstacles opposed to the concert and accomplishment of the secret wishes of an unjust and interested majority? Here, again, the extent of the Union gives it the most palpable advantage.

The influence of factious leaders may kindle a flame within their par-

ticular States, but will be unable to spread a general conflagration
through the other States. . . .

  . . .

In the extent and proper structure of the Union, therefore, we behold
a *republican remedy* [italics added] for the diseases most incident to republican government. And according to the degree of pleasure and pride
we feel in being republicans, ought to be our zeal in cherishing the spirit
and supporting the character of Federalists.

Source: The Federalist, ed. Jacob E. Cooke (Cleveland: World Publishing Company,
1961), *Federalist* Number 10, pp. 56–65. For further understandings of James Madison's view regarding the relationships between state and national governments
see Madison's comments in 1791 and 1792 published in the *National Gazette*. His
call for a balanced federal system of government can be found in Lance Banning,
Jefferson and Madison: Three Conversations from the Founding (Madison, Wis.: Madison House, 1995), pp. 199–202. See also *Federalist* Numbers 14 and 39. In *Federalist* Number 39, Madison wrote, "[t]he proposed Constitution . . . is . . . neither a
national nor federal Constitution, but a composition of both."

DOCUMENT 20: Agrippa Writes a Letter to the People in Opposition to an Extended Republic and the Constitution of the United States, December 3, 1787

The Antifederalist Agrippa wrote a critical assessment of James Madison's call for an "extended republic" as a means to protect individuals'
rights and liberties. In a letter to the Boston *Massachusetts Gazette*,
Agrippa reemphasized the arguments of Montesquieu that a republican
government operated best in a small geographic entity and questioned
whether legislation could be uniformly applied across large and varied
territories. Despotism and misery, Agrippa predicted, would result from
a uniform national state. Most scholars believe that James Winthrop, a
librarian of Harvard, a postmaster of Cambridge, and eventual Judge
of Common Pleas, was the author of essays written under the pseudonym Agrippa.

* * *

To the People.

Having considered some of the principal advantages of the happy
form of government under which it is our peculiar good fortune to live,
we find by experience, that it is the best calculated of any form hitherto
invented, to secure to us the right of our persons and of our property,

and that the general circumstances of the people shew an advanced state of improvement never before known. . . .

. . .

Let us now consider how far it is practicable consistent with the happiness of the people and their freedom. It is the opinion of the ablest writers on the subject, that no extensive empire can be governed upon republican principles, and that such a government will degenerate to a despotism, unless it be made up of a confederacy of smaller states, each having the full powers of internal regulation. This is precisely the principle which has hitherto preserved our freedom. No instance can be found of any free government of considerable extent which has been supported upon any other plan. Large and consolidated empires may indeed dazzle the eyes of a distant spectator with their splendour, but if examined more nearly are always found to be full of misery. The reason is obvious. In large states the same principles of legislation will not apply to all the parts. The inhabitants of warmer climates are more dissolute in their manners, and less industrious, than in colder countries. A degree of severity is, therefore, necessary with one which would cramp the spirit of the other. We accordingly find that the very great empires have always been despotick. They have indeed tried to remedy the inconveniences to which the people were exposed by local regulations; but these contrivances have never answered the end. The laws not being made by the people, who felt the inconveniences, did not suit their circumstances. It is under such tyranny that the Spanish provinces languish, and such would be our misfortune and degradation, if we should submit to have the concerns of the whole empire managed by one legislature. To promote the happiness of the people it is necessary that there should be local laws; and it is necessary that those laws should be made by the representatives of those who are immediately subject to the want of them. By endeavouring to suit both extremes, both are injured.

It is impossible for one code of laws to suit Georgia and Massachusetts. They must, therefore, legislate for themselves. Yet there is, I believe, not one point of legislation that is not surrendered in the proposed plan. Questions of every kind respecting property are determinable in a continental court, and so are all kinds of criminal causes. The continental legislature has, therefore, a right to make rule *in all cases* by which their judicial courts shall proceed and decide causes. Nor rights are reserved to the citizens. The laws of Congress are in all cases to be the supreme law of the land, and paramount to the constitutions of the individual states. The Congress may institute what modes of trial they please, and no plea drawn from the constitution of any state can avail. This new system is, therefore, a *consolidation* [italics added] of all states into one large mass, however diverse the parts may be of which it is to be composed. The idea of an uncompounded republick . . . containing six millions of white inhabitants all reduced to the same standards of morals, or habits, and of laws, is in itself an absurdity, and contrary to the whole experience of mankind. . . .

Source: The Anti-Federalist: Writings of the Opponents of the Constitution, ed. Herbert J. Storing, An Abridgement, by Murray Dry (Chicago: University of Chicago Press, 1985), pp. 234–236 and *The Debate on the Constitution: Federalist and Antifederalist Speeches, Articles, and Letters during the Struggle over Ratification* (New York: The Library of America, 1993), 1:448–450.

Part II

Federalism and the Meaning of the Tenth Amendment, 1789–1835

Sitting in the House chamber in the late spring of 1789, James Madison prepared to address his First Congress colleagues on the issue of a Bill of Rights. Many of the amendment proposals were designed overtly to check the power of the national government and would severely damage the structure of government designed by Madison and others in Philadelphia. Although the Constitution had been ratified, threats still loomed that the structure of government as conceived by Madison and prescribed in the Constitution could be altered by the amendatory process. Antifederalist suggestions for amendments did precisely that. Their proposals included strategies to turn loyalty away from the strengthened general government and redirect loyalty to the states. During the ratification period of the Constitution, Antifederalists had even suggested a second general convention. This action, Madison realized, would have undermined the "great work" completed at the Constitutional Convention in Philadelphia.

A separate Bill of Rights, omitted in the Constitution, served as a focal point of opposition for Antifederalists during ratification debates. Now, in 1789, even antifederalists were divided on the importance of a Bill of Rights. A faction of them sincerely thought a Bill of Rights was important. Another faction used the issue of a Bill of Rights as a means to reopen the debates surrounding the Constitution. This group wished to return to a structure of government that elevated the importance and the power of the states and diminished the role of the central government. As Madison stood before his congressional colleagues on June 8, 1789, James Jackson of Georgia upbraided the Virginia representative for interrupting "the more important business" before the House. Jackson curtly responded to Madison's Bill of Rights proposals with a sharp statement: "[T]his is not the time for bringing forward amendments."[1]

Throughout the humiliating ordeal, Madison remained steadfast in seeking to protect liberties without destroying the achievements of the Philadelphia convention. On June 8, he stated before his congressional colleagues that amendments were necessary to "satisfy the public mind that their liberties will be perpetual, and this without endangering any part of the Constitution" (see Document 22). On August 13, Madison insisted that despite the urgency of other business, the people were "also anxious to secure those rights which they are apprehensive are endangered." It was "incumbent" on his colleagues, he said, that "in point of candor and good faith, as well as policy," to "make such alterations in the Constitution as will give satisfaction, without injuring or destroying any of its vital principles."[2]

By the end of the summer of 1789, twelve amendments had emerged from the House of Representatives and the U.S. Senate and were sent to the states for approval. By December 15, 1791, a Bill of Rights (ten of the twelve amendments proposed) had been formally approved by the required number of states and became a distinct part of the Constitution. The First through Ninth Amendments protect the rights of the individual from the national government and prohibit the national government from placing an individual in jeopardy. The Tenth Amendment stresses power relationships in and between state and national governments.

IMPORTANCE OF THE BILL OF RIGHTS IN STATE AND NATIONAL GOVERNMENTS

The Bill of Rights are a prohibition against certain powers of government, not a granting of rights. Enlightenment belief in natural law and common law principles assumes that human beings are rational. In a state of nature, humans have basic rights, but others may intrude upon them. The social contract suggests that human beings must have rules and laws. A tension exists between popular will and the universal proposition of natural or fundamental rights. The majority must have the right to speak, but it might do so by trampling on the rights of the minority. The Constitution has a commitment to popular sovereignty. However, the tension between majority rule and minority rights does not disappear. Article III of the Constitution provides that the law can transcend what people want because the law itself is just. Moreover, rights have fluidity. Although rights are constant, they are filtered through a social order; that is, it may be said that there are no rights without an assertion of them. In different times, then, there is the potential for different rights depending on the energy of those who claim their right has been abused.

Five points are essential to an understanding of rights protection and the relationship to state and national governments. First, it is important to remember that the purpose of a Bill of Rights is to limit government in favor of the individual. Second, the Supreme Court would rule in 1833 that the Bill of Rights applied only against the national government. This application of the Bill of Rights existed during the period 1789 to 1835, would be maintained for the most part through the remainder of the nineteenth century, and would continue well into the twentieth century. Beginning in the 1920s, the Supreme Court would apply the Bill of Rights to the states. The actions of state governments would now be constrained by the rights of individuals as defined in the Bill of Rights. The Supreme Court justices incorporated the Bill of Rights through the Fourteenth Amendment. Such judicial decisions prohibited states from violating an individual's right to life, liberty, and property without due process of law. Third, both state and national governments provided bills of rights, although state bills of rights varied in their quality and capacity to protect individuals. Fourth, when individuals felt their rights were abused, they appealed to either the courts of state or the national government, depending on which would better serve to protect their interests. And fifth, the Tenth Amendment was crucial in establishing the relationship between state and national governments.

APPLICATION OF THE BILL OF RIGHTS

Congress's decision to reject a proposed amendment of Madison against state infringements of essential rights was of historic importance. This decision, made during the first session of the First Congress in 1789, meant that the Bill of Rights applied only to the national government for over one hundred years of the nation's existence. In a very important 1833 Supreme Court case, *Barron v. Baltimore* (see Document 27), the court ruled that the Fifth Amendment did not apply against the states; nor did the other rights in the Bill of Rights apply to the various states. Supreme Court chief justice John Marshall clarified which government was restricted in the relations between the state and federal government by the Bill of Rights.

John Marshall revisited the debate over the Bill of Rights that occurred in Congress in 1789. He recognized that Madison's proposed amendment, which would apply the Bill of Rights against the states, had been rejected and concluded that Congress had settled the matter. His opinion bolstered the states concerning such social issues as retention of slavery and ignoring women's rights. In circumstances concerning the rights and interests of the individual, John Marshall preferred to keep the issue a local concern. He did this because Congress seemingly intended it to be so.

IMPORTANCE OF THE TENTH AMENDMENT

Another issue that involved the Bill of Rights concerned state and national government relations. The issue focused on the importance of the Tenth Amendment.

The first nine amendments deal mainly with the rights of the people relative to the federal government. The Tenth Amendment accommodated states' rights advocates who were upset by the balance of power between the states and the federal government. States' rights advocates pointed directly at two sections of the Constitution that worked against their interests. The first section is the "necessary and proper" clause, which states that Congress has the power "to make all Laws which shall be *necessary and proper* [italics added] for carrying into Execution [its] Powers, and all other Powers vested by this Constitution in the Government of the United States, or in any Department or Officer thereof." The necessary-and-proper clause, found in Article I, section 8, clause 18 of the Constitution, was disturbing to states' rights advocates, who feared it gave too much power to the national government. Their fears were further alarmed by a second section in the Constitution, the supremacy clause (Article VI, section 2):

This Constitution, and the Laws of the United States which shall be made in Pursuance thereof; and all Treaties made, or which shall be made, under the Authority of the United States, shall be the *supreme Law of the Land* [italics added]; and the Judges in every State shall be bound thereby, any Thing in the Constitution or Laws of any State to the Contrary notwithstanding.

States' rights advocates saw these clauses as allocating far too much power to the national government.

Congressional foes of a stronger national government tried to revert the power of the national government to its pre–Constitutional Convention days. They looked to weaken the strength of the new national government by using the language of the Articles of Confederation. Specifically, they employed the language of Article II of the former constitution, which read:

Each state retains its sovereignty, freedom and independence, and every Power, Jurisdiction and right, which is not by this confederation *expressly* [italics added] delegated to the United States, in Congress assembled.

Had states' rights advocates been successful, they would have undone what Madison and others had accomplished at the Constitutional Convention. The success or failure of a stronger national government hinged on one word, *expressly*. Opponents of a more invigorated national government tried to enervate the national government by inserting *expressly* between *not* and *delegated* in the Tenth Amendment. The use of "powers not *expressly* [italics added] delegated to the United States by the Constitution" would have negated the necessary-and-proper clause of the Constitution.

James Madison withstood this alteration that could have changed the scope of the national government's powers and ultimately the direction of state and national government relations. Because of his efforts, the Tenth Amendment read:

The powers not delegated to the United States by the Constitution, nor prohibited by it to the States, are reserved to the States respectively, or to the people.

Madison's actions prompted states' rights advocates in the House to express their reservations with a Bill of Rights that maintained a stronger central government. William Grayson of Virginia summarized their anguish with the comment that "nothing had changed." Grayson further expressed his disappointment with the Bill of Rights as proposed by Madison with the frustrated statement that this was not the Bill of Rights he and his colleagues had called for. James Madison did not permit *structural* changes in the plan of government to occur from the proposed amendments.

Madison's efforts to prevent a reversion to conditions under the Articles of Confederation ultimately led to use of both the general-welfare clause and the necessary-and-proper clause to expand the power of the national government continually. Madison would not agree with Alexander Hamilton's zealous use of the invigorating clauses in the Constitution. Later, Madison felt these clauses enlarged executive authority and legislative authority beyond what he felt were appropriate.

The Tenth Amendment stresses the power relationship that exists between state and national governments. Often referred to as *reserved powers*, the Tenth Amendment provides that powers not given to the national government and at the same time not denied to the states belong to the states. These powers can be large in scope and are often involved in citizens' everyday lives. For instance, the reserved powers permit states to determine the legal age of marriage and the licensing of physicians, lawyers, teachers, beauticians, electricians, and plumbers, to name a few.

The Tenth Amendment raises two important issues. Would the states' reserved powers include authority established prior to the writing of the Constitution? What relationship would the powers of the states have to rights of the individual? Rights of individuals are a characteristic of American legal traditions. Protections to free speech, religious freedom, a jury trial, and the right against self-incrimination are crucial to all individuals. As part of the Bill of Rights, the Tenth Amendment may be regarded as a rights amendment. That is, the words *power* and *rights* are interchanged. Thus, the Tenth Amendment may be used to express the view that "rights not granted to the states are *reserved* to the people."[3] The current emphasis on individual rights has caused jurists to reconceive views regarding the Tenth Amendment. Among the leading scholars, Justice Sandra Day O'Connor has suggested that the Tenth Amendment stresses the protection of dual citizenship rights of state residents rather than protection of traditional states' rights.[4]

Behind the ratified amendments, including the Tenth Amendment, flowed a powerful strain of popular sovereignty. During the 1790s majority rule proved problematic for the constitutional system when the Federalist party passed the Alien and Sedition Acts. The national legislature seemingly violated the First Amendment rights of those who held an opposing political view.[5] In this instance, Madison turned to the states in 1798, as a result of the Sedition Act, to protect individual rights. Madison wrote the Virginia Resolutions; his colleague Thomas Jefferson wrote the Kentucky Resolutions (see Document 24). Both provided a basis for the subsequent compact theory (the Union was created by a compact of the states and the federal government; it could not be the judge of its own powers), that would emerge in the 1830s as a result of John C. Calhoun and his states' rights leadership in South Carolina.

James Madison was ambiguous about the compact theory. In the 1830s he insisted that he never intended this result to follow the logic of nullifiers. Nor would he have agreed to what would eventually occur as acts of secession in the 1860s. Nevertheless, he turned in 1798 to the states to protect individual rights and to keep federal legislative power within its limits. He did this just as he had turned to the national government a decade earlier when states had exercised too much power and he had felt that individual rights were then jeopardized within the sphere of state legislation.

NOTES

1. *The Debates and Proceedings in the Congress of the United States,* compiled by Joseph Gales (Washington, D.C.: Gales and Seaton, 1834–1856), 1:425, 444.

2. Ibid., 433, 706.

3. Linda K. Kerber, "The Meanings of Citizenship," *Journal of American History* 84 (December 1997): 835.

4. John Kincaid, "The Devolution Tortoise and the Centralization Hare," *New England Economic Review* (May–June 1998): 29.

5. John C. Miller, *Crisis in Freedom: The Alien and Sedition Acts* (Boston: Little Brown and Company, 1951).

DOCUMENT 21: George Mason's Objections to the Proposed Constitution, October 1, 1787

George Mason had attended the Constitutional Convention as a delegate from Virginia. Toward the end of the convention, he proposed that a Bill of Rights be added. His proposal was defeated by a unanimous vote, 10–0. As a result, Mason refused to sign the Constitution on September 17. Two weeks later, on October 1, he sent a draft letter expressing his opposition to the new plan of government. His criticism of the new plan set the stage for the major argument of Antifederalists: there was no Bill of Rights. Mason opposed the new Constitution because he felt it gave too much power to the general government. At the forefront of his opposition was the lack of a declaration of rights. The lack of a Bill of Rights was intertwined in state and national government relations and the rights of the individual.

* * *

There is no Declaration of Rights: and the Laws of the general Government being paramount to the Laws and Constitutions of the several States, the Declaration of Rights in the separate States are no Security. Nor are the people secured even in the Enjoyment of the Benefits of the common law: which stands here upon no other Foundation than its having been adopted by the respective Acts forming the Constitutions of the several States.

In the House of Representatives there is not the Substance, but the Shadow only of Representation; which can never produce proper Information in the Legislature, or inspire confidence in the People. . . .

The Senate have the Power of altering all Money-Bills, and of originating Appropriations of Money and the Sallerys of the Officers of their own Appointment in Conjunction with the President of the United States; although they are not the Representatives of the People, or amenable to them.

These with their other great Powers (viz. Their Power in the Appointment of Ambassadors and all public Officers, in making Treaties, and in trying all Impeachments) their Influence upon and Connection with the supreme Executive from these Causes, their Duration of Office, and their being a constant existing Body almost continually sitting, joined with their being one compleat Branch of the Legislature, will destroy any Balance in the Government, and enable them to accomplish what Usurpations they please upon the Rights and libertys of the People.

The Judiciary of the United States is so constructed and extended, as to absorb and destroy the Judiciarys of the several States. . . .

The President of the United States has no constitutional Council (a thing unknown in any safe and regular Government) he will therefore be unsupported by proper Information and Advice; and will generally be directed by Minions and Favourites. . . .

From this fatal Defect of a constitutional Council has arisen the improper Power of the Senate, in the Appointment of public Officers, and the alarming Dependence and Connection between the Branch of the Legislature, and the supreme Executive. . . .

. . .

There is no Declaration of any kind for preserving the Liberty of the Press, the Tryal by Jury in civil Causes; nor against the Danger of standing Armys in time of Peace.

The State Legislatures are restrained from laying Export Duties on their own Produce.

The general Legislature is restrained from prohibiting the further Importation of Slaves for twenty odd Years; though such Importations render the United States weaker, more vulnerable, and less capable of Defence.

Both the general Legislature and the State Legislatures are expressly prohibited [from] making ex post facto Laws; though there never was, or can be a Legislature but must and will make such Laws, when necessity and the public Safety require them; which will hereafter be a Breach of all the Constitutions in the Union, and afford precedents for other Innovations. . . .

Source: Kermit L. Hall, *Major Problems in American Constitutional History* (Lexington, Mass.: D.C. Heath, 1992), 1:182–184 and *The Debates on the Constitution: Federalist and Antifederalist Speeches, Articles, and Letters during the Struggle over Ratification* (New York: The Library of America, 1993), 1:346–349.

DOCUMENT 22: James Madison's Proposal to Congress for a Bill of Rights, June 8, 1789

James Madison was the principal author of the Bill of Rights, a declaration that protects individual liberties from government. Constitutional scholars refer to rights that cannot be taken away as *negative rights*; that is, the government did not give these rights to individuals but individuals possess these rights because they are human beings. Government has no power to bestow or revoke the Bill of Rights.

This document was a response to the list of criticisms originating among Antifederalists. Although Madison initially had opposed a Bill of Rights during and shortly after the Constitutional Convention because he believed there were sufficient protections already in the Constitution, he came to support a declaration of rights as long as it did not alter the structure of government and still secure the rights of the individual. To ensure that no alteration occurred, Madison culled through over two hundred amendment proposals and then submitted a Bill of Rights to members of the House of Representatives on June 8, 1789. Former Antifederalists criticized his proposals and denounced him for wasting their time on trivial matters.

As proposed by Madison, the Bill of Rights would have protected citizens from both state and national government encroachments. Significantly, the Congress rejected Madison's fifth proposal that individual rights should be protected from the actions of state governments. Thus, the rights of the individual were protected only from the actions of the national government. This decision in later years would affect protections of citizens from the state. For example, in *Barron v. Baltimore* (1833) (see Document 27), the Supreme Court ruled that Fifth Amendment protections did not extend to the encroachment of state and local governments. Not until the Fourteenth Amendment, passed after the Civil War, did individuals enjoy protection from state governments, and such protections were not applied until the 1920s.

Throughout James Madison's proposal for a declaration of rights, he linked the relationship of individual rights to state and national governments. His eighth proposal set the stage for the reserved powers clause in what would become the Tenth Amendment to the Constitution.

* * *

It is a fortunate thing that the objection to the Government has been made on the ground I stated; because it will be practicable, on that ground, to obviate the objection, so far as to satisfy the public mind that their liberties will be perpetual, and this without endangering any part of the Constitution, which is considered as essential to the existence of the Government by those who promoted its adoption.

The amendments which have occurred to me proper to be recommended by Congress to the State Legislatures, are these:

First. That there be prefixed to the Constitution a declaration, that all power is originally vested in, and consequently derived from, the people.

That Government is instituted and ought to be exercised for the benefit of the people; which consists in the enjoyment of life and liberty, with the right of acquiring and using property, and generally of pursuing and obtaining happiness and safety.

That the people have an indubitable, unalienable, and indefeasible right to reform or change their Government, whenever it be found adverse or inadequate to the purposes of its institution.

Secondly, That in article 1st, section 2, clause 3, these words be struck out, to wit: "The number of Representatives shall not exceed one for every thirty thousand, but each State shall have at least one Representative, and until such enumeration shall be made," and that in place thereof be inserted these words, to wit: "After the first actual enumeration, there shall be one Representative for every thirty thousand, until the number amount to ____, after which the proportion shall be so regulated by Congress, that the number shall never be less than ____, nor more than ____, but each State shall, after the first enumeration, have at least two Representatives; and prior thereto."

Thirdly. That in article 1st, section 6, clause 1, there be added to the end of the first sentence these words, to wit: "But no law varying the compensation last ascertained shall operate before the next ensuing election of Representatives."

Fourthly. That in article 1st, section 9, between clauses 3 and 4, be inserted these clauses, to wit: The civil rights of none shall be abridged on account of religious belief or worship, nor shall any national religion be established, nor shall the full and equal rights of conscience be in any manner, or on any pretext, infringed.

The people shall not be deprived or abridged of their right to speak, to write, or to publish their sentiments; and the freedom of the press, as one of the great bulwarks of liberty, shall be inviolable.

The people shall not be restrained from peaceably assembling and consulting for their common good; not from applying to the Legislature by petitions, or remonstrances, for redress of their grievances.

The right of the people to keep and bear arms shall not be infringed; a well armed and well regulated militia being the best security of a free country: but no person religiously scrupulous of bearing arms shall be compelled to render military service in person.

No soldier shall in time of peace be quartered in any house without the consent of the owner; nor at any time, but in a manner warranted by law.

No person shall be subject, except in cases of impeachment, to more than one punishment or one trial for the same offence; nor shall be compelled to be a witness against himself; nor be deprived of life, liberty, or property, without due process of law; nor be obliged to relinquish his property, where it may be necessary for public use, without a just compensation.

Excessive bail shall not be required, nor excessive fines imposed, nor cruel and unusual punishments inflicted.

The rights of the people to be secured in their persons, their houses, their papers, and their other property, from all unreasonable searches and seizures, shall not be violated by warrants issued without probable cause, supported by oath or affirmation, or not particularly describing the places to be searched, or the persons or things to be seized.

In all criminal prosecutions, the accused shall enjoy the right to a speedy and public trial, to be informed of the cause and nature of the accusation, to be confronted with his accusers, and the witnesses against him; to have a compulsory process for obtaining witnesses in his favor; and to have the assistance of counsel for his defence.

The exceptions here or elsewhere in the Constitution, made in favor of particular rights, shall not be so construed as to diminish the just importance of other rights retained by the people, or as to enlarge the powers delegated by the Constitution; but either as actual limitations of such powers, or as inserted merely for greater caution.

Fifthly. That in article 1st, section 10, between clauses 1 and 2, be inserted this clause, to wit:

No State shall violate the equal rights of conscience, or the freedom of the press, or the trial by jury in criminal cases.

Sixthly. That, in article 3d, section 2, be annexed to the end of clause 2d, these words, to wit: But no appeal to such court shall be allowed where the value in controversy shall not amount to _____ dollars: nor shall any fact triable by jury, according to the course of common law, be otherwise re-examinable than may consist with the principles of common law.

Seventhly. That in article 3d, section 2, the third clause be struck out, and in its place be inserted the clauses following, to wit:

The trial of all crimes (except in cases of impeachments, and cases arising in the land or naval forces, or the militia when on actual service, in time of war or public danger) shall be by an impartial jury of freeholders of the vicinage, with the requisite of unanimity for conviction, of the right of challenge, and other accustomed requisites; and in all crimes punishable with loss of life or member, presentment or indictment by a grand jury shall be an essential preliminary, provided that in cases of crimes committed within any county which may be in possession of an enemy, or in which a general insurrection may prevail, the trial may by law be authorized in some other county of the same State, as near as may be to the seat of the offence.

In cases of crimes committed not within any county, the trial may by law be in such county as the laws shall have prescribed. In suits at common law, between man and man, the trial by jury, as one of the best securities to the rights of people, ought to remain inviolate.

Eighthly. That immediately after article 6th ... the clauses following, to wit:

The powers delegated by this Constitution are appropriated to the departments to which they are respectively distributed: so that the Legislative Department shall never exercise the powers vested in the Executive or Judicial, nor the Executive exercise the powers vested in the Legislative or Judicial, nor the Judicial exercise the powers vested in the Legislative or Executive Departments.

The powers not delegated by this Constitution nor prohibited by it to the States, are reserved to the States respectively. [italics added]

Ninthly. That article 7th be numbered as article 8th.

The first of these amendments relates to what may be called a bill of rights. I will own that I never considered this provision so essential to the Federal Constitution as to make it improper to ratify it, until such an amendment was added; at the same time, I always conceived, that in a certain form, and to a certain extent, such a provision was neither improper nor altogether useless. I am aware that a great number of the most respectable friends to the Government, and champions for republican liberty, have thought such a provision not only unnecessary, but even improper; nay, I believe some have gone so far as to think it even dangerous. Some policy has been made use of, perhaps, by gentlemen on both sides of the question: I acknowledge the ingenuity of those arguments which were drawn against the Constitution, by a comparison with the policy of Great Britain, in establishing a declaration of rights; but there is too great a difference in the case to warrant the comparison: therefore, the arguments drawn from that source were in a great measure inapplicable.

. . .

I wish, also, in revising the Constitution, we may throw into that section, which interdicts the abuse of certain powers in the State Legislatures, some other provisions of equal, if not greater importance than those already made. The words, "No State shall pass any bill of attainder, *ex post facto* law," &c., were wise and proper restrictions in the Constitution. I think there is more danger of those powers being abused by the State Governments than by the Government of the United States. The same may be said of other powers which they possess, if not controlled by the general principle, that laws are unconstitutional which infringe the rights of the community. I should, therefore, wish to extend this interdiction, and add, as I have stated in the 5th resolution, that no State shall violate the equal right of conscience, freedom of the press, or trial by jury in criminal cases; because it is proper that every Government should be disarmed of powers which trench upon those particular rights.

I know, in some of the State constitutions, the power of the Government is controlled by such a declaration; but others are not. I cannot see any reason against obtaining even a double security on those points; and nothing can give a more sincere proof of the attachment of those who opposed this Constitution to these great and important rights, than to see them join in obtaining the security I have now proposed; because it must be admitted, on all hands, that the *State Governments are as liable to attack these invaluable privileges as the General Government is, and therefore ought to be as cautiously guarded against*. . . . [italics added]

Source: The Debates and Proceedings in the Congress of the United States, compiled by Joseph Gale (Washington, D.C.: Gales and Seaton, 1834–1856), 1:433–442.

DOCUMENT 23: The Sedition Act, July 14, 1798

In 1798, the United States nearly engaged in war with France. Followers of Thomas Jefferson's political party, the Democratic-Republicans, criticized in newspapers the policies of the Federalist party as led by John Adams and Alexander Hamilton. The Federalist political party, not to be confused with the Federalists who had supported the Constitution, controlled both houses of the Congress and used its power to legislate at the national level by means of the Alien and Sedition Acts.

There were three parts to the Alien and Sedition Acts: a Naturalization Act, an Alien Act, and a Sedition Act. Federalists justified passage of the Sedition Act to combat pro-French views hostile to the policies of the national government. The Sedition Act was passed and signed by the president on July 14, 1798—Bastille Day in France. This document was never overturned. It died out because it was not renewed in 1801.

* * *

Sec. 1. *Be it enacted* . . . [t]hat if any persons shall unlawfully combine or conspire together, with intent to oppose any measure or measures of the government of the United States, which are or shall be directed by proper authority, or to impede the operation of any law of the United States, or to intimidate or prevent any person holding a place or office in or under the government of the United States, from undertaking, performing or executing his trust or duty; and if any person or persons, with intent as aforesaid, shall counsel, advise or attempt to procure any insurrection, riot, unlawful assembly, or combination, whether such conspiracy, threatening, counsel, advice, or attempt shall have the proposed effect or not, he or they shall be deemed guilty of a high misdemeanor, and on conviction, before any court of the United States having jurisdiction thereof, shall be punished by a fine not exceeding five thousand dollars, and by imprisonment during a term not less than six months nor exceeding five years; and further, at the discretion of the court may be holden to find sureties for his good behaviour in such sum, and for such time, as the said court may direct.

Sec. 2. That if any person shall write, print, utter, or publish, or shall cause or procure to be written, printed, uttered or published, or shall knowingly and willingly assist or aid in writing, printing, uttering or publishing any false, scandalous and malicious writing or writings against the government of the United States, or either house of the Congress of the United States, or the President of the United States, with intent to defame the said government, or either house of the said Congress, or the said President, or to bring them, or either of them, into contempt or disrepute; or to excite against them or either or any of them, the hatred of the good people of the United States, or to stir up sedition within the United States, or to excite any unlawful combinations therein, for opposing or resisting any law of the United States, or any act of the President of the United States, done in pursuance of any such law, or of the powers in him vested by the constitution of the United States, or to resist, oppose, or defeat any such law or act, or to aid, encourage or abet any hostile designs of any foreign nation against the United States, their people or government, then such person, being thereof convicted before any court of the United States having jurisdiction thereof, shall be punished by a fine not exceeding two thousand dollars, and by imprisonment not exceeding two years.

Sec. 3. That if any person shall be prosecuted under this act, for the writing or publishing any libel aforesaid, it shall be lawful for the defendant, upon the trial of the cause, to give in evidence in his defence, the truth of the matter contained in the publication charged as a libel. And the jury who shall try the cause, shall have a right to determine the law and the fact, under the direction of the court, as in other cases.

Sec. 4. That this act shall continue to be in force until March 3, 1801, and no longer. . . .

Source: Henry Steele Commager, ed., *Documents of American History* (New York: Appleton-Century-Crofts, 1963), 1:177–178.

DOCUMENT 24: The Kentucky Resolutions, November 16, 1798

In response to the Alien and Sedition Acts, James Madison and Thomas Jefferson wrote the Virginia and Kentucky Resolutions, respectively. The U.S. Supreme Court had established the principle of judicial review; however, it had not yet applied that power in a way that invalidated an act of Congress. Madison and Jefferson, viewing the Alien and Sedition Acts as an abuse of First Amendment rights, responded with resolutions that gave state governments the power to act on behalf of citizens.

The Virginia and Kentucky declarations called for local intervention in the federal sphere. State interposition was at the forefront of the Virginia and Kentucky Resolutions, with the latter slightly more assertive in the role of states than Madison's declaration. Madison regretted his carelessness in preparing the Virginia Resolution and went to the Virginia legislature to clarify his language.

The Kentucky Resolution suggested that state legislatures had the power to negate national legislation. When circulated among the states for approval, the Virginia and Kentucky Resolutions were rejected. One can only speculate what would have happened had the states supported the declarations. Would their acceptance have returned the federal system to the days of the Confederation? The reasoning behind the resolutions would serve as a foundation for the Hartford Convention during the War of 1812 (see Document 26) and the theory of nullification as proposed and articulated by John C. Calhoun in the 1830s (see Document 29).

* * *

I. *Resolved*, that the several States composing the United States of America, are not united on the principle of unlimited submission to their general government; but that by compact under the style and title of a Constitution for the United States and of amendments thereto, they constituted a general government for special purposes, delegated to that government certain definite powers, reserving each State to itself, the residuary mass of right to their own self-government; and that whensoever the general government assumes undelegated powers, its acts are unauthoritative, void, and of no force: That to this compact each State acceded as a State, and is an integral party, its co-States forming, as to itself, the other party: That the government created by this compact was not made the exclusive or final judge of the extent of the powers delegated to itself; since that would have made its discretion and not the Constitution, the measure of its powers; but that as in all other cases of compact among parties having no common Judge, *each party has an equal right to judge for itself, as well of infractions as of the mode and measure of redress.*

II. *Resolved*, that the Constitution of the United States having delegated to Congress a power to punish treason, counterfeiting the securities and current coin of the United States, piracies and felonies committed on the high seas, and offenses against the laws of nations, and no other crimes whatever, and it being true as a general principle, and one of the amendments to the Constitution having also declared "that the powers not delegated to the United States by the Constitution, nor prohibited by it to the States, are reserved to the States respectively, or to the people," therefore also [the Sedition Act of July 14, 1798]; as also the act passed by them on the 27th day of June, 1798, entitled "An act to punish frauds committed on the Bank of the United States" (and all other their acts which assume to create, define, or punish crimes other than those enumerated in the Constitution), are altogether void and of no force, and that the power to create, define, and punish such other crimes is reserved, and of right appertains solely and exclusively to the respective States, each within its own Territory.

III. *Resolved*, that it is true as a general principle, and is also expressly declared by one of the amendments to the Constitution that "the powers not delegated to the United States by the Constitution, nor prohibited by it to the States, are reserved to the States respectively or to the people; " and that no power over the freedom of religion, freedom of speech, or freedom of the press being delegated to the United States by the Constitution, nor prohibited by it to the States, all lawful powers respecting the same did of right remain, and were reserved to the States, or to the people: That thus was manifested their determination to retain to themselves the right of judging how far the licentiousness of speech and of the press may be abridged without lessening their useful freedom, and how far those abuses which cannot be separated from their use should be tolerated rather than the use be destroyed; and thus also they guarded against all abridgment by the United States of the freedom of religious opinions and exercises, and retained to themselves the right of protecting the same, as this State, by a law passed on the general demand of its citizens, had already protected them from all human restraint or interference: And that in addition to this general principle and express declaration, another and more special provision has been made by one of the amendments to the Constitution which expressly declares, that "Congress shall make no law respecting an establishment of religion, or prohibiting the free exercise thereof, or abridging the freedom of speech, or of the press," thereby guarding in the same sentence, and under the same words, the freedom of religion, of speech, and of the press, insomuch, that whatever violates either, throws down the sanctuary which covers the others, and that libels, falsehoods, defamation equally with heresy and false religion, are withheld from the cognizance of Federal tribunals. That therefore [the Sedition Act], which does abridge the freedom of the press, is not law, but is altogether void and of no effect.

IV. *Resolved*, that alien friends are under the jurisdiction and protection of the laws of the State wherein they are; that no power over them has been delegated to the United States, nor prohibited to the individual States distinct from their power over citizens; and it being true as a general principle, and one of the amendments to the Constitution having also declared that "the powers not delegated to the United States by the Constitution, nor prohibited by it to the States, are reserved to the States respectively, or to the people," the [Alien Act of June 22, 1798], which assumes power over alien friends not delegated by the Constitution, is not law, but is altogether void and of no force.

V. *Resolved*, that in addition to the general principle as well as the express declaration, that powers not delegated are reserved, another and more special provision inserted in the Constitution form abundant caution has declared, "that the migration or importation of such persons as any of the States now existing shall think proper to admit, shall not be prohibited by the Congress prior to the year 1808." That this Commonwealth does admit the migration of alien friends described as the subject of the said act concerning aliens; that a provision against prohibiting their migration is a provision against all acts equivalent thereto, or it would be nugatory; that to remove them when migrated is equivalent to a prohibition of their migration, and is therefore contrary to the said provision of the Constitution, and void.

VI. *Resolved*, that the imprisonment of a person under the protection of the laws of this Commonwealth on his failure to obey the simple order of the President to depart out of the United States, as is undertaken by the said act entitled "An act concerning aliens," is contrary to the Constitution, one amendment to which has provided, that "no person shall be deprived of liberty without due process of law," and that another having provided "that in all criminal prosecutions, the accused shall enjoy the right to a public trial by an impartial jury, to be informed of the nature and cause of the accusation, to be confronted with the witnesses against him, to have compulsory process for obtaining witnesses in his favour, and to have the assistance of counsel for his defense," the same act undertaking to authorize the President to remove a person out of the United States who is under the protection of the law, on his own suspicion, without accusation, without jury, without public trial, without confrontation of the witnesses against him, without having witnesses in his favour, without defense, without counsel, is contrary to these provisions also of the Constitution, is therefore not law, but utterly void and of no force. That transferring the power of judging any person who is under the protection of the laws, from the courts to the President of the United States, as is undertaken by the same act concerning aliens, is against the article of the Constitution which provides, that "the judicial power of the United States shall be vested in courts, the judges of which shall hold their offices during good behavior," and that the said act is void for that reason also; and it is further be noted, that this transfer of judiciary power is to that magistrate of the general government who already possesses all the executive, and a qualified negative in all the legislative powers.

VII. *Resolved*, that the construction applied by the general government (as is evinced by sundry of their proceedings) to those parts of the Constitution of the United States which delegate to Congress a power to lay and collect taxes, duties, imposts, and excises; to pay the debts, and provide for the common defense, and general welfare of the United States, and to make all laws which shall be necessary and proper for carrying into execution the powers vested by the Constitution in the government of the United States, or any department thereof, goes to the destruction of all the limits prescribed to their power by the Constitution: That words meant by that instrument to be subsidiary only to the execution of the limited powers ought not to be so construed as themselves to give unlimited powers, nor a part so to be taken as to destroy the whole residue of the instrument: That the proceedings of the general government under color of these articles will be a fit and necessary subject for revisal and correction at a time of greater tranquillity, while those specified in the preceding resolutions call for immediate redress.

VIII. *Resolved*, that the preceding Resolutions be transmitted to the Senators and Representatives in Congress from this Commonwealth, who are hereby enjoined to present the same to their respective Houses, and to use their best endeavors to procure, at the next session of Congress, a repeal of the aforesaid unconstitutional and obnoxious acts.

IX. *Resolved*, lastly, that the Governor of this Commonwealth be, and is hereby authorized and requested to communicate the preceding Resolutions to the Legislatures of the several States, to assure them that this Commonwealth considers Union for specified National purposes, and particularly for those specified in their late Federal Compact, to be friendly to the peace, happiness, and prosperity of all the States: that faithful to that compact according to the plain intent and meaning in which it was understood and acceded to by the several parties, it is sincerely anxious for its preservation: that it does also believe, that to take from the States all the powers of self-government, and transfer them to a general and consolidated government, without regard to the special delegations and reservations, solemnly agreed to in that compact, is not for the peace, happiness, or prosperity of these States: And that, therefore, this Commonwealth is determined as it doubts not its co-States are, tamely to submit to undelegated and consequently unlimited powers in no man or body of men on earth: that if the acts before specified should stand, these conclusions would flow from them; that the general government may place any act they think proper on the list of crimes and punish it themselves, whether enumerated or not enumerated by the Constitution as cognizable by them: that they may transfer its cognizance to the President or any other person, who may himself be the accuser, counsel, judge, and jury, whose suspicions may be the evidence, his order the sentence, his officer the executioner, and his breast the sole record of the transaction: that a very numerous and valuable description of the inhabitants of these States being by this precedent reduced as outlaws to the absolute dominion of one man, and the barrier of the Constitution thus swept away from us all, no rampart now remains against the passions and the powers of a majority of Congress, to protect from a like exportation or other more grievous punishment the minority of the same body, the legislatures, judges, governors, and counselors of the States, nor their other peaceable inhabitants who may venture to reclaim the constitutional rights and liberties of the State and people, or who for other causes, good or bad, may be obnoxious to the views or marked by the suspicions of the President, or be thought dangerous to his or their elections or other interests, public or personal: that the friendless alien has indeed been selected as the safest subject of a first experiment, but the citizen will soon follow, or rather has already followed: for, already has a sedition act marked him as its prey: that these and successive acts of the same character, unless arrested on the threshold, may tend to drive these States into revolution and blood, and will furnish new calumnies against Republican governments, and new pretexts for those who wish it to be believed, that man cannot be governed but by a rod of iron: that it would be a dangerous delusion were a confidence in the men of our choice to silence our fears for the safety of our rights: that confidence is everywhere the parent of despotism: free government is founded in jealousy and not in confidence; it is jealousy and not confidence which prescribes limited Constitutions to bind down those whom we are obliged to trust with power: that our Constitution has accordingly fixed the limits to which and no further our confidence may go; and let the honest advocate of confidence read the alien and sedition acts, and say if the constitution has not been wise in fixing limits to the government it created, and whether we should be wise in destroying those limits; let him say what the government is if it be not a tyranny, which the men of our choice have conferred on the President, and the President of our choice has assented to and accepted over the friendly strangers, to whom the mild spirit of our country and its laws had pledged hospitality and protection: that the men of our choice have more respected the bare suspicions of the President than the solid rights of innocence, the claims of justification, the sacred force of truth, and the forms and substance of law and justice. In questions of power then let no more be heard of confidence in man, but bind him down from mischief by the claims of the Constitution. That this Commonwealth does therefore call on its co-States for an expression of their sentiments on the acts concerning aliens, and for the punishment of certain crimes herein before specified, plainly declaring whether these acts are or are not authorized by the Federal Compact. And it doubts not that their sense will be so announced as to prove their attachment unaltered to limited government, whether general or particular, and that the rights and liberties of their co-States will be exposed to no dangers by remaining embarked on a common bottom with their own: That they will concur with this Commonwealth in considering the said acts so palpably against the Constitution as to amount to an undisguised declaration, that the compact is not meant to be the measure of the powers of the general government, but that it will proceed in the exercise over these States of all powers whatsoever: That they will view this as seizing the rights of the States and consolidating them in the hands of the general government with a power assumed to bind the States (not merely in cases made Federal) but in all cases whatsoever, by laws made, not with their consent, but by others against their consent: That this would be to surrender the form of government we have chosen, and to live under one deriving its powers from its own will, and not from our authority; and that the co-States, recurring to their natural right in cases not made Federal, will concur in declaring these acts void and of no force, and will each unite with this Commonwealth in requesting their repeal at the next session of Congress.

Source: Henry Steele Commager, ed., *Documents of American History*, 7th ed. (New York: Appleton-Century-Crofts, 1963), 1:178–182.

DOCUMENT 25: *United States v. Peters*, 1809

During the American Revolution, an American crew captured a British ship. It seized the ship's cargo and claimed it as its prize. Later, the colony of Pennsylvania seized the ship and claimed that Pennsylvania had the right to both the ship and its cargo. David Rittenhouse, a treasurer who represented Pennsylvania, sold the ship without turning over the money to the state. Instead, he deposited the money in a bank and spent the interest.

After nearly thirty years, in 1808, heirs of the crew made a claim against the Rittenhouse estate. The state of Pennsylvania passed a law protecting its access to that part of the estate and refused to allow a federal court of appeals to carry out its decision, which had been to support the claim of the heirs of the crew. Upon hearing the case, the Marshall Court decided in favor of national supremacy. States were not allowed to nullify acts of the federal government.

* * *

February 20. *Marshall, Ch. J.*, delivered the opinion of the court as follows:

With great attention, and with serious concern, the court has considered the return made by the judge for the District of Pennsylvania to the *mandamus* [a court order] directing him to execute the sentence pronounced by him in the case of *Gideon Olmstead and others* v. *Rittenhouse's Executrixes*, or to show cause for not so doing. The cause shown is an act of the legislature of Pennsylvania, passed subsequent to the rendition of his sentence. This act authorizes and requires the governor to demand, for the use of the state of Pennsylvania, the money which had been decreed to Gideon Olmstead and others; and which was in the hands of the executrixes of David Rittenhouse; and in default of payment, to direct the Attorney General to institute a suit for the recovery thereof. This act further authorizes and requires the governor to use any further means he may think necessary for the protection of what it denominates "the just rights of the state," and also to protect the persons and properties of the said executrixes of David Rittenhouse, deceased, against any process whatever, issued out of any federal court in consequence of their obedience to the requisition of the said act.

If the legislatures of the several states may, at will, annul the judgment of the courts of the United States, and destroy the rights acquired under those judgments, the constitution itself becomes a solemn mockery, and the nation is deprived of the means of enforcing its laws by the instrumentality of its own tribunals. So fatal a result must be deprecated by all; and the people of Pennsylvania, not less than the citizens of every other state, must feel a deep interest in resisting principles so destructive of the Union, and in averting consequences so fatal to themselves.

The act in question does not, in terms, assert the universal right of the state to interpose in every case whatever; but assigns, as a motive for its interposition in this particular case, that the sentence, the execution of which it prohibits, was rendered in a cause over which the federal courts have no jurisdiction.

If the ultimate right to determine the jurisdiction of the courts of the Union is placed by the constitution in the several state legislatures, then this act concludes the subject; but if that power necessarily resides in the supreme judicial tribunal of the nation, then the jurisdiction of the District Court of Pennsylvania, over the case in which that jurisdiction was exercised, ought to be most deliberately examined; and the act of Pennsylvania, with whatever respect it may be considered, cannot be permitted to prejudice the question. . . .

While this suit was depending, the state of Pennsylvania forbore to assert its title, and, in January, 1803, the court decreed in favor of the libellants; soon after which, the legislature passed the act which has been stated.

It is contended that the federal courts were deprived of jurisdiction, in this cause, by that amendment [Eleventh Amendment] of the constitution which exempts states from being sued in those courts by individuals. This amendment declares, "that the judicial power of the United States shall not be construed to extend to any suit, in law or equity, commenced or prosecuted against one of the United States by citizens of another state, or by citizens or subjects of any foreign state."

The right of a state to assert, as plaintiff, any interest it may have in a subject, which forms the matter of controversy between individuals, in one of the courts of the United States, is not affected by this amendment; nor can it be so construed as to oust the court of its jurisdiction, should such claim be suggested. The amendment simply provides, that no suit shall be commenced or prosecuted against a state. The state cannot be made a defendant to a suit brought by an individual; but it remains the duty of the courts of the United States to decide all cases brought before them by citizens of one state against citizens of a different state, where a state is not necessarily a defendant. In this case, the suit was not instituted against the state or its treasurer, but against the executrixes of David Rittenhouse, for the proceeds of a vessel condemned in the court of admiralty, which were admitted to be in their possession. If these proceeds had been the actual property of Pennsylvania, however wrongfully acquired, the disclosure of that fact would have presented a case on which it is unnecessary to give an opinion. . . .

Source: Joseph P. Cotton, Jr., ed., *The Constitutional Decisions of John Marshall* (New York: Da Capo Press, 1971), 1:219–225. For further reading on the Marshall Court and its relationship to national supremacy, see the 1816 decision, *Martin v. Hunter's Lessee*. In one of the most nationalistic opinions ever rendered, Justice Joseph Story asserted that in matters of ultimate constitutional authority the Supreme Court could reverse the decisions of the highest state courts. Justice Joseph Story rejected the principle of equal sovereignty between the states and the federal government. Story argued that the people, not the states, had created the national government and therefore the Supreme Court was the "final constitutional authority over all other elements of government, including state courts." As constitutional historian Charles Warren would later observe, Story's opinion for the Marshall Court in *Martin v. Hunter's Lessee* (1816) established the "keystone of the whole arch of Federal judicial power." Charles Warren, *The Supreme Court in United States History* (Boston: Little, Brown, 1922) 1:449.

DOCUMENT 26: Report and Resolutions of the Hartford Convention, January 1815

Many New Englanders were opposed to the War of 1812. Commerce had been adversely affected, and they felt that the northern states were bearing a disproportionate cost of the war. The Hartford Convention was the high point of New England's disaffection for the war, which they pejoratively called "Mr. Madison's War."

In October 1814, Federalists met in Massachusetts and voted to hold a convention for the purposes of taking independent action. State legislatures from Massachusetts, Rhode Island, Connecticut, Vermont, and New Hampshire chose delegates to meet in Hartford, Connecticut. The attendance of the twenty-two delegates implied that the northeastern section of the nation considered secession, although no formal pronouncement was ever made.

The Hartford Convention proved to be ill-timed. When its resolutions were announced, the War of 1812 had come to an end, embarrassing the Federalist party, whose members had attended.

* * *

THEREFORE RESOLVED.

That it be and hereby is recommended to the legislatures of the several states represented in this Convention, to adopt all such measures as may be necessary effectually to protect the citizens of said states from the operation and effects of all acts which have been or may be passed by the Congress of the United States, which shall contain provisions, subjecting the militia or other citizens to forcible drafts, conscriptions, or impressments not authorised by the constitution of the United States.

Resolved, That it be and hereby is recommended to the said Legislatures, to authorize an immediate and earnest application to be made to the government of the United States, requesting their consent to some arrangement, whereby the said states may, separately or in concert, be empowered to assume upon themselves the defence of their territory against the enemy; and a reasonable portion of the taxes, collected within said states, may be paid into the respective treasuries thereof, and appropriated to the payment of the balance due said states, and to the future defence of the same. The amount so paid into the said treasuries to be credited, and the disbursements made as aforesaid to be charged to the United States.

Resolved, That it be, and hereby is, recommended to the legislatures of the aforesaid states, to pass laws (where it has not already been done) authorizing the governors or commanders-in-chief of their militia to make detachments from the same, or to form voluntary corps, as shall be most convenient and conformable to their constitutions, and to cause the same to be well armed, equipped and disciplined, and held in readiness for service; and upon the request of the governor of either of the other states to employ the whole of such detachment or corps, as well as the regular forces of the state, or such part thereof as may be required and can be spared consistently with the safety of the state, in assisting the state, making such request to repel any invasion thereof which shall be made or attempted by the public enemy.

Resolved, That the following amendments of the constitution of the United States be recommended to the states represented as aforesaid, to be proposed by them for adoption by the state legislatures, and in such cases as may be deemed expedient by a convention chosen by the people of each state.

First. Representatives and direct taxes shall be apportioned among the several states which may be included within this Union, according to their respective numbers of free persons, including those bound to serve for a term of years, and excluding Indians not taxed, and all other persons.

Second. No new state shall be admitted into the Union by Congress, in virtue of the power granted by the constitution, without the concurrence of two thirds of both houses.

Third. Congress shall not have power to lay any embargo on the ships or vessels of the citizens of the United States, in the ports or harbours thereof, for more than sixty days.

Fourth. Congress shall not have power, without the concurrence of two thirds of both houses, to interdict the commercial intercourse between the United States and any foreign nation or the dependencies thereof.

Fifth. Congress shall not make or declare war, or authorize acts of hostility against any foreign nation, without the concurrence of two thirds of both houses, except such acts of hostility be in defence of the territories of the United States when actually invaded.

Sixth. No person who shall hereafter be naturalized, shall be eligible as a member of the senate or house of representatives of the United States, nor capable of holding any civil office under the authority of the United States.

Seventh. The same person shall not be elected president of the United States a second time; nor shall the President be elected from the same state two terms in succession.

Resolved, That if the application of these states to the government of the United States, recommended in a foregoing resolution, should be unsuccessful and peace should not be concluded, and the defence of these states should be neglected, as it has been since the commencement of the war, it will, in the opinion of this convention, be expedient for the legislatures of the several states to appoint delegates to another convention, to meet at Boston . . . with such powers and instructions as the exigency of a crisis so momentous may require.

Source: Henry Steele Commager, ed., *Documents of American History*, 7th ed. (New York: Appleton-Century-Crofts, 1963), 1:209–211.

DOCUMENT 27: *Barron v. Baltimore* (1833)

In 1833 the Supreme Court made a decision concerning the application of the Bill of Rights to states. John Barron and John Craig, the plaintiffs, were owners of a highly productive wharf in Baltimore. The city of Baltimore decided to upgrade streets and because of its concern for health conditions diverted streams of water. The diversion caused deposits along the wharf and led to shallow water in the wharf. Craig and Barron claimed that local authorities had taken their property away from them. They sued and sought protection based on the Fifth Amendment to the Constitution, which protected private property and a "just compensation" for its loss.

The John Marshall Court was compelled to rule on the Fifth Amendment's application to the states. The Marshall Court decided that the Fifth Amendment to the Constitution did not apply because the Bill of Rights did not apply to the states. Marshall referred to the debates when James Madison proposed a Bill of Rights in the summer of 1789, including an amendment that would protect rights from the states. The U.S. Congress rejected the proposed amendment. Marshall therefore concluded that the Fifth Amendment and other protections in the Bill of Rights applied only to actions of the national government. The Marshall Court decision outraged many abolitionists who argued that *Barron* was incorrectly decided and that the Bill of Rights did apply to the states. This minority position did not take hold, however, until after the Civil War and the writing of the Fourteenth Amendment, in part written to apply the Bill of Rights to the states.

The decision held throughout the nineteenth century and into the twentieth. In the 1920s, the Supreme Court incorporated First Amendment rights through the Fourteenth Amendment to apply to states. The decision of Congress in 1789 to limit the Bill of Rights to the national government had important consequences for citizens in state and national government relations.

* * *

The judgment brought up by this writ of error having been rendered by the court of a state, this tribunal can exercise no jurisdiction over it, unless it be shown to come within the provisions of the 25th section of the judiciary act. The plaintiff in error contends, that it comes within that clause in the fifth amendment to the constitution, which inhibits the taking of private property for public use, without just compensation. He insists, that this amendment being in favor of the liberty of the citizen, ought to be so construed as to restrain the legislative power of a state, as well as that of the United States. If this proposition be untrue, the court can take no jurisdiction of the cause.

The question thus presented is, we think, of great importance, but not of much difficulty. The constitution was ordained and established by the people of the United States for themselves, for their own government, and not for the government of the individual states. Each state established a constitution for itself, and in that constitution, provided such limitations and restrictions on the powers of its particular government, as its judgement dictated. The people of the United States framed such a government for the United States as they supposed best adapted to their situation and best calculated to promote their interests. The powers they conferred on this government were to be exercised by itself; and the limitations on power, if expressed in general terms, are naturally, and, we think, necessarily, applicable to the government created by the instrument. They are limitations of power granted in the instrument itself; not of distinct governments, framed by different persons and for different purposes.

If these propositions be correct, the fifth amendment must be understood as restraining the power of the general government, not as applicable to the states. . . .

. . .

[I]t is universally understood, it is part of the history of the day, that the great revolution which established the constitution of the United States, was not effected without immense opposition. Serious fears were extensively entertained, that those powers which the patriot statesmen, who then watched over the interests of our country, deemed essential to union, and to the attainment of those unvaluable objects for which union was sought, might be be exercised in a manner dangerous to liberty. In almost every convention by which the constitution was adopted, amendments to guard against the abuse of power were recommended. These amendments demanded security against the apprehended encroachments of the general government—not against those of the local governments. In compliance with a sentiment thus generally expressed, to quiet fears thus extensively entertained, amendments were proposed by the required majority in congress, and adopted by the states. These amendments contain no expression indicating an intention to apply them to the state governments. This court cannot so apply them.

We are of the opinion, that the provision in the fifth amendment to the constitution, declaring that private property shall not be taken for public use, without just compensation, is intended solely as a limitation on the exercise of power by the government of the United States, and is not applicable to the legislation of the states. . . .

Source: Barron v. City of Baltimore, 32 U.S. 243 (1833), http://caselaw.findlaw. com/cgi-bin/getcase/pl?navby=case&court=US&vol=32&involv=243.

Part III

States' Rights in the Antebellum Period and the Civil War, 1828–1865

In 1850 during a senatorial debate between two spokespersons, one from the North and one from the South, the issue of states' rights and American federalism took a new turn. John C. Calhoun of South Carolina had been the leading spokesperson for the South since the 1830s. William H. Seward of New York was a rising leader in the Senate and symbolized the views of many people in the North. Central to the 1850 debates was the discourse that took place between Calhoun representing the South and Seward representing the North. The Calhoun-Seward exchange heralded the intractable North-South polarization concerning the nature of federalism (see Documents 34 and 35). Moreover, it contrasted two models in the 1850s that reflected what had transpired throughout the nineteenth century leading up to the Civil War: the nineteenth century was a battle over the constitutional direction of states' rights and federalism that would ultimately be decided by the Civil War.

Calhoun believed that rights were a product of social circumstances—intelligence, patriotism, and virtue.[1] A society composed of citizens who were ignorant, unpatriotic, and vicious would produce a government that was inferior. The individual, he argued, must have society for self-preservation, and government was necessary as the controlling power to maintain society. The government, the South Carolinian firmly believed, should correspond to the character of the citizenry.

What was necessary was to ensure that citizens were composed of intelligent, patriotic, and virtuous members.

Representing the southern view, Calhoun urged a community of states to allow for control of their social and economic interests. He summarized the southern model with the observation that "the separate governments of the States [should] maintain and protect the powers reserved to them, and among others, the sovereign powers by which they ordained and established, not only their separate State constitutions and governments, but also the Constitution and Government of the United States."[2] Clearly Calhoun shared the views of Antifederalists of the previous century concerning the powers and roles of state and national governments.[3]

Senator William H. Seward of New York challenged his South Carolina adversary on two points. First, the "Wizard of the North" (as Seward was called by southern opponents) opposed the southern leader on federalism; and second, he wanted to condemn slavery from the point of view of appealing to a higher law. Representing the northern view, Seward found a national community of individuals to be indispensable. He forthrightly challenged states' rights theory and slavery, with a reference to higher law. In particular, he criticized protections of slavery that were lodged in the Constitution. Article IV, section 2 of the Constitution permitted a fugitive slave law, which Seward believed violated higher law. Thus, Seward turned to the Declaration of Independence and the belief that "all men are created equal" to expose and condemn southern violations of higher law.

Seward's elevation of the Declaration of Independence to constitutional status meant that the Declaration would supersede all other constitutional documents, such as the Articles of Confederation, all state constitutions, and the U.S. Constitution. The inclusion of higher law caused Seward's contemporaries to ask several questions concerning states' rights and federalism in the antebellum period. Does popular sovereignty mean the people will make decisions within their respective states or within the national community of sovereign individuals? Does a state have the power to nullify national policies when it believes the policies are adverse to state interests? Can the national government enforce its policies over the objections of a state? Answers to these questions were ultimately resolved with the outcome of the Civil War. Yet from 1828 to 1865, state or national supremacy was yet to be determined.

POWER AT THE LOCAL, STATE, AND SECTIONAL LEVELS

The logic of local democracy, fervently expressed by Antifederalists during the ratification of the Constitution, lay behind states' rights doctrine. States' rights proponents situate power in local authority that is sympathetic to the culture, experiences, and the dispositions of its people. Spokesmen of states' rights such as John Taylor of Caroline, Thomas Jefferson, and John C. Calhoun understood that local control over political decisions would encourage their particular vision of republican government. States' rights, they argued, give voice and power to local virtues and is more responsive, as well as understanding, of the needs and demands of its citizens.

States' rights may suffer, however, from the problem of parochialism. Local prejudices and beliefs, whether on race or other issues, can dominate the actions of local majorities, which can manifest a tyrannical intimidation over minorities and individuals and coerce them through legislation.

JOHN C. CALHOUN'S SECTIONAL AND STATES' RIGHTS POSITION

In 1828, John C. Calhoun quietly authored (written but not signed by him) *South Carolina's Exposition and Protest*, which championed federal compact theory. *Exposition and Protest* contains both theory and means of implementation. The theory was not Calhoun's original idea; it was drawn from previous states' rights doctrines contained in the Virginia (the right to repeal) and Kentucky (the right to threaten nullification) Resolutions. States have rights, according to the theory. Under the constitutional compact, states participated in a voluntary partnership of the states. If the national government violated the compact, states could declare a congressional legislative act unconstitutional. If a state questions a congressional law, its legislature can call for a special convention to determine the constitutionality of the law. If the state approves the law, then the law may be enforced. On the other hand, if the state disapproves of the law, then the federal compact has been violated and the special convention can move for remedial interposition, which would invoke nullification. Thus, the state authority interposes itself between the federal law and local enforcement of the law. In essence, the state could veto an act of the federal legislature.

Calhoun was well aware the North (and West) controlled the terms of government by an absolute majority and that the South was in the perpetual minority, so he devised this plan to protect his section of the country from northern dominance. In order to prevent dictatorship by the North, the Congress, according to Calhoun, had two alternatives. The first was to accept the decision of the nullifying state. The law would then exist in full force in all the states except the state where it was nullified. The second option could be taken if the Congress felt strongly about the law. If so, the Congress could call for a constitutional amendment and submit it to the states for ratification. If approved by two-thirds of the states, all states—including the state that nullified the federal act—would have to live with it. Thus, Calhoun created a concurrent majority that expressly protected states' rights.

Calhoun recognized the slow and tedious nature of his states' rights–compact theory. It was conceived that way to protect the state and the numerical minority against the majority in constitutional terms. Calhoun knew that implementation of his compact theory would overturn the working basis of the federal system of government. However, he defended these states' rights ideas to provide alternatives because, in his and other southerners' view, the South was being overrun by "consolidation" or majority sentiment expressed through the voice of a powerful national government. He believed that minority sections would see his model of implementation for states' rights as a good way to defend against the majority in the national community. The South Carolina spokesperson knew it was revolutionary because he was challenging the sacred idea of majority rule in the context of the national community. He was also drawing from defiant Antifederalist thought, which had been rejected by the more urban and populous sections of the nation.

In the 1830s John C. Calhoun and Robert Y. Hayne, a colleague of Calhoun, vociferously advanced the social compact theory during the nullification crisis. It resulted in one of the most stirring debates in American history. In the ensuing Webster-Hayne debate, Robert Y. Hayne of South Carolina and Daniel Webster of Massachusetts sharpened the lines between states' rights and the concept of Union (see Document 28). Ultimately the issue of states' rights contributed to a rift in relations between President Andrew Jackson and John C. Calhoun, a member of the Jackson cabinet. Their split centered on South Carolina's ordinance of nullification directed against high protective tariffs and Jackson's firm response to threats of secession.

The idea of nullification was certainly not a uniquely southern perspective. Over thirty years earlier, following the national government's passage of the Alien and Sedition Acts of 1798, James Madison and Thomas Jefferson had written the Virginia and Kentucky Resolutions as a response to national violations on individual rights. Madison and, especially, Jefferson raised the specter of nullification. Later, during the War of 1812, New England opponents to the conflict met in December 1814 in Hartford, Connecticut, to voice their dissatisfaction with national policy. At the Hartford Convention (see Document 26), New England Federalists offered amendments that would limit the power of the national government in foreign affairs, bar immigrants from government positions, and imply the threat of secession. By the 1830s only southern spokespersons articulated the states' rights–compact theory with its right of nullification. Initially southern state leaders protested that northern encroachments concerning tariff policies threatened the welfare of the South. John C. Calhoun of South Carolina wrote the *South Carolina Exposition and Protest* and expressed the right of interposition to protect the rights of a minority against imposition by the majority (see Documents 29 and 30).

Ultimately the southern states took the compact theory to its extreme by seceding from the Union. On the eve of the Civil War, southern leaders argued that the Constitution represented a mutual contract between the states and the federal government. They tenaciously believed that the states had created the national government and that when the national government (or North) abrogated its part of the agreement, the contract was no longer valid. The Civil War, fought between 1861 and 1865, brought to an end this specific argument concerning federalism when the Union prevailed.

ROGER B. TANEY AND THE SUPREME COURT ON STATES' RIGHTS AND FEDERALISM IN THE ANTEBELLUM PERIOD

How did the Supreme Court in the mid-nineteenth century respond to the states' rights challenge to national sovereignty? Slavery had become a moral and political issue intertwined with popular sovereignty. In 1857 the Supreme Court reached a decision in what would later be characterized as the Court's great "self-inflicted wound." The Supreme Court attempted to impose a judicial solution to the political and moral issue of slavery. Chief Justice Roger Taney and the rest of the Supreme Court justices wanted to prevent any constitutional doctrine that would endanger a state's absolute authority over slavery as an institution, slaves, and freedmen. Thus, Taney hoped to do two things when the *Dred Scott* case came before the Court. First, he hoped to keep African Americans in a state of subjection to the white race. And second, he wanted to remove all other constitutional theories that opposed those of John C. Calhoun. Through him, southern slaveholding demands would have constitutional support.

Before 1850, the Supreme Court rarely heard cases involving slavery. Sometimes the cases they did hear concerning the commerce clause in the Constitution raised slavery questions, since abolitionists hoped to use the law to prohibit interstate slave trade. A major issue came before the Court based on the antislavery doctrine of "once free always free." Dred Scott, a slave owned by Peter Blow and purchased by John Emerson, an army physician, had traveled from Missouri to Illinois and Wisconsin. Both of the latter were free states. When Emerson died in 1843, he left Scott (as legal chattel property) to his widow. Three years later, Scott (aided by abolitionists) sued for his freedom on the grounds that his earlier residence in Illinois had liberated him from slavery.

When the case came before the Supreme Court, Taney and the eight other justices all wrote separate opinions. They decreed that any African American, slave or free, had no right to sue in a federal court because no African Americans could be a "citizen." Taney denied the assertion that any African American could ever attain the status of citizenship. Thus he precluded African Americans from ever enjoying any constitutional rights guaranteed in the U.S. Constitution.

Taney made a second important decision in the *Dred Scott* case. He shifted the importance of individual rights to a conflict over states' rights and federalism (see Document 37). His interpretation coincided with the ideas of John C. Calhoun. Taney ruled that Congress did not have the power to prevent slaveholders with their slaves from settling in the territories. He then ruled that popular sovereignty, when related to the issue of slavery, had no merit: neither the people in a free state nor settlers in a western territory could decide on the issue of slavery. While Republicans, on the eve of the Civil War, reaffirmed their belief in free-soil (no slavery in the western territories). Taney and the Supreme Court held to the rigid dogma of racial inequality. No doubt some Republicans shared a belief in racial inequality, but what they wanted was a free-soil environment, which would not allow slave labor, to improve their free economic system. The *Dred Scott* decision upheld the concept of slave labor, thus abrogating the free-soil principle and popular sovereignty.

John C. Calhoun had articulated a states' rights–compact theory of government, and Taney bolstered Calhoun's arguments with the *Dred Scott* decision. Northerners, however, viewed Taney's national court authority as a violation of *their* states' rights because it did not allow a state to exclude slavery from its land. Popular sovereignty was thus endangered. William H. Seward, having spoken for the Declaration of Independence as a higher law, urged national supremacy. The states were subordinate to the national government in Seward's mind. Unfortunately, the issue of state or national supremacy would be resolved on the battlefield.

NOTES

1. John C. Calhoun, "Speech on the Oregon Bill," in *Union and Liberty: The Political Philosophy of John C. Calhoun*, ed. Ross M. Lence (Indianapolis: Liberty Fund, 1992), 568.

2. John C. Calhoun, *Congressional Globe*, 31st Cong., 1st sess., 1850, p. 452.

3. John C. Calhoun challenged Publius in the *Federalist* essays, particularly the extended republic in the Tenth *Federalist*, numerical majority in the Twenty-Second *Federalist*, the compound government of the Thirty-ninth *Federalist*, and limited government through separation of powers in the Fifty-first *Federalist*. Calhoun also criticized judicial review as described in the Seventy-eighth *Federalist*.

DOCUMENT 28: Liberty and Union, Now and Forever, One and Inseparable, January 1830

In 1830 Daniel Webster rose to answer a speech given by a Senator Robert Y. Hayne of South Carolina on the tariff issue, which had angered the South. Senator Hayne had expressed his belief, formulated by John C. Calhoun, that the Constitution was a creation of the states and therefore the states retained the right to judge the constitutionality of laws passed by Congress and to nullify laws they found unconstitutional. Webster summarized the position that the Constitution was a creation of the people, not the creation of a compact among the states.

* * *

THERE YET REMAINS to be performed, Mr. President, by far the most grave and important duty which I feel to be devolved on me by this occasion. It is to state, and to defend, what I conceive to be the true principles of the Constitution under which we are here assembled. I might well have desired that so weighty a task should have fallen into other and abler hands. I could have wished that it should have been executed by those whose character and experience give weight and influence to their opinions, such as cannot possibly belong to mine. But, sir, I have met the occasion, not sought it; and I shall proceed to state my own sentiments, without challenging for them any particular regard, with studied plainness, and as much precision as possible.

I understand the honorable gentleman from South Carolina to maintain, that it is a right of the state legislatures to interfere whenever, in their judgment, this government transcends its constitutional limits and to arrest the operation of its laws.

I understand him to maintain this right as a right existing under the Constitution, not as a right to overthrow it on the ground of extreme necessity, such as would justify violent revolution.

. . .

What he contends for is that it is constitutional to interrupt the administration of the Constitution itself, in the hands of those who are chosen and sworn to administer it, by the direct interference, in form of law of the states, in virtue of their sovereign capacity. The inherent right in the people to reform their government I do not deny; and they have another right, and that is to resist unconstitutional laws without overturning the government. It is no doctrine of mine that unconstitutional laws bind the people. The great question is—Whose prerogative is it to decide on the constitutionality or unconstitutionality of the laws? On that, the main debate hinges.

The proposition that, in case of a supposed violation of the Constitution by Congress, the states have a constitutional right to interfere and annul the law of Congress is the proposition of the gentleman. . . .

I say, the right of a state to annul a law of Congress cannot be maintained but on the ground of the inalienable right of man to resist oppression; that is to say, upon the ground of revolution. I admit that there is an ultimate violent remedy, above the Constitution and in defiance of the Constitution, which may be resorted to when a revolution is to be justified. But I do not admit that, under the Constitution and in conformity with it, there is any mode in which a state government, as a member of the Union, can interfere and stop the progress of the general government, by force of her own laws, under any circumstances whatever.

This leads us to inquire into the origin of this government and the source of its power. Whose agent is it? Is it the creature of the state legislatures, or the creature of the people? If the government of the United States be the agent of the state governments, then they may control it, provided they can agree in the manner of controlling it; if it be the agent of the people, then the people alone can control it, restrain it, modify, or reform it. It is observable enough that the doctrine for which the honorable gentleman contends leads him to the necessity of maintaining, not only that this general government is the creature of the states, or that it is the creature of each of the states severally, so that each may assert the power for itself of determining whether it acts within the limits of its authority. It is the servant of four-and-twenty masters, of different wills and different purposes, and yet bound to obey all.

This absurdity (for it seems no less) arises from a misconception as to the origin of this government and its true character. It is, sir, the people's Constitution, the people's government, made for the people, made by the people, and answerable to the people. The people of the United States have declared that this Constitution shall be the supreme law. We must either admit the proposition or dispute their authority. The states are, unquestionably, sovereign, so far as their sovereignty is not affected by this supreme law. But the state legislatures, as political bodies, however sovereign, are yet not sovereign over the people. . . . We are all agents of the same supreme power, the people. The general government and the state governments derive their authority from the same source. Neither can, in relation to the other, be called primary, though one is definite and restricted, and the other general and residuary. The national government possesses those powers, which it can be shown the people have conferred on it, and no more. All the rest belongs to the state governments, or to the people themselves. So far as the people have restrained state sovereignty, by the expression of their will, in the Constitution of

the United States, so far, it must be admitted, state sovereignty is effectually controlled.

. . .

. . . Where do they [the states] find the power to interfere with the
laws of the Union? Sir, the opinion which the honorable gentleman maintains is a notion found in a total misapprehension, in my judgment, of
the origins of this government, and of the foundation on which it stands.
I hold it to be a popular government, erected by the people. . . . It is as
popular, just as truly emanating from the people, as the state governments. It is created for one purpose; the state governments for another.
It has its own powers; they have theirs. There is no more authority with
them to arrest the operation of a law of Congress than with Congress to
arrest the operation of their laws.

We are here to administer a Constitution emanating immediately from
the people, and trusted by them to our administration. It is not the creature of the state governments. It is of no moment to the argument that
certain acts of the state legislatures are necessary to fill our seats in this
body. That is not one of their original state powers, a part of the sovereignty of the state. It is a duty which the people, by the Constitution
itself, have imposed on the state legislatures. . . .

. . .

. . . The Constitution has itself pointed out, ordained, and established
that authority. How has it accomplished this great and essential end? By
declaring, sir, that *"the Constitution, and the laws of the United States made
in pursuance thereof, shall be the supreme law of the land, anything in the
constitution or laws of any state to the contrary notwithstanding."*

This sir, was the first great step. By this, the supremacy of the Constitution and laws of the United States is declared. The people so will it.
No state law is to be valid which comes in conflict with the Constitution,
or any law of the United States passed in pursuance of it. But who shall
decide this question of interference? To whom lies the last appeal? This
sir, the Constitution itself decides also, by declaring, *"that the judicial
power shall extend to all cases arising under the Constitution and laws of the
United States."* These two provisions cover the whole ground. They are,
in truth, the keystone of the arch! With these it is a government; without
them it is a confederation. . . .

. . .

God grant that in my day, at least, that curtain may not rise! God
grant that on my vision never may be opened what lies behind! When
my eyes shall be turned to behold for the last time the sun in heaven,
may I not see him shining on the broken and dishonored fragments of
a once glorious Union; on states dissevered, discordant, belligerent; on
a land rent with civil feuds, or drenched, it may be, in fraternal blood!
Let their last feeble and lingering glance rather behold the gorgeous en-

sign of the republic, now known and honored throughout the earth, still full high advanced, its arms and trophies streaming in their original luster, not a stripe erased or polluted, nor a single star obscured, bearing for its motto, no such miserable interrogatory as "What is all this worth?" nor those words of delusion and folly, "Liberty first and Union afterwards"; but everywhere, spread all over the land, and in every wind under the whole heavens, that other sentiment, dear to every true American heart—Liberty and Union, now and forever, one and inseparable!

Source: http://www.dartmouth.edu/~dwebster/speeches/hayne-speech.html.

DOCUMENT 29: John C. Calhoun's Fort Hill Address, 1831

By 1831, it was common knowledge that Senator John C. Calhoun from South Carolina was the author of "Exposition and Protest." In 1831, at his plantation near Clemson University, Calhoun gave the Fort Hill Address, a strong expression of a states' rights position in a federal system of government. Calhoun referred throughout his address to the Virginia and Kentucky Resolutions. While Calhoun advocated the natural right of a state to interpose itself between the people and the national government, he was guarded in this address because of his position as vice president in the Jackson administration. Although he had expressed his views of states' rights secretly in "Exposition and Protest," the Fort Hill Address was his first public pronouncement of his belief about state and federal relations.

* * *

The question of the relation which the States and General Government bear to each other is not one of recent origin. From the commencement of our system, it has divided public sentiment. Even in the Convention, while the Constitution was struggling into existence, there were two parties as to what this relation should be, whose different sentiments constituted no small impediment in forming that instrument. After the General Government went into operation, experience soon proved that the question had not terminated with the labors of the Convention. The great struggle that preceded the political revolution of 1801, which brought Mr. Jefferson into power, turned essentially on it; and the doctrines and arguments on both sides were embodied and ably sustained— On the one, in the Virginia and Kentucky Resolutions, and the Report

to the Virginia Legislature—and on the other, in the replies of the Legislature of Massachusetts and some of the other States. . . .

. . .

The great and leading principle is, that the General Government emanated from the people of the several States, forming distinct political
communities, and acting in their separate and sovereign capacity, and
not from all of the people forming one aggregate political community;
that the Constitution of the United States is, in fact, a compact, to which
each State is a party, in the character already described; and that the
several States, or parties, have a right to judge of its infractions; and . . .
they have the right, in the last resort, to use the language of the Virginia
Resolutions, "to interpose for arresting the progress of the evil, and for
maintaining, within their respective limits, the authorities, rights, and
liberties appertaining to them." This right of interposition, thus solemnly
asserted by the State of Virginia, be it called what it may—State-right,
veto, nullification, or by any other name—I conceive to be the fundamental principle of our system, resting on facts historically as certain as
our revolution itself, and deductions as simple and demonstrative as that
of any political, or moral truth whatever; and I firmly believe that on its
recognition depend the stability and safety of our political institutions.

Source: "The Fort Hill Address: On the Relations of the States and Federal Government," in Ross M. Lence, ed., *Union and Liberty: The Political Philosophy of John
C. Calhoun* (Indianapolis: Liberty Fund, 1992), pp. 369–371.

DOCUMENT 30: John C. Calhoun against the Force Bill, February 15, 1833

John C. Calhoun developed the states' rights argument surrounding
the position that the Constitution was the creation of the sovereign
states. The immediate events surrounding this speech were the tariff
acts Congress passed in 1828 and 1832, South Carolina's resistance to
those tariffs, and the debate involving the force bill, which gave President Jackson the power to use military force to coerce South Carolina
into compliance with the tariff measures. This speech in the Senate
raised central questions that continued to define the debate of states'
rights up to the eve of the Civil War and during Reconstruction, when
Americans were forced to confront the issue of whether the Confederate states ever left the Union. Senator Calhoun's central concern was
whether the power of judicial review resided solely in the Supreme
Court or whether state courts had the power to judge actions of the

national government as unconstitutional. Central to this issue of judicial review were Calhoun's view of the United States as a confederation
and his fear of a consolidated government.

* * *

. . .

All must admit that there are delegated and reserved powers, and that
the powers reserved are reserved to the States respectively. The powers,
then, of the system are divided between the General and the State governments; and the point immediately under consideration is, whether a
State has any right to judge as to the extent of its reserved powers, and
to defend them against the encroachments of the General Government. . . .

But it is contended that the Constitution has conferred on the Supreme
Court the right of judging between the States and the General Government. Those who make this objection overlook, I conceive, an important
provision of the Constitution. By turning to the tenth amended article
[Tenth Amendment], it will be seen that the reservation of power to the
States is not only against the powers delegated to Congress, but against
the United States themselves, and extends, of course, as well to the judiciary as to the other departments of the government. The article provides that all powers not delegated to the United States, or prohibited
by it to the States, are reserved to the States respectively, or to the people.
This presents the inquiry: What powers are delegated to the United
States? They may be classed under four divisions: First, those that are
delegated by the States to each other, by virtue of which the Constitution
may be altered or amended by three-fourths of the States, when, without
which, it would have required the unanimous vote of all; next, the powers conferred on Congress; then, those on the President; and, finally,
those on the judicial department—all of which are particularly enumerated in the parts of the Constitution which organize the respective departments. The reservation of powers to the States is, as I have said,
against the whole, and is as full against the judicial as it is against the
executive and legislative departments of the government meet. It cannot
be claimed for the one without claiming it for the whole, and without,
in fact, annulling this important provision of the Constitution.

Against this, as it appears to me, conclusive view of the subject, it has
been urged that this power is expressly conferred on the Supreme Court
by that portion of the Constitution which provides that the judicial
power shall extend to all cases in law and equity arising under the Constitution, the laws of the United States, and treaties made under their
authority. I believe the assertion to be utterly destitute of any foundation.
It obviously is the intention of the Constitution simply to make the ju-

dicial power commensurate with the law-making and treaty-making powers; and to vest it with the right of applying the Constitution, the laws, and the treaties, to the cases which might arise under them, and not to make it the judge of the Constitution, the laws, and the treaties themselves. In fact, the power of applying the laws to the facts of the case, and deciding upon such application, constitutes, in truth, the judicial power. . . .

. . .

The very point at issue between the two parties there, is, whether nullification is a peaceable and an efficient remedy against an unconstitutional act of the General Government, and may be asserted as such through the State tribunals. . . . They . . . tell us that the Supreme Court is the appointed arbiter of all controversies between a State and the General Government. Why, then, do they not leave this controversy to that tribunal?

. . .

In reviewing the ground over which I have passed, it will be apparent that the question in controversy involves that most deeply important of all political questions, whether ours is a federal or a consolidated government—a question, on the decision of which depend, as I solemnly believe, the liberty of the people, their happiness, and the place which we are destined to hold in the moral and intellectual scale of nations. . . .

Source: http://douglass.speech.nwu.edu/calh__a30.htm.

DOCUMENT 31: Andrew Jackson's Second Inaugural Address, March 4, 1833

President Jackson's Second Inaugural Address summarized his thoughts on the nullification crisis in presenting his view of states' rights within a general government. While not addressing Calhoun by name, he raised the specter of the loss of peace, prosperity, and good government, which he believed would accompany the act of nullification.

* * *

THE will of the American people, expressed through their unsolicitated suffrages, calls me before you to pass through the solemnities preparatory to taking upon myself the duties of President of the United States for another term. . . .

So many events have occurred within the last four years which have necessarily called forth—sometimes under circumstances the most delicate and painful—my views of the principles and policy which ought to be pursued by the General Government that I need on this occasion but allude to a few leading considerations connected with some of them.

. . .

In the domestic policy of this Government there are two objects which especially deserve the attention of the people and their representatives, and which have been and will continue to be the subjects of my increasing solicitude. They are the preservation of the rights of the several States and the integrity of the Union.

These great objects are necessarily connected, and can only be attained by an enlightened exercise of the powers of each within its appropriate sphere in conformity with the public will constitutionally expressed. To this end it becomes the duty of all to yield a ready and patriotic submission to the laws constitutionally enacted, and thereby promote and strengthen a proper confidence in those institutions of the several States and of the United States which the people themselves have ordained for their own government.

My experience in public concerns and the observation of a life somewhat advanced confirm the opinions long since imbibed by me, that the destruction of our State governments or the annihilation of their control over the local concerns of the people would lead directly to revolution and anarchy, and finally to despotism and military domination. In proportion, therefore, as the General Government encroaches upon the rights of the States, in the same proportion does it impair its own power and detract from its ability to fulfill the purposes of its creation. Solemnly impressed with these considerations, my countrymen will ever find me ready to exercise my constitutional powers in arresting measures which may directly or indirectly encroach upon the rights of the States or tend to consolidate all political power in the General Government. But of equal, and, indeed, of incalculable, importance is the union of these States, and the sacred duty of all to contribute to its preservation by a liberal support of the General Government in the exercise of its just powers. You have been wisely admonished to "accustom yourselves to think and speak of the Union as of the palladium [safeguard] of your political safety and prosperity, watching for its preservation with jealous anxiety, discountenancing whatever may suggest even a suspicion that it can in any event be abandoned, and indignantly frowning upon the first dawning of any attempt to alienate any portion of our country from the rest or to enfeeble the sacred ties which now link together the various parts." Without union our independence and liberty would never have been achieved; without union they never can be maintained. . . . The loss of liberty, of all good government, of peace, plenty, and happiness, must inevitably follow a dissolution of the Union. . . .

The time at which I stand before you is full of interest. The eyes of all nations are fixed on our Republic. The event of the existing crisis will be decisive in the opinion of mankind of the practicability of our federal system of government. Let us realize the importance of the attitude in which we stand before the world. . . .

Deeply impressed with the truth of these observations, and under the obligation of that solemn oath which I am about to take, I shall continue to exert all my faculties to maintain the just powers of the Constitution and to transmit unimpaired to posterity the blessings of our Federal Union. At the same time, it will be my aim to inculcate by my official acts the necessity of exercising by the General Government those powers only that are clearly delegated. . . . [I]t will be my desire so to discharge my duties as to foster with our brethren in all parts of the country a spirit of liberal concession and compromise, and, by reconciling our fellow-citizens to those partial sacrifices which they must unavoidably make for the preservation of a greater good, to recommend our invaluable government and Union to the confidence and affections of the American people.

Finally, it is my most fervent prayer to that Almighty Being . . . that He will so overrule all my intentions and actions and inspire the hearts of my fellow-citizens that we may be preserved from dangers of all kinds and continue forever a united and happy people.

Source: http://www.columbia.edu/~sv12/inaugural/pres24.html.

DOCUMENT 32: Abraham Lincoln's Address before the Young Men's Lyceum of Springfield, Illinois, January 27, 1838

In 1838, Abraham Lincoln spoke before the Young Men's Lyceum of Springfield, Illinois. Lincoln, with a growing and influential law practice, was concerned about the rule of law. His speech addressed the issue of mob violence and its widespread effects on civil society. The lawyer and eventual Whig party congressman appealed to citizens to abide by the rule of law.

Lincoln warned of ambitious individuals who stirred up others for their own self-interest. A people "attached to the government and laws" was essential for a civil society to exist. Lincoln pointed to the Constitution as a bedrock. A civil society required voluntary associations such as lyceums, which encouraged education, self-improvement, and moral commitment. Such informal associations for self-improvement were an essential link connecting the individual citizen to the remote and distant government, and Lincoln used the opportunity to invigorate the belief in the importance of the rule of law.

* * *

AS A SUBJECT for the remarks of the evening, "The perpetuation of our political institutions" is selected.

In the great journal of things happening under the sun, we, the American people, find our account running under date of the nineteenth century of the Christian era. We find ourselves in the peaceful possession of the fairest portion of the earth as regards extent of territory, fertility of soil, and salubrity of climate. We find ourselves under the government of a system of political institutions conducing more essentially to the ends of civil and religious liberty than any of which the history of former times tells us. We, when mounting the stage of existence, found ourselves the legal inheritors of these fundamental blessings. . . . This task of gratitude to our fathers, justice to ourselves, duty to our posterity, and love for our species in general, all imperatively require us faithfully to perform.

How then shall we perform it? At what point shall we expect the approach of danger? By what means shall we fortify against it? Shall we expect some transatlantic military giant to step the ocean and crush us at a blow? Never! . . .

At what point, then, is the approach of danger to be expected? I answer, If it ever reach us it must spring up amongst us; it cannot come from abroad. If destruction be our lot we must ourselves be its author and finisher. As a nation of freemen we must live through all time, or die by suicide.

I hope I am over wary; but if I am not, there is even now something of ill omen amongst us. I mean the increasing disregard for law which pervades the country—the growing disposition to substitute the wild and furious passions in lieu of the sober judgment of courts, and the worse than savage mobs for the executive ministers of justice. This disposition is awfully fearful in any community; and that it now exists in ours, though grating to our feelings to admit, it would be a violation of truth and an insult to our intelligence to deny. Accounts of outrages committed by mobs . . . have pervaded the country from New England to Louisiana . . . ; neither are they confined to the slaveholding or the non-slaveholding States. Alike they spring up among the pleasure-hunting masters of Southern slaves, and the order-loving citizens of the land of steady habits. Whatever then their cause may be, it is common to the whole country.

It would be tedious as well as useless to recount the horrors of all of them. Those happenings in the State of Mississippi and at St. Louis are perhaps the most dangerous in example and revolting to humanity. In the Mississippi case they first commenced by hanging the regular gamblers. . . . Next, negroes suspected of conspiring to raise an insurrection were caught up and hanged in all parts of the State; then, white men supposed to be leagued with the negroes; and finally, strangers from neighboring States, going thither on business, were in many instances subjected to the same fate. . . .

Turn, then, to that horror-striking scene at St. Louis. A single victim was only sacrificed there. . . . A mulatto man . . . was seized in the street, dragged to the suburbs of the city, chained to a tree, and actually burned to death; and all within a single hour from the time he had been a freeman attending to his own business and at peace with the world.

Such are the effects of mob law. . . .

But you are perhaps ready to ask, "What has this to do with the perpetuation of our political institutions?" I answer, "It has much to do with it." Its direct consequences are, comparatively speaking, but a small evil, and much of its danger consists in the proneness of our minds to regard its direct as its only consequences. . . . [B]y the operation of this mobocratic spirit which all must admit is now abroad in the land, the strongest bulwark of any government, and particularly of those constituted like ours, may effectually be broken down and destroyed—I mean the attachment of the people. Whenever this effect shall be produced among us . . . this government cannot last. . . .

. . .

The question recurs, "How shall we fortify against it?" The answer is simple. Let every American, every lover of liberty, every well-wisher to his posterity swear by the blood of the Revolution never to violate in the least particular the laws of the country, and never to tolerate their violation by others. As the patriots of seventy-six did to the support of the Declaration of Independence, so to the support of the Constitution and laws let every American pledge his life, his property, and his sacred honor. . . .

. . .

There is no grievance that is a fit object of redress by mob law. In any case that may arise, as, for instance, the promulgation of abolitionism, one of two positions is necessarily true—that is, the thing is right within itself, and therefore deserves the protection of all law and all good citizens, or it is wrong, and therefore proper to be prohibited by legal enactments; and in neither case is the interposition of mob law either necessary, justifiable, or excusable.

But it may be asked, "Why suppose danger to our political institutions? Have we not preserved them for more than fifty years? And why may we not for fifty times as long?"

. . . That our government should have been maintained in its original form, from its establishment until now, is not much to be wondered at. I had many props to support it through that period, which are now decayed and crumbled away. . . .

. . .

. . . Passion has helped us, but can do no more. It will in future be our enemy. Reason—cold, calculating, unimpassioned reason—must furnish all the materials for our future support and defense. Le those materials be molded into general intelligence, sound morality, and, in particular, a reverence for the Constitution and laws. . . .

Source: http://douglass.speech.nwu.edu/line__a69.htm.

DOCUMENT 33: The Seventh of March Speech: Daniel Webster and the Compromise of 1850

Senator Daniel Webster's speech in the U.S. Senate addressed the issue of fugitive slaves and the prospects of southern secession from the Union. His initial argument indirectly addressed the southern argument for nullification by confessing that while believing that the issue of the return of fugitive slaves to owners was primarily a responsibility of state authorities, he urged northerners to assume their constitutional obligations to return slaves to their owners. Second, Webster examined the issue of whether "peaceful secession" was possible. He concluded that it was not.

* * *

I wish to speak to-day, not as a Massachusetts man, nor as a Northern man, but as an American, and a member of the Senate of the United States. It is fortunate that there is a Senate of the United States; a body not yet removed from its propriety, not lost to a just sense of its own dignity and its own high responsibilities, and a body to which the country looks, with confidence, for wise, moderate, patriotic, and healing counsels. . . .

. . . [I]n the excited times in which we live, there is found to exist a state of crimination and recrimination between the North and South. There are lists of grievances produced by each; and those grievances, real or supposed, alienate the minds of one portion of the country from the other, exasperate the feelings, and subdue the sense of fraternal affection, patriotic love, and mutual regard. . . . I will not answer . . . the general statements of the honorable Senator from South Carolina [Calhoun], that the North has prospered at the expense of the South ... in the collecting of its revenues. .... But I will allude to the other complaints of the South ... that there has been found at the North, among individuals and among legislators, a disinclination to perform fully their constitutional duties in regard to the return of persons bound to service who have escaped into the free States. In that respect, the South, in my judgment, is right, and the North is wrong. Every member of every Northern legislature is bound by oath, like every other officer in the country, to support the Constitution of the United States; and the article of the Constitution which says to these States that they shall deliver up fugitives from service is as binding in honor and conscience as any other article. ....

. . .

Mr. President, I should much prefer to have heard from every member on this floor declarations of opinion that this Union could never be dissolved, than the declaration of opinion by any body, that, in any case, under the pressure of any circumstances, such a dissolution was possible. I hear with distress and anguish the word "secession," especially when it falls from the lips of those who are patriotic, and known to the country, and known all over the world, for their political services. Secession! Peaceable secession! Sir, your eyes and mine are never destined to see that miracle. The dismemberment of this vast country without convulsion! ... Sir, he who sees these States, now revolving in harmony around a common centre, and expects to see them quit their places and fly off without convulsion, may look the next hour to see heavenly bodies rush from their spheres, and jostle against each other in the realms of space, without causing the wreck of the universe. There can be no such thing as peaceable secession. .... Is the great Constitution under which we live, covering this whole country, is it to be thawed and melted away by secession, as the snows on the mountain melt under the influence of a vernal sun, disappear almost unobserved, and run off? No, Sir! No, Sir! I will not state what might produce the disruption of the Union; but, sir, I see as plainly as I see the sun in heaven what that disruption itself must produce; I see that it must produce war, and such a war as I will not describe, *in its twofold character*.

Peaceable secession! Peaceable secession! The concurrent agreement of all the members of this great republic to separate! A voluntary separation, with alimony on one side and on the other. Why, what should be the result? Where is the line to be drawn? What States are to be seceded? What is to remain American? What am I to be? An american no longer? Am I to become a sectional man, a local man, a separatist, with no country in common with the gentlemen who sit around me here, or who fill the other house of Congress? ... Why, sir, our ancestors ... would rebuke and reproach us; and our children and our grandchildren would cry out shame upon us, if we of this generation should dishonor these ensigns of the power of the government and the harmony of that Union which is every day felt among us with so much joy and gratitude....

. . .

And now, Mr. President, instead of speaking of the possibility or utility of secession . . . let us enjoy the fresh air of Liberty and Union. . . . Let us make our generation one of the strongest and brightest links in that golden chain which is destined, I fondly believe, to grapple the people of all the States to this Constitution for ages to come. . . . No monarchical throne presses these States together, no iron chain of military power encircles them; they live and stand under a government popular in its form, representative in its character, founded upon principles of equality, and so constructed, we hope, as to last for ever. In all its history it has been beneficent; it has trodden down no man's liberty; it has crushed no State. Its daily respiration is liberty and patriotism; its yet youthful veins are full of enterprise, courage, and honorable love of glory and renown. . . .

Source: http://www.dartmouth.edu/~dwebster/speeches/seventh-march.html.

DOCUMENT 34: John C. Calhoun, the Compromise of 1850, and State Autonomy, First Session of Congress, 1850

In 1850, controversy over the territory the United States acquired during the Mexican War came to a head and nearly led to disunion. In a speech before Senate colleagues, John C. Calhoun of South Carolina addressed the causes of disunion. He warned that the causes were beyond the issue of slavery, although he found that issue to be at the heart of disagreement between the North and the South. At the center of his concern about the threat of disunion was the encroachment of the national government on the rights of the states.

As a leading politician and political theorist for the South and its most eminent spokesperson, Calhoun outlined the causes of the threat of disunion. He framed the frustrations of the South in the context of the change in equilibrium between the South and the North and the radical change in the national government's character. He referred to the shift from a federal system to a consolidated system as a primary cause of the threat of disunion. His reference to documents of the 1780s reinvigorated the ideas expressed by Federalists and Antifederalists during the debates surrounding ratification.

* * *

Mr. Calhoun: I have Senators, believed from the first that the agitation of the subject of slavery would, if not prevented by some timely and effective measure, end in disunion. Entertaining this opinion, I have, on all proper occasions, endeavored to call the attention of each of the two great parties which divide the country to adopt some measure to prevent so great a disaster, but without success. The agitation has been permitted to proceed, with almost no attempt to resist it, until it has reached a period when it can no longer be disguised or denied that the Union is in danger. You have thus had forced upon you the greatest and the gravest questions that can ever come under your consideration: How can the Union be preserved?

To give a satisfactory answer to this mighty question, it is indispensable to have an accurate and thorough knowledge of the nature and the character of the cause by which the Union is endangered. Without such knowledge it is impossible to pronounce, with any certainty, by what measure it can be saved; just as it would be impossible for a physician to pronounce in the case of some dangerous disease, with any certainty, by what remedy the patient could be saved, without familiar knowledge of the nature and character of the cause of the disease. The first question, then, presented for consideration, in the investigation I propose to make, in order to obtain such knowledge, is: What is it that has endangered the Union?

To this question there can be but one answer: that the immediate cause is the almost universal discontent which pervades all the States composing the southern section of the Union. This widely-extended discontent is not of recent origin. It commenced with the agitation of the slavery question, and has been increasing ever since. The next question, going one step further back, is: What has caused this widely-diffused and almost universal discontent?

It is a great mistake to suppose, as is by some, that it originated with demagogues, who excited the discontent with the intention of aiding their personal advancement, or with the disappointed ambition of certain politicians, who resorted to it as the means of retrieving their fortunes. On the contrary, all the great political influences of the section were arrayed against excitement, and exerted to the utmost to keep the people quiet. The great mass of the people of the South were divided, as in the other section, into Whigs and Democrats. The leaders and the presses of both parties in the South were very solicitous to prevent excitement and to preserve quiet; because it was seen that the effects of the former would necessarily tend to weaken, if not destroy, the political ties which united them with their respective parties in the other section. Those who know the strength of party ties will readily appreciate the immense forces which this cause exerted against agitation and in favor of preserving quiet. But, as great as it was, it was not sufficiently so to prevent the wide-spread discontent which now pervades the section. No; some cause, far deeper and more powerful than the one supposed, must exist, to account for discontent so wide and deep. The question, then, recurs: What is the cause of this discontent? It will be found in the belief of the people of the southern States, as prevalent as the discontent itself, that they cannot remain, as things now are, consistently with honor and safety, in the Union. The next question to be considered is: What has caused this belief?

One of the causes is, undoubtedly, to be traced to the long-continued agitation of the slavery question on the part of the North, and the many aggressions which they have made on the rights of the South during the time. . . .

There is another, lying back of it, with which this is intimately connected, that may be regarded as the great and primary cause. That is to be found in the fact that the equilibrium between the two sections in the Government, as it stood when the constitution was ratified and the Government put in action, has been destroyed. At that time there was nearly a perfect equilibrium between the two, which afforded ample means to each to protect itself against the aggression of the other; but, as it now stands, one section has the exclusive power of controlling the Government, which leaves the other without any means of protecting itself against its encroachment and oppression. . . .

. . .

The result of the whole is to give the northern section a predominance in every part of the Government, and thereby concentrate in it the two elements which constitute the Federal Government—a majority of States and a majority of their population, estimated in federal numbers. Whatever section concentrates the two in itself possesses the control of the entire Government.

. . . [The] great increase of Senators, added to the great increase of members in the House of Representatives and the electoral college on the part of the North, which must take place under the next decade, will effectually and irretrievably destroy the equilibrium which existed when the Government was commenced.

Had this destruction been the operation of time, without the interference of Government, the South would have had no reason to complain; but such was not the fact. It was caused by the legislation of this Government. . . . [T]he original character of the Government has been radically changed. . . . [T]he equilibrium between the two sections has been destroyed [by a series of government acts], and the whole powers of the system centered in a sectional majority.

The first of the series of acts by which the South was deprived of its due share of the territories, originated with the Confederacy, which preceded the existence of the Government. It is to be found in the [Northwest] ordinance of 1787. . . . The next of the series is the Missouri compromise, which excluded the South from that large part portion of Louisiana. . . . The last of the series excluded the South from the whole of the Oregon Territory. . . .

I have not included the territory recently acquired by the treaty with Mexico. The North is making the most strenuous efforts to appropriate the whole to herself, by excluding the South from every foot of it. . . .

Such is the first and great cause that has destroyed the equilibrium between the two sections in the Government. . . .

. . .

But while these measures were destroying the equilibrium between the two sections, *the action of the Government was leading to a radical change in its character, by concentrating all the power of the system in itself* [italics added]. . . .

That the Government claims, and practically maintains, the right to decide in the last resort as to the extent of its powers, will scarcely be denied by any one conversant with the political history of the country. That it also claims the right to resort to force to maintain whatever power she claims, against all opposition, is equally certain. Indeed, it is apparent, from what we daily hear, that this has become the prevailing and fixed opinion of a great majority of the community. Now, I ask, what limitation can possibly be placed upon the powers of a Government claiming and exercising such rights? And, if none can be, *how can the separate governments of the States maintain and protect the powers reserved to them by the Constitution* [italics added], or the people of the several States maintain those which are reserved to them, and among others, the sovereign powers by which they ordained and established, not only their separate State constitutions and governments, but also the Constitution and Government of the United States? But, if they have no constitutional means of maintaining them against the right claimed by this Government, it necessarily follows that they hold them at its pleasure and discretion, and that all the powers of the system are in reality concentrated in it. It also follows that the character of the Government has been changed, in consequence, from a Federal Republic, as it originally came from the hands of its framers, and that it has been changed into a great national consolidated Democracy. It has indeed, at present, all the characteristics of the latter, and not one of the former, although it still retains its outward form.

The result of the whole of these causes combined is, that, the North has acquired a decided ascendancy over every department of this Government, and through it a control over all the powers of the system. . . .

Source: Speech of John C. Calhoun, *Congressional Globe*, 31st Congress, 1st session, 1850, pp. 451–452.

DOCUMENT 35: William H. Seward, the Compromise of 1850, and an Appeal to a Higher Law, First Session of Congress, 1850

William H. Seward was a U.S. senator from New York. The "Wizard of the North" entered into debate with Senator John C. Calhoun of South Carolina during the Compromise of 1850. Although the debate between Calhoun and Seward centered around whether the Mexican cession lands would be slave or free, their discourse ultimately focused on the issue of states' rights and federalism. Seward described the origins of the Constitution as an equilibrium but in a different way than Calhoun did (see Document 34). Seward argued that an acceptance of Calhoun's plan would return the nation to the period of the Articles of Confederation.

* * *

Allowing due consideration to the increasing density of our population, we are safe in assuming, that long before this mass shall have attained the maximum numbers indicated, the entire width of our possessions, from the Atlantic to the Pacific ocean, will be covered by it, and be brought into social maturity, and complete political organization.

The question now arises, Shall this one great people, having a common origin, a common language, a common religion, common sentiments, interests, sympathies, and hopes, remain one political State, one nation, one Republic, or shall it be broken into two conflicting, and probably hostile nations or Republics? There cannot ultimately be more than two; for the habit of association is already formed, as the interests of mutual intercourse are being formed. It is already ascertained where the centre of political power must rest; it must rest in the agricultural interests and masses, who will occupy the interior of the continent. These masses, if they cannot all command access to both oceans, will not be obstructed in their approaches to that one which offers the greatest facilities to their commerce.

Shall the American people then be divided? Before deciding on this question, let us consider our position, our power, and capabilities.

The world contains no seat of empire so magnificent as this.... The nation thus situated ... must command the empire of the seas, which alone is real empire.

We think, that we may claim to have inherited physical and intellectual vigor, courage, invention, and enterprise, and the systems of education prevailing among us, open to all the stores of human science and art.

The Old World and the past were allotted by Providence to the pupilage of mankind, under the hard discipline of arbitrary power, quelling the violence of human passions. The New World and the future seem to have been appointed for the maturity of mankind with the development of self-government operating in obedience to reason and judgment.

We have thoroughly tried our novel system of democratic Federal Government, with its complex, yet harmonious and effective, combination of distinct local elective agencies, for the conduct of domestic affairs, and its common central elective agencies, for the regulation of internal interests, and of intercourse with foreign nations; and we know, that it is a system equally cohesive in its parts, and capable of all desirable expansion; and that it is a system, moreover, perfectly adapted to secure domestic tranquility, while it brings into activity all the elements of national aggrandizement [glorification]. . . .

And now it seems to me, that the perpetual unity of our empire hangs on the decision of this day and of this hour.

California is already a State—a complete and fully-appointed State. She never again can be less than that. . . .

        . . .

It is now avowed by the honorable Senator from South Carolina, (Mr. Calhoun,) that nothing will satisfy the slave States but a compromise that will convince them that they can remain in the Union consistently with their honor and their safety. And what are the concessions which will have that effect? . . .

        . . .

These terms amount to this: that the free States having already, or although they may hereafter have, majorities of States, majorities of population, and majorities in both houses of Congress, shall concede to the slave States, being in a minority in both, the unequal advantage of an equality—that is, that we shall alter the Constitution so as to convert the Government from a national democracy, operating by a constitutional majority of voices, into a Federal alliance, in which the minority shall have a veto against the majority. And this is to return to the original Articles of Confederation!

I will not stop to protest against the injustice or the inexpediency of an innovation which, if it was practicable, would be so entirely subversive of the principle of democratic institutions. It is enough to say, that it is totally impracticable. The free States, northern and western acquiesced, in the long and nearly unbroken ascendancy of the slave States under the Constitution, because the result happened under the Constitution. But they have honor and interests to preserve; and there is nothing in the nature of mankind, or in the character of that people, to induce an expectation that they, loyal as they are, are insensible to the duty of defending them. But the scheme would still be impracticable, even if this difficulty were overcome. What is proposed, is a political equilibrium. Every political equilibrium requires a physical equilibrium to rest upon, and is valueless, without it. To constitute a physical equilibrium between the slave States, and the free States, requires first an equality of territory or some near approximation; and this is already lost. But it requires much more than this; it requires an equality or a proximate equality, in the number of slaves and freemen. And this must be perpetual! . . .

. . .

. . . The theory of a new political equilibrium claims that it once existed, and has been lost. When lost, and how? It began to be lost in 1787, when preliminary arrangements were made to admit five new free States in the Northwest territory, two years before the Constitution was finally adopted—that it, it began to be lost two years before it began to exist!

Sir, the equilibrium if restored, would be lost again, and lost more rapidly than it was before. The progress of the free population is to be accelerated by increased emigration from Europe and Asia, while that of the slaves is to be checked and retarded by inevitable partial emancipation. "Nothing (says Montesquieu) reduces a man so low as always to see freemen, and yet not be free. Persons in that condition are natural enemies of the State, and their numbers would be dangerous, if increased too high." Sir, the fugitive slave colonies and the emancipated slave colonies in the free States, in Canada, and in Liberia, are the best guarantees South Carolina has for the perpetuity of slavery. . . .

. . .

. . . The Constitution contains only a compact, which rests for its execution on the States. Not content with this, the slave States induced legislation by Congress; and the Supreme Court of the United States have virtually decided that the whole subject is within the province of Congress, and exclusive of State authority—nay, not merely as persons to be claimed, but as property and chattels, to be seized without any legal authority or claim whatever. The compact is thus subverted by the procurement of the slave States. . . .

. . .

. . . Relying on the perversion of the Constitution, which makes slaves mere chattels, the slave States have applied to them the principles of the criminal law, and have held that he who aided the escape of his fellow man from bondage, was guilty of a larceny in stealing him. I speak of what I know. . . .

. . .

. . . There are constitutions and statutes, codes mercantile and codes civil; but when we are legislating for States, especially when we are founding States, all these laws must be brought to the standard of the laws of God, and must be tried by that standard, and must stand or fall by it. . . .

. . .

But even if the States continue as States, they surrendered their equality as States, and submitted themselves to the sway of the numerical majority, with qualifications of checks—first, of the representation of three fifths of slaves in the ratio of representation and taxation; and secondly, of the equal representation of States in the Senate. . . .

. . .

. . . [W]hen the Constitution was adopted, twelve of the thirteen States were slave States, and so there was no equilibrium. And so as to the classification of States as northern States and southern States. It is the maintenance of slavery by law in a State, not parallels of latitude, that makes it a southern State; and the absence of this, that makes it a northern State. And so all the States, save one, were southern States, and there was no equilibrium. But the Constitution was made, not only for southern and northern States, but for States neither northern nor southern—the western States, their coming in being foreseen and provided for. . . .

. . .

. . . The Constitution regulates our stewardship; the Constitution devotes the domain to union, to justice, to defence, to welfare, and to liberty.

But there is a higher law than the Constitution, which regulates our authority over the domain, and devotes it to the same noble purposes. The territory is a part—no inconsiderable part—of the common heritage of mankind, bestowed upon them by the Creator of the universe. We are his stewards, and must so discharge our trust as to secure, in the highest attainable degree, their happiness.

Source: Speech of William H. Seward, *Congressional Globe*, 31st Congress, 1st session, 1850, appendix, pp. 262–265.

DOCUMENT 36: William H. Seward and the Declaration of Independence: An Appeal to Higher Law, 1856

In 1856, the United States experienced a mini–civil war over the issue of slavery in Kansas. What resulted was the Kansas-Nebraska Act, a piece of legislation that many historians believe exacerbated the tension between southern and northern states. Popular sovereignty—the natural rights concept that ultimate political authority rests with the people—was the strategy that came from the 1848 election and the Compromise of 1850; it was implemented in the Kansas-Nebraska

Act of 1856. It fueled the tensions of settlement in Kansas as both slave-holders and freeholders rushed to settle Kansas and determine the direction of its state constitution.

In this speech before the Senate, William H. Seward of New York addressed the issue of slavery. After noting the global changes that had occurred regarding the issue, he appealed to the Declaration of Independence as a constitutional document espousing higher law. The implications of this link to the Declaration of Independence were profound concerning state and national government relations.

* * *

... Shall we confess before the world, after so brief a trial, that this great political system of ours is inadequate either to enable the majority to control through the operation of opinion, without force, or to give security to the citizen against tyranny and domestic violence? Are we prepared so soon to relinquish our simple and beautiful systems of republican government, and to substitute in their place the machinery of usurpation and despotism?

The Congress of the United States can refuse admission to Kansas only on the ground that it will not relinquish the hope of carrying African slavery into that new Territory. If you are prepared to assume that ground, why not do it manfully and consistently, and establish slavery there by a direct and explicit act of Congress? But have we come to that stage of demoralization and degeneracy so soon?—we, who commenced our political existence and gained the sympathies of the world by proclaiming to other nations that we held "these truths to be self-evident: that all men are created equal, and have certain inalienable rights; and that among these rights are life, liberty, and the pursuit of happiness;" we who, in the spirit of that declaration, have assumed to teach and to illustrate, for the benefit of mankind, a higher and better civilization than they have hitherto known! If the Congress of the United States shall persist in this attempt, then they shall at least allow me to predict its results: Either you will not establish African slavery in Kansas, or you will do it at the cost of the sacrifice of all the existing liberties of the American people. Even if slavery, were, what it is not, a boon to the people of Kansas, they would reject it if enforced upon their acceptance by Federal bayonets. The attempt is in conflict with all the tendencies of the age.

Source: Speech of William H. Seward, *Congressional Globe*, 34th Congress, 1st session, 1856, appendix, pp. 404–405.

DOCUMENT 37: *Dred Scott v. Sandford* (1857): Roger B. Taney and States' Rights

Issues of individual rights, states' rights, the status of slaves, and the nature of the U.S. Constitution converged in the *Dred Scott* decision of the Roger B. Taney Court in 1857. The case brought before the Supreme Court concerned the legal status of Dred Scott, a man born into slavery who had since resided in the free states of Illinois, Wisconsin, and the territory of Minnesota. The larger issues included the authority of the federal government to limit the extension of slavery in the territories. The Taney Court, comprising primarily southern justices, supported John C. Calhoun's constitutional principles in a decision that found Dred Scott to be a slave because Congress did not have the authority to exclude the use of a person's property from any territory of the United States. Furthermore, the Court reiterated the principle that Scott, and all other slaves, were property and therefore had no recourse to sue for redress in court.

The decision, delivered by Chief Justice Taney, overturned legislative acts found in the Missouri Compromise, the Compromise of 1850, and the Kansas-Nebraska Act and supported strongly the institution of slavery, disallowing citizenship on the basis of color.

* * *

The question is simply this: Can a negro, whose ancestors were imported into this country, and sold as slaves, become a member of the political community formed and brought into existence by the constitution of the United States, and as such become entitled to all the rights, and privileges, and immunities, guaranteed by that instrument to the citizen? One of which rights is the privilege of suing in a court of the United States in the cases specified in the constitution.

. . .

. . . We think they are not, and that they are not included, and were not intended to be included, under the word "citizens" in the constitution, and can therefore claim none of the rights and privileges which that instrument provides for and secures to citizens of the United States. On the contrary, they were at that time considered as a subordinate and inferior class of beings, who had been subjugated by the dominant race, and, whether emancipated or not, yet remained subject to their authority, and had no rights or privileges but such as those who held the power and the government might choose to grant them.

...

... The duty of the court is, to interpret the instrument they have framed, with the best lights we can obtain on the subject, and to administer it as we find it, according to its true intent and meaning when it was adopted.

In discussing this question, we must not confound the rights of citizenship which a State may confer within its own limits, and the rights of citizenship as a member of the Union. ... But this character of course was confined to the boundaries of the State, and gave him no rights or privileges in other States beyond those secured to him by the laws of nations and the comity of States. Nor have the several States surrendered the power of conferring these rights and privileges by adopting the constitution of the United States. ...

It is very clear, therefore, that no State can, by any act or law of its own, passed since the adoption of the constitution, introduce a new member into the political community created by the constitution of the United States. It cannot make him a member of this community by making him a member of its own. ...

...

In the opinion of the court, the legislation and histories of the times, and the language used in the declaration of independence, show, that neither the class of persons who had been imported as slaves, nor their descendants, whether they had become free or not, were then acknowledged as a part of the people, nor intended to be included in the general words used in that memorable instrument. ...

The act of Congress, upon which the plaintiff relies, declares that slavery and involuntary servitude, except as a punishment for crime, shall be forever prohibited in all that part of the territory ceded by France, under the name of Louisiana, which lies north of thirty-six degrees thirty minutes north latitude and not included within the limits of Missouri. ...

...

... All we mean to say on this point is that, as there is no express regulation in the Constitution defining the power which the general government may exercise over the person or property of a citizen in a territory thus acquired, the Court must necessarily look to the provisions and principles of the Constitution, and its distribution of powers, for the rules and principles by which its decision must be governed.

Taking this rule to guide us, it may be safely assumed that citizens of the United States who migrate to a territory belonging to the people of the United States cannot be ruled as mere colonists, dependent upon the will of the general government, and to be governed by any laws it may think proper to impose. The principle upon which our governments rest, and upon which alone they continue to exist, is the union of states, sovereign and independent within their own limits in their internal and domestic concerns, and bound together as one people by a general government, possessing certain enumerated and restricted powers, delegated to it by the people of the several states, and exercising supreme authority within the scope of the powers granted to it, throughout the dominion of the United States. . . . Whatever it acquires, it acquires for the benefit of the people of the several states who created it. . . .

But the power of Congress over the person or property of a citizen can never be a mere discretionary power under our Constitution and form of government. . . . The territory, being a part of the United States, the government and the citizen both enter it under the authority of the Constitution, with their respective rights defined and marked out; and the federal government can exercise no power over his person or property, beyond what that instrument confers, nor lawfully deny any right which it has reserved. . . .

. . . Thus the rights of property are united with the rights of person and placed on the same ground by the Fifth Amendment to the Constitution, which provides that no person shall be deprived of life, liberty, and property without due process of law. . . .

. . .

. . . [The federal government] has no power over the person or property of a citizen but what the citizens of the United States have granted. . . .

. . .

Upon these considerations it is the opinion of the Court that the act of Congress which prohibited a citizen from holding and owning property of this kind in the territory of the United States . . . is not warranted by the Constitution and is therefore void; and that neither Dred Scott himself, nor any of his family, were made free by being carried into this territory; even if they had been carried there by the owner with the intention of becoming a permanent resident. . . .

Source: Kermit Hall, *Major Problems in American Constitutional History* (Lexington, Mass.: D.C. Heath, 1992), pp. 463–470.

DOCUMENT 38: James Buchanan's Fourth Annual Message: States and Withdrawal from the Union, December 3, 1860

Following the 1860 election, the outgoing president, James Buchanan, delivered his fourth annual message to Congress. Buchanan confronted the threat of secession by offering his views concerning how the federal government could respond to secession of one or more states.

* * *

Fellow-Citizens of the Senate and House of Representatives:

... [I]it is beyond the power of any President, no matter what may be his own political proclivities, to restore peace and harmony among the States. Wisely limited and restrained as is his power under our Constitution and laws, he alone can accomplish but little for good or for evil on such a momentous question. . . .

The question fairly stated is, Has the Constitution delegated to Congress the power to coerce a State into submission which is attempting to withdraw or has actually withdrawn from the Confederacy [Federal Union]? If answered in the affirmative, it must be on the principle that the power has been conferred upon Congress to declare and to make war against a State. After much serious reflection I have arrived at the conclusion that no such power has been delegated to Congress or to any other department of the federal government. It is manifest upon an inspection of the Constitution that this is not among the specific and enumerated powers granted to Congress, and it is equally apparent that its exercise is not "necessary and proper for carrying into execution" any of these powers. . . .

. . .

The fact is that our Union rests upon public opinion, and can never be cemented by the blood of its citizens shed in civil war. . . .

. . .

Congress can contribute much to avert it [civil war] by proposing and recommending to the legislatures of the several States the remedy for existing evils which the Constitution has itself provided for its own preservation. . . .

This is the very course which I earnestly recommend in order to obtain an "explanatory amendment" of the Constitution on the subject of slavery. . . . Such an explanatory amendment would, it is believed, forever terminate the existing dissensions, and restore peace and harmony among the States.

Source: Fred L. Israel, ed., *The State of the Union Messages of the Presidents, 1790–1966* (New York: Chelsea House, 1967).

DOCUMENT 39: Resolutions of Secession: Mississippi (January 11, 1861), South Carolina (December 20, 1860), and Virginia (April 17, 1861)

In the tradition of the Declaration of Independence, the southern states summarized their grievances with the Union in documents variously known as resolutions or ordinances of secession. Mississippi and South Carolina provided detailed reasons for severing ties with the Union. The principle of state sovereignty, the U.S. Constitution as the creation of the states, and a list of grievances against the national government, state governments of free states, and abolitionist groups provided a rationale for the separation of Mississippi and South Carolina from the Union. In contrast, the Virginia Ordinance of Secession was relatively brief and more dispassionate; it listed the circumstances of Virginia in joining the Union in 1788 and observed that secession was the result of the federal government's "injury and oppression" through the perversion of its powers.

* * *

Mississippi Resolutions

Whereas, the constitutional Union was formed by the several states in their separate sovereign capacity for the purpose of mutual advantage and protection;

That the several states are distinct sovereignties, whose supremacy is limited so far only as the same has been delegated by voluntary compact to a federal government, and, when it fails to accomplish the ends for which it was established, the parties to the compact have the right to resume, each state for itself, such delegated powers;

That the institution of slavery existed prior to the formation of the federal Constitution, and is recognized by its letter, and all efforts to impair its value or lessen its duration by Congress, or any of the free states, is a violation of the compact of Union and is destructive of the ends for which it was ordained, but in defiance of the principles of the Union thus established, the people of the Northern states have assumed a revolutionary position toward the Southern states;

That they have set at defiance that provision of the Constitution which was intended to secure domestic tranquility among the states and promote the general welfare, namely: "No person held to service or labor in one state, under the laws thereof, escaping into another shall, in consequence of any law or regulation therein, be discharged from such service or labor, but shall be delivered up, on claim of the party to whom such service or labor may be due";

That they have by voluntary associations, individual agencies, and state legislation interfered with slavery as it prevails in the slaveholding states;

That they have enticed our slaves from us and, by state intervention, obstructed and prevented their rendition under the Fugitive Slave Law;

That they continue their system of agitation obviously for the purpose of encouraging other slaves to escape from service . . . ;

That they claim the right and demand its execution by Congress, to exclude slavery from the territories . . . ;

That they declare in every manner in which public opinion is expressed their unalterable determination to exclude from admittance into the Union any new state that tolerates slavery in its constitution . . . ;

That they thus seek by an increase of Abolition state . . . for the purpose of preparing an amendment to the Constitution of the United States abolishing slavery in the states . . . ;

That they have . . . insulted and outraged our citizens . . . ;

That to encourage the stealing of our property . . . ;

That they have sought to create domestic discord in the Southern states by incendiary publications;

That they encouraged a hostile invasion of a Southern state . . . ;

That they have deprived Southern citizens of their property . . . ;

We of the Southern states alone made an exception to that universal quiet;

That they have elected a majority of electors for President and Vice-President . . . ;

Be it resolved by the legislature of the state of Mississippi that, in the opinion of those who now constitute the said legislature, the secession of each aggrieved state is the proper remedy for these injuries.

South Carolina Declarations

THE PEOPLE of the state of South Carolina, in convention assembled, on the 2nd day of April, A.D. 1852, declared that the frequent violations of the Constitution of the United States by the federal government, and its encroachments upon the reserved rights of the states, fully justified this state in their withdrawal from the federal Union; but in deference to the opinions and wishes of the other slaveholding states, she forebore at that time to exercise this right. Since that time, these encroachments have continued to increase, and further forbearance ceases to be a virtue.

And, now, the state of South Carolina, having resumed her separate and equal place among nations, deems it due to herself, to the remaining United States of America, and to the nations of the world, that she should declare the immediate causes which have led to this act.

In the year 1765, that portion of the British empire embracing Great Britain undertook to make laws for the government of that portion composed of the thirteen American colonies. A struggle for the rights of self-government ensued, which resulted, on the 4th of July, 1776, in a Declaration, by the colonies. . . .

They further solemnly declared that whenever any "form of government becomes destructive of the ends for which it was established, it is the right of the people to alter or abolish it, and to institute a new government. . . ."

In pursuance of this Declaration of Independence, each of the thirteen states proceeded to exercise its separate sovereignty. . . . [T]hey entered into a league known as the Articles of Confederation. . . .

Under this Confederation, the War of the Revolution was carried on. . . .

. . .

Thus were established the two great principles asserted by the colonies, namely, the right of a state to govern itself; and the right of a people to abolish a government when it becomes destructive of the ends for which it was instituted. And concurrent with the establishment of these principles was the fact that each colony became and was recognized by the mother country as a free, sovereign, and independent state.

In 1787, deputies were appointed by the states to revise the Articles of Confederation; and on Sept. 17, 1787, these deputies recommended, for the adoption of the states, the Articles of Union, known as the Constitution of the United States.

The parties to whom this Constitution was submitted were the sovereign states; they were to agree or disagree, and when nine of them agreed, the compact was to take effect among those concurring; and the general government, as the common agent, was then to be invested with their authority.

If only nine of the thirteen states had concurred, the other four would have remained as they then were—separate, sovereign states, independent of any of the provisions of the Constitution. . . .

By this Constitution, certain duties were imposed upon the several states, and the exercise of certain of their powers was restrained, which necessarily impelled their continued existence as sovereign states. But, to remove all doubt, an amendment was added which declared that the powers not delegated to the United States by the Constitution, nor prohibited by it to the states, are reserved to the states respectively, or to the people. On the 23rd of May, 1788, South Carolina, by a convention of her people, passed an ordinance assenting to the Constitution, and afterward altered her own constitution to conform herself to the obligations she had undertaken.

Thus was established, by compact between the states, a government with defined objects and powers, limited to the express words of the grant. This limitation left the whole remaining mass of power subject to the clause reserving it to the states or the people, and rendered unnecessary any specification of reserved rights. We hold that the government thus established is subject to the two great principles asserted in the Declaration of Independence; and we hold further that the mode of its formation subjects it to a third fundamental principle, namely, the law of compact. . . .

In the present case, the fact is established with certainty. We assert that fourteen of the states have deliberately refused for years past to fulfill their constitutional obligations, and we refer to their own statutes for the proof.

The Constitution of the United States, in its 4th Article, provides as follows: "No person held to service or labor in one state, under the laws thereof, escaping into another shall, in consequence of any law or regulation therein, be discharged from such service or labor, but shall be delivered up, on claim of the party to whom such service or labor may be due."

This stipulation was so material to the compact that without it that compact would not have been made. . . . The states of Maine, New Hampshire, Vermont, Massachusetts, Connecticut, Rhode Island, New York, Pennsylvania, Illinois, Indiana, Michigan, Wisconsin, and Iowa have enacted laws which either nullify the acts of Congress or render useless any attempt to execute them. In many of these states the fugitive is discharged from the service of labor claimed, and in none of them has the state government complied with the stipulation made in the Constitution.

The state of New Jersey, at an early day, passed a law in conformity with her constitutional obligation; but the current of antislavery feeling has led her more recently to enact laws which render inoperative the remedies provided by her own laws and by the laws of Congress. In the state of New York even the right of transit for a slave has been denied by her tribunals; and the states of Ohio and Iowa have refused to surrender to justice fugitives charged with murder and with inciting servile insurrection in the state of Virginia. Thus the constitutional compact has been deliberately broken and disregarded by the nonslaveholding states; and the consequence follows that South Carolina is released from her obligation.

The ends for which this Constitution was framed . . . endeavored to accomplish by a federal government in which each state was recognized as an equal and had separate control over its own institutions. . . .

We affirm that these ends for which this government was instituted have been defeated, and the government itself has been destructive of them by the action of the nonslaveholding states. . . . For twenty-five years this agitation has been steadily increasing, until it has now secured to its aid the power of the common government. Observing the forms of the Constitution, a sectional party has found, within that article establishing the Executive Department, the means of subverting the Constitution itself. A geographical line has been drawn across the Union, and all the states north of that line have united in the election of a man to the high office of President of the United States whose opinions and purposes are hostile to slavery. . . .

This sectional combination for the subversion of the Constitution has been aided, in some states, by elevating to citizenship persons who, by the supreme law of the land, are incapable of becoming citizens. . . .

On the 4th of March next this party will take possession of the government. It has announced that the South shall be excluded from the common territory, that the judicial tribunal shall be made sectional, and that a war must be waged against slavery until it shall cease throughout the United States.

The guarantees of the Constitution will then no longer exist; the equal rights of the states will be lost. . . .

Sectional interest and animosity will deepen the irritation. . . .

We, therefore, the people of South Carolina, by our delegates in convention assembled, appealing to the Supreme Judge of the world for the rectitude of our intentions, have solemnly declared that the Union heretofore existing between this state and the other states of North America is dissolved; and that the state of South Carolina has resumed her position among the nations of the world, as [a] separate and independent state, with full power to levy war, contract alliances, establish commerce, and to do all other acts and things which independent states may of right do.

Virginia Ordinance of Secession

An ORDINANCE to repeal the ratification of the Constitution of the United States of America, by the State of Virginia, and to resume, all rights and powers granted under said Constitution.

The people of Virginia, in their ratification of the constitution of the United States of America, adopted by them in convention on the twenty-fifth day of June in the year of our Lord one thousand seven hundred and eighty-eight, having declared that the powers granted under the said constitution were derived from the people of the United States, and might be resumed whensoever the same should be perverted to their injury and oppression; and the federal government having perverted said powers, not only to the injury of the people of Virginia, but to the oppression of the southern, slaveholding states:

Now, therefore, we the people of Virginia do declare and ordain, that the ordinance adopted by the people of this state in convention on the twenty-fifth day of June in the year of our Lord one thousand seven hundred and eighty-eight, whereby the constitution of the United States of America was ratified, and all acts of the general assembly of this state ratifying or adopting amendments to said constitution, are hereby repealed and abrogated; that the union between Union between the state of Virginia and the other states under the constitution aforesaid is hereby dissolved, and that the state of Virginia is in the full possession and exercise of all the rights of sovereignty which belong and appertain to a free and independent state.

And they do further declare, that said constitution of the United States of America is no longer, binding on any of the citizens of this state.

This ordinance shall take effect and be an act of this day, when ratified by a majority of the votes of the people of this state, cast at a poll to be taken thereon the fourth Thursday in May, next, in pursuance of a schedule hereafter to be enacted.

Done in convention, in the city of Richmond, on the seventeenth day of April, in the year of our Lord one thousand eight hundred and sixty-one, and in the eighty-fifth year of the commonwealth of Virginia.

Source: http://www.nv.cc.va.us/~nvsageh/SecessionDocs.htm.

DOCUMENT 40: Abraham Lincoln's First Inaugural Address, March 4, 1861

In preparation for his First Inaugural Address, Abraham Lincoln requested from his law partner, William Herndon, a number of books containing speeches made during the preceding three decades. Among the speeches Lincoln wished to consult were Daniel Webster's reply to Robert Hayne, Andrew Jackson's Proclamation Against Nullification, and Henry Clay's speech of 1850.

Lincoln hoped his remarks would quell southern fears. He promised to respect states' rights and assured the South that he would not interfere with slavery where it already existed. Moreover, he hoped to satisfy southern suspicions regarding the issue of fugitive slaves. Yet Lincoln provided his notion of the government, which was perpetual and did not allow states to withdraw from the Union. Lincoln implied the importance of the Declaration of Independence with the important observation, "The Union is much older than the Constitution." He also referenced throughout his address the importance of majority rule–minority rights and warned the South that under its plan of protecting minority rights, perpetual fragmentation of governments and territories would result.

Lincoln concluded his address with reference to the "mystic chords of memory, stretching from every battlefield and patriot grave." His literary metaphor of "mystic chords of memory" was a reference to Publius's "sacred knot" in *Federalist* Number 15. The Union, in Lincoln's view, was perpetual and binding.

* * *

Fellow-Citizens of the United States:

In compliance with a custom as old as Government itself, I appear before you to address you briefly and to take in your presence the oath prescribed by the Constitution of the United States to be taken by the President "before he enters on the execution of this office."

. . .

Apprehension seems to exist among the people of the Southern States that by the accession of a Republican Administration their property and their peace and personal security are to be endangered. There has never been any reasonable cause for such apprehension. . . .

I have no purpose, directly or indirectly, to interfere with the institution of slavery in the States where it exists. I believe I have no lawful right to do so, and I have no inclination to do so.

Those who nominated and elected me did so with full knowledge that I had made this and many similar declarations and had never recanted them. . . .

. . . I add, too, that all the protection which, consistently with the Constitution and the laws, can be given will be cheerfully given to all the States when lawfully demanded, for whatever cause—as cheerfully to one section as to another.

There is much controversy about the delivering up of fugitives from service or labor. . . .

. . .

There is some difference of opinion whether this [fugitive slave] clause [in Article IV of the Constitution] should be enforced by national or by State authority, but surely that difference is not a very material one. If the slave is to be surrendered, it can be of little consequence to him or to others by which authority it is done. . . .

. . .

It is seventy-two years since the first inauguration of a President under our National Constitution. . . . Yet, with all this scope of precedent, I now enter upon the same task for the brief constitutional term of four years under great and peculiar difficulty. A disruption of the Federal Union, heretofore only menaced, is now formidably attempted.

I hold that in contemplation of universal law and of the Constitution the Union of these States is perpetual. Perpetuity is implied, if not expressed, in the fundamental law of all national governments. It is safe to assert that no government proper ever had a provision in its organic law for its own termination. . . .

Again: If the United States be not a government proper, but an association of States in the nature of contract merely, can it, as a contract, be peaceably unmade by less than all the parties who made it? One party to a contract may violate it—break it, so to speak—but does it not require all to lawfully rescind it?

Descending from these general principles, we find the proposition that in legal contemplation the Union is perpetual confirmed by the history of the Union itself. . . .

But if destruction of the Union by one or by a part only of the States be lawfully possible, the Union is less perfect than before the Constitution, having lost the vital element of perpetuity.

It follows from these views that no State upon its mere motion can lawfully get out of the Union; that resolves and ordinances to that effect are legally void, and that acts of violence within any State or States against the authority of the United States are insurrectionary or revolutionary, according to circumstances.

I therefore consider that in view of the Constitution and the laws the Union is unbroken, and to the extent of my ability, I shall take care, as the Constitution itself expressly enjoins upon me, that the laws of the Union be faithfully executed in all the States. . . . I trust this will not be regarded as a menace, but only as the declared purpose of the Union that it will constitutionally defend and maintain itself.

. . .

That there are persons in one section or another who seek to destroy the Union at all events and are glad of any pretext to do it I will neither affirm nor deny; but if there be such, I need address no word to them. . . .

. . .

All profess to be content in the Union if all constitutional rights can be maintained. . . . If by the mere force of numbers a majority should deprive a minority of any clearly written constitutional right, it might in a moral point of view justify revolution; certainly would if such a right were a vital one. But such is not our case. All the vital rights of minorities and individuals are so plainly assured to them by affirmations and negations, guarantees and prohibitions, in the Constitution that controversies arise concerning them. . . .

. . .

I do not forget the position assumed by some that constitutional questions are to be decided by the Supreme Court. . . .

One section of our country believes slavery is right and ought to be extended, while the other believes it is wrong and ought not to be extended. This is the only substantial dispute, The fugitive slave clause of the Constitution and the law for the suppression of the foreign slave trade are each as well enforced, perhaps, as any law can ever be in a community where the moral sense of the people imperfectly supports the law itself. . . .

Physically speaking, we can not separate. We can not remove our respective sections from each other nor build an impassable wall between them. . . .

This country, with its institutions, belongs to the people who inhabit it. Whenever they shall grow weary of the existing Government, they can exercise their constitutional right of amending it or their revolutionary right to dismember or overthrow it. . . .

. . .

My countrymen, one and all, think calmly and well upon this whole subject. . . .

In your hands, my dissatisfied fellow-countrymen, and not in mine, is the momentous issue of civil war. . . .

I am loath to close. We are not enemies, but friends. We must not be enemies. Though passion may have strained it must not break our bonds of affection. The mystic chords of memory, stretching from every battlefield and patriot grave to every living heart and hearthstone all over this broad land, will yet swell the chorus of the Union, when again touched, as surely they will be, by the better angels of our nature.

Source: http://douglass.speech.nwu.edu/linc_a73.htm.

DOCUMENT 41: The Emancipation Proclamation, January 1, 1863

The Emancipation Proclamation added a moral dimension to the Civil War when it confirmed that the purpose of the war for the Union had become a war for freedom. President Abraham Lincoln's decision to announce the proclamation provided a moral compass, although not complete, for the eventual direction emancipation would take. At the time of its pronouncement, the proclamation applied only to the states that were in rebellion. With the Emancipation Proclamation, however, African Americans legitimately liberated themselves from slavery.

* * *

By the President of the United States of America:
A Proclamation.

Whereas on the twenty-second day of September, in the year of our Lord one thousand eight hundred and sixty-two, a proclamation was issued by the President of the United States, containing, among other things, the following, to wit:

"That on the first day of January, in the year of our Lord one thousand eight hundred and sixty-three, all persons held as slaves within any State or designated part of a State, the people whereof shall then be in rebellion against the United States, shall be then, thenceforward, and forever free; and the Executive Government of the United States, including the military and naval authority thereof, will recognize and maintain the freedom of such persons, and will do no act or acts to repress such persons, or any of them, in any efforts they may make for their actual freedom.

"That the Executive will, on the first day of January aforesaid, by proclamation, designate the States and parts of States, if any, in which the people thereof, respectively, shall then be in rebellion against the United States; and the fact that any State, or the people thereof, shall on that day be, in good faith, represented in the Congress of the United States by members chosen thereto at elections wherein a majority of the qualified voters of such State shall have participated, shall, in the absence of strong countervailing testimony, be deemed conclusive evidence that such State, and the people thereof, are not then in rebellion against the United States."

Now, therefore I, Abraham Lincoln, President of the United States, by virtue of the power in me vested as Commander-in-Chief, of the Army and Navy of the United States in time of actual armed rebellion against the authority and government of the United States, and as a fit and necessary war measure for suppressing said rebellion, do, on this first day of January, in the year of our Lord one thousand eight hundred and sixty-three, and in accordance with my purpose so to do publicly proclaimed for the full period of one hundred days, from the day first above mentioned, order and designate as the States and parts of States wherein the people thereof respectively, are this day in rebellion against the United States, the following, to wit:

Arkansas, Texas, Louisiana, (except the Parishes of St. Bernard, Plaquemines, Jefferson, St. John, St. Charles, St. James Ascension, Assumption, Terrebonne, Lafourche, St. Mary, St. Martin, and Orleans, including the City of New Orleans) Mississippi, Alabama, Florida, Georgia, South Carolina, North Carolina, and Virginia, (except the forty-eight counties designated as West Virginia, and also the counties of Berkley, Accoumac, Northampton, Elizabeth City, York, Princess Ann, and Norfolk, including the cities of Norfolk and Portsmouth), and which excepted parts, are for the present, left precisely as if this proclamation were not issued.

And by virtue of the power, and for the purpose aforesaid, I do order and declare that all persons held as slaves within said designated States, and parts of States, are, and henceforward shall be free; and that the Executive government of the United States, including the military and naval authorities thereof, will recognize and maintain the freedom of said persons.

And I hereby enjoin upon the people so declared to be free to abstain from all violence, unless in necessary self-defence; and I recommend to them that, in all cases when allowed, they labor faithfully for reasonable wages.

And I further declare and make known, that such persons of suitable condition, will be received into the armed service of the United States to garrison forts, positions, stations, and other places, and to man vessels of all sorts in said service.

And upon this act, sincerely believed to be an act of justice, warranted by the Constitution, upon military necessity, I invoke the considerate judgment of mankind, and the gracious favor of Almighty God.

In witness whereof, I have hereunto set my hand and caused the seal of the United States to be affixed.

Done at the City of Washington, this first day of
January, in the year of our Lord one thousand eight
hundred and sixty three, and of the Independence of the
United States of America the eighty-seventh.
By the President: ABRAHAM LINCOLN
WILLIAM H. SEWARD, Secretary of State

Source: http://www.nara.gov/exhall/featured-document/eman/emanproc.html.

Part IV

Changes Involving States' Rights and Federalism from the Civil War to the New Deal, 1865–1940

In 1895 Booker T. Washington prepared to address the public at the Atlanta Cotton States and International Exposition held in Georgia (see Document 43). His speech would become a provocative commentary on the status of African Americans as citizens in the federal system. As he prepared for his speech to a predominantly white southern audience, the recognized leader of African Americans recalled the changes in American society during the post–Civil War period. Ever the realist, Washington knew full well the precarious situation of his people in southern political, economic, and social life. The North had not only withdrawn from southern battlefields but had also retreated from the Reconstruction of the South in 1877. Beginning in the 1880s and continuing into the 1890s and beyond, the northern population was altered as immigrants from southern and eastern Europe came in increasing numbers to the United States. Industrial development, stimulated by the Civil War, had transformed the character of American life. Northern, western, and southern cities were growing rapidly as larger numbers of Americans earned their livelihood in commerce and industry. Washington considered other events as he prepared his speech. Most African Americans lived in the South during the 1890s, and state legislatures had systematically disfranchised black voters through grandfather clauses, literacy tests, and poll taxes. He was aware of the role the Supreme Court might play either confirming segregation or overturning that practice. Washington would call for gradualism in his speech, whereby economic advancement would serve as a precursor to full political rights for African Americans.

Washington echoed older themes as to whether citizenship is confirmed to a person as a result of his on her being or whether the exercise of citizenship in its various forms, including voting, is a responsibility that requires drawing on a wealth of knowledge, experience, and dispositions. Washington's proposal was a logical accommodation to the existing physical threats such as lynching, frequent in the 1890s and early 1900s. The North too had become inattentive to the cause of civil rights as state and national politicians were drawn to concerns presented by industrial cities and an ever more interdependent economy. Their waning zeal for the cause of African American political equality left people of color in a vulnerable position. Furthermore, several intellectual currents of the time supported the racist belief of African American inferiority.

Two major intellectual movements captured the mind of many Americans in the late nineteenth century. Social Darwinism, as defined in the writings of Englishman Herbert Spencer, characterized life as a struggle and explained differences in social position as a result of the struggle of individuals and groups for status and survival. Sociologists rationalized the inequality of races, as did geographers, whose theory of environmental determinism justified racial inequality based on the struggle of individuals to survive in harsh or mild climates. Environmental determinists such as Ellsworth Huntington and Ellen Semple claimed that individuals living in harsh climates, such as that of northern Europe, developed more elaborate cultures and higher intelligence than individuals and races inhabiting tropical climes. Following the German influence of her mentor Friedrich Ratzel, Semple established the importance of the environment in determining culture in American intellectual thought. European influence, then, provided a lens for Americans to understand social, economic, and racial inequalities. American conclusions, largely viewed as racist today, were based on the struggle of individuals over centuries of time in less than hospitable conditions.

The foundation for liberal beliefs in gradualism was based on the principle that African Americans needed ethical and economic advances as prerequisites for political equality. This belief structure had its roots in the racial climate of the South in the 1890s in which lynching and racist intellectual thought stemming from Social Darwinism prevailed. Brutal actions by whites upon African Americans denigrated their very qualities as human beings. Social Darwinism questioned their capacities to participate in American society. Booker T. Washington's policy of gradualism and accommodation was created in this hostile climate as a survival tactic not only for him and Tuskegee Institute, a postcivil war missionary schools and a leading college for people of color, but all other members of his race.[1]

In contrast to the policy of gradualism, W.E.B. Du Bois called for immediate recognition of the full citizenship rights of African Americans. Educated at Harvard and in Germany, Du Bois was a founder of the Niagara Movement, a group that had met since 1905 at a place associated with the antislavery movement, to denounce discrimination. Du Bois became a founder of the National Association for the Advancement of Colored People's (NAACP) and served as director of publicity and editor of its journal, *The Crisis*. Appealing to the founding documents, Du Bois argued that there was no need for African Americans to prove their worth as individuals in order to justify conferring the rights of citizenship on the group. The Constitution, including the civil rights amendments—the Thirteenth, Fourteenth, and Fifteenth—clearly ended slavery, provided citizenship to former slaves, and extended to them equal protection of the laws and empowered voting rights.

Thus, two diametrically opposed strategies emerged in the early twentieth century concerning the achievement of full civil rights for African Americans. The struggles of African Americans became embedded in the fabric of nineteenth- and twentieth-century events such as Reconstruction after the Civil War, World Wars I and II, and the Great Depression. So too, African American rights were intertwined within the movement to obtain equal rights for women.

In the Reconstruction era, federal protection of civil rights focused on three civil rights amendments to the Constitution and legislation passed by Radical Republicans in Congress. The Supreme Court, however, protected southern states from "reforms" intended to improve the status of African Americans. One historian of the Court, Charles Warren, commented on the Supreme Court's decisions to invalidate post–Civil War civil rights legislation. Warren wrote that if the Court had ruled otherwise, "the States would have largely lost their autonomy and become, as political entities, only of historical interest." He further observed that if civil rights legislation had been upheld immediately after the Civil War, "the boundary lines between States and the National Government would be practically abolished."[2]

In a series of cases from the 1870s through the 1890s, the Supreme Court upheld southern state segregation laws that prescribed separate but equal facilities. The Court's ruling in *Plessy v. Ferguson* (1896) affirmed the principle that legally established racial distinctions did not violate the provisions of the Thirteenth and Fourteenth Amendments. The separate-but-equal doctrine would remain a guiding principle for the Court until civil rights cases of the late 1940s, which culminated in the landmark decision of *Brown v. Topeka Board of Education* (1954).

During the late nineteenth and early twentieth centuries, southern white leaders were divided by social class as well as race in reasserting control of their state governments. The Bourbons or Redeemers represented upper class antebellum southern leadership and the effort to recapture the position that they once held as the political and economic leaders of the South. These wealthy merchants and plantation owners did not wish to surrender the control of their local governments to black majorities or poor white voters. The Southern Populist Alliance, in contrast, was composed of poor whites and freedmen who were temporarily joined by agricultural issues and concerns. Their unity was short-lived and breached as white southern politicians capitalized on racial divisions and racial antipathies fanned by programs of radical reconstruction. The passage of Jim Crow laws entrenched the government in the hands of white southerners, segregated the races, worked to turn back the principles of the Civil Rights Amendments, and endangered the lives of blacks via lynchings and other acts of violence and personal intimidation.

World War I changed the composition of American society when African Americans migrated from the rural South to the urban North in search of jobs. Following the war, African Americans for the most part remained in northern cities as a major component of the workforce. African Americans settled in their own communities resulting in a segregated pattern of housing and discrimination.

The Great Depression of the 1930s resulted in an unemployment rate that rose to 25 percent in 1933. The New Deal of Franklin D. Roosevelt, which emphasized relief, recovery, and reform, did little to end racial discrimination as white southern Democrats felt uneasy and threatened by African American participation in the politics of the Democratic party. FDR's policy of pragmatism sacrificed the rights of African Americans to what he believed were more pressing needs.

WOMEN'S SUFFRAGE IN STATE AND NATIONAL RELATIONS

Throughout the nineteenth and twentieth centuries there had been a link between African American rights and women's rights as leaders in one reform movement frequently served as leaders in the other movement or populated their ranks. Reform movements were inextricably linked often referencing the same principles of the founding documents to justify the changes they advocated in American society.

In 1848, the Seneca Falls, New York, convention of women had announced formal efforts to achieve equality between the sexes. Reforms in the women's movement and the abolition of slavery both involved the issue of equality. A series of efforts were made in the 1850s to forward the issue of women's equality when Wendell Phillips, a noted abolitionist, spoke in Worcester, Massachusetts on women's suffrage. He advocated dramatic changes in the legal system that prevented fairness and consistency in the law as applied to women. Phillips supported women's rights in what was then considered an unpopular cause in the interests of justness and fairness. He offered the following resolution in 1851: "That, while we would not undervalue other methods, the right of suffrage for women is . . . the corner-stone of this enterprise, since we do not seek to protect woman, but rather to place her is a position to protect herself."[3]

Women's suffrage generated three disparate groups. Suffragists were women (with the support of some men) who supported national and state amendments that extended the franchise to women. States' rights suffragists, mostly in the southern states, framed the cause as a states' rights issue. While they supported amendments to state constitutions, they opposed an amendment to the Constitution of the United States. Generally, states' rights suffragists broke with the national group, fearing that a constitutional amendment would enfranchise African Americans and extend federal power into a domain they believed was reserved for state action. The third group opposed the extension of the franchise to women. Anti-suffragists, at least in the South, expressed alarm that women suffrage would undermine the existing social order, that is lose their special and protected place in American society, and impair the family structure, which they viewed as the primary unit of society.[4]

Immediately following the Civil War, the unity of the women's movement was shattered by the question of whether suffrage was the paramount issue. Susan B. Anthony and Elizabeth Cady Stanton founded the National Woman Suffrage Association to promote a woman suffrage amendment to the Constitution as one of many feminist concerns. In contrast, Lucy Stone and Julia Ward Howe established the American Woman Suffrage Association, which stressed the single issue of suffrage as the first and foremost basic reform for women's rights. For a half-century this rift over strategy dominated and, possibly, postponed the women's movement to equality. The Nineteenth Amendment proved to be the cause decided upon, and states ratified the woman's suffrage amendment before and during World War I. Yet, the strategy of securing the right to vote for women via a national amendment raised strong opposition including the resistance of white southern women who, from their point of view, expressed aversion to an amendment that violated states' rights (see Documents 49 and 50).

The New Orleans white states' rights feminist Kate Gordon, who historian Marjorie Spruill Wheeler described as "negrophobic," did not want a break down in racial barriers that excluded African Americans from exercising the right to vote. Gordon, for example, wanted suffrage for women, but if a national amendment proved to enforce the African Americans' right to vote she adamantly opposed that initiative. As one of her colleagues Belle Kearney wrote, "The world is scarcely beginning to realize the enormity of the situation that faces the south in its grapple with the negro problem which was thrust upon it at the close of the civil war when 4,500,000 ex-slaves, illiterate and semi-barbarous, were enfranchised." Kearney continued, "Such a situation has no parallel in history. . . . The South has struggled under its death-weight for over thirty years bravely and magnanimously."[5]

Clearly many white southern women held views regarding race in the South during the late nineteenth and early twentieth centuries. The extent of their racial animosity even led to the exclusion of African American suffragist Adella Hunt Logan who was a life-long member of the National American Woman Suffrage Association. Logan, a contributor to *Woman's Journal* and the *Crisis*, was barred from attending women's conventions in the South.[6] Many white southern suffragists were willing to sacrifice the possibility of extending the franchise to women, if that extension involved an amendment to the national constitution and thereby opened the possibility of enforcing equal rights for African Americans. Given that choice, they valued states' rights more highly.

By 1915, differences over states' rights divided the southern suffrage movement as competing groups—the National American Woman Suffrage Association, the Southern States Woman Suffrage Conference, and the National Woman's Party—vied for the allegiance of southern women. In 1920, when the 19th Amendment was ratified, many southern suffragists were troubled that their enfranchisement was won at the cost of states' sovereignty.[7]

FEDERALISM IN THE POSTBELLUM PERIOD

On the eve of the Civil War, southern state leaders argued that the Constitution represented a mutual contract between the states and the federal government and then carried out the threats that had been made some thirty years earlier. Southern leaders tenaciously believed that the states created the national government and that when the national government (or North) abrogated its part of the agreement, the contract was no longer valid. When the Union prevailed in the Civil War, fought between 1861 and 1865, it brought to an end the specific argument concerning federalism.

During the war, five positions regarding the nature of Reconstruction emerged: the "Southern," the "Conquered Provinces," the "Presidential," the "State Suicide," and the theory of "Forfeited Rights." These positions hold beliefs, from the moderate view, that the southern states had never left the Union, to the extreme, that southern states should be treated as conquerored territories. Radical Republicans, such as Thaddeus Stevens and Charles Sumner, supported the position that the states were conquered territory and subject to the will of the conqueror. Sumner also believed that the seceded states had committed suicide and that Union control was needed similar to the control Congress exercised over territories.[8]

After fighting on the battlefields had subsided, the U.S. Supreme Court helped resolve the dispute over the nature of the Union with its ruling in *Texas v. White* (1869). Chief Justice of the Supreme Court Salmon P. Chase wrote on the meaning of the "State" and the nature of the Union. He stated, "The Constitution looks to an indestructible Union, composed of indestructible States."[9] In the view of the Court, the Confederate States had never left the Union.

INCREASED ROLE OF THE NATIONAL GOVERNMENT

The Civil War stimulated industrialization and large-scale enterprises, which increased the role of the national government. Abraham Lincoln's Republican party assumed the mantle of fostering national interest. Lincoln's prosecution of the war challenged the South's emphasis on the Constitution as a framework of negative restraints on the government. He assumed the responsibility to sustain the Union. The Constitution had guaranteed a republican form of government in every state in Article IV, section 4, and it also guaranteed the "general welfare" in Article I, section 8. Congress had the power to respond to situations, such as rebellions, even though there were no specific prescriptions concerning the best course of action. The Preamble to the Constitution, as interpreted some fifty years earlier by strong nationalists Alexander Hamilton, John Marshall, and Joseph Story, required the national government to maintain the guarantee of republican governments in the states and the general welfare. Their views defined federalism as expanding the role of the national government at the expense of state governments.

The rise of corporations challenged the abilities of state and national governments to regulate commerce. This phenomenon had existed since the 1820s when Supreme Court decisions such as that in *Dartmouth College v. Woodward* (1818) supported private enterprise. Interstate commerce grew dramatically with the organization of the Northwest and Southwest territories into states. Using the river system, cities such as Cincinnati, Ohio, grew rapidly in the 1820s. Goods from all over the nation were transported via the Ohio-Mississippi River system, and roads, canals, and railroads followed in succession as means to carry interstate commerce.

In the 1880s, the growth of large corporations stimulated by the Civil War and the volume of trade made possible by the internal improvements (created during the previous fifty years) challenged the nineteenth-century laissez-faire policy. There was a strong faith in capitalism in the early decades of the 1800s characterized by large numbers of independent producers who took advantages of opportunities to establish businesses. The capitalism of small-scale enterprise did not require regulation, and it was supported by the belief that capitalism and democracy were consistent with one another. It was assumed that individuals could enter the marketplace as producers and succeed or fail based on their intellect and character. By the end of the nineteenth century, however, questions arose concerning the ability to compete within an economic environment dominated by large, corporate enterprises.

Theodore Roosevelt strove to increase the power of the federal government greatly. First touted as the "Square Deal" and then as "New Nationalism," TR dismissed the agrarian-oriented populism of Democrat William Jennings Bryan. Roosevelt saw the need for federal intervention to solve or ameliorate problems stemming from trusts, the exploitation of natural resources, labor unrest, recession cycles, and the need for conservation. In strengthening federal power, TR also increased executive power.

Woodrow Wilson, in his role as a strong party leader, converted the Democratic party into a political entity with a national focus of positive liberalism. The negative liberalism of the nineteenth century emphasized the restraint of government involvement in the economy in order to maximize freedom and individual initiative. Negative liberalism had envisioned a small national government and the support of state governments that were closer to the people and considered avenues to democratic expression of citizens. The positive liberalism of Wilson and his successors emphasized the involvement of the national government in economic affairs as a means to mediate the harsh conditions of modern life. Positive liberalism called for a much larger national government, one that was actively involved in the lives of all citizens.

Wilson's New Freedom established a national agenda for reform. The enormous amount of significant legislation enacted during his presidency continued to expand the role of the federal government and the power of the executive office. His domestic reforms caused the formation of huge bureaucracies. All of this, coupled with the exigencies of World War I, shifted more power from the states to the federal government. The era of big government had begun and would continue, albeit not without debate and opposition, to expand even more under the presidency of Franklin D. Roosevelt and the New Deal.

NOTES

1. Edgar Gardner Murphy to Booker T. Washington, July 28, 1903, Booker T. Washington Papers, Library of Congress, quoted in Hugh C. Bailey, *Edgar Gardner Murphy: Gentle Progressive* (Coral Gables, Fla.: University of Miami Press, 1968), pp. 118–120.

2. Charles Warren, *The Supreme Court in United States History*, rev. ed., 2 vols. (Boston: Little, Brown, 1922), II:547–548.

3. Extract from George William Curtis Eulogy on Wendell Phillips before the Municipal Authorities of Boston, April 18, 1884. http://memory.loc.gov/cgi-bin/query/r?ammem/naw:@field+(SOURCE+@band(rbnawsa+n8344)):@@@REF.

4. Marjorie Spruill Wheeler, *New Women of the New South: The Leaders of the Woman Suffrage Movement in the Southern States* (New York: Oxford University Press, 1993).

5. Belle Kearney, *A Slaveholder's Daughter* (Westport, Conn.: Greenwood Press, 1969), 97. As quoted in Marjorie Spruill Wheeler, *New Women of the New South* (New York: Oxford University Press, 1993), 102–103.

6. Ibid., p. 111.

7. Ibid., pp. xv–xvi.

8. Rozann Rothman, "The American Civil War and Reconstruction: A Crisis in Political Integration," in Daniel J. Elazar, ed., *Federalism and Political Integration* (Lanham, Md.: University Press of America, 1984), pp. 98–199.

9. *Texas v. White*, 7 Wall. 700, at 725 (1869).

DOCUMENT 42: Women's Suffrage Petition to Congress, December 1871

The women's suffrage movement had been an important part of nineteenth-century reform efforts. Women were prominent leaders in efforts to establish public schools, create women's seminaries and colleges, advocate humane treatment for the insane, and lead in the efforts of abolition. Intertwined with these other reform efforts was the movement for women to gain the right to vote.

Women were split regarding the issue of women's suffrage. The group who wrote this document represented individuals who believed this right would best be obtained through an amendment to the U.S. Constitution. The women who signed the petition to Congress were active advocates of women's equality. Elizabeth Cady Stanton's political activism spanned most of the nineteenth century. Stanton protested against the belief that women were inferior intellectually to men. She participated vigorously in the abolitionist movement and was an organizer of the Seneca Falls convention, drafting resolutions in the Declaration of Sentiments. Stanton tested the constitutional right for women to seek public office by running for Congress. Isabella Beecher Hooker, daughter of the Reverend Lyman Beecher, disliked notoriety but rose to leadership in the cause of women's rights. She gained a national reputation when she spoke at the convention of the National Suffrage Association in 1870. Isabella Beecher Hooker worked diligently to create popular support for a federal suffrage amendment. Olympia Brown was a Universalist minister who advocated woman's suffrage. Influenced by Susan B. Anthony and Elizabeth Cady Stanton, she joined the American Equal Rights Association. Olympia Brown was particularly active in Wisconsin where she became the president of the state Woman Suffrage Association. Susan B. Anthony, like Elizabeth Cady Stanton, was active in the abolitionist movement as the principal New York agent for William Lloyd Garrison's Anti-Slavery Society. Anthony feared that male African American voters would join the opponents of women's suffrage. Josephine Sophia White Griffing maintained her commitment to attaining equal status for African Americans. Her work to achieve emancipation did not end with the close of the Civil War. Griffing was concerned about the lives of African Americans after slavery ended. She held to the conviction that both public and private agencies should support the newly freed African Americans as they struggled to attain political equality and economic security.

Other individuals, especially southern women, confined their efforts to obtaining the right by amendment to their state constitutions. Still other women and men opposed women's suffrage. A frequent argument these individuals used was that women's sphere of influence was primarily domestic: the raising of children and the running of the household. Politics, including voting, was considered in the male domain.

* * *

To the Honorable the Senate and House of Representatives of the United States in congress assembled:

The undersigned, Citizens of the United States, believing that under the present Federal constitution all women who are citizens of the United States have the right to vote, pray your Honorable Body to enact a law during the present Session that shall assist and protect them in the exercise of that right.

And they pray further that they be permitted in person, and in behalf of the thousands of other women who are petitioning Congress to the same effect, to be heard upon this Memorial before the Senate and House at an early day in the present Session.

We ask your Honorable Body to bear in mind that while men are represented on the floor of Congress and so may be said to be heard there, women who are allowed no vote and therefore no representation cannot truly be heard except as congress shall open its doors to us in person.

Elizabeth Cady Stanton
Isabella Beecher Hooker
Olympia Brown
Susan B. Anthony
Josephine S. Griffing
(One Signature indecipherable)

Source: http://www.nara.gov/education/teaching/woman/ldoc2p1.g:f.

DOCUMENT 43: Booker T. Washington, Atlanta Exposition Address, 1895

Booker T. Washington, a former slave in Malden, Virginia, which eventually became West Virginia, advocated a policy of gradualism consistent with the nineteenth century belief that the right to vote was equated with hard work and integrity. In 1895, Washington made a speech at the Atlanta Cotton States and International Exposition held in Georgia. Washington faced a predominantly white crowd in Atlanta. Washington fully understood that his remarks could inflame white animosities toward blacks or they could help African Americans establish themselves as part of southern society. Given the decade's experiences in lynchings, race riots, legislation of Jim Crow laws throughout the southern states, and the coming decision of the Supreme Court in *Plessy v. Ferguson* (1896), which lent sanction to de jure segregation, Washington advocated the path of gradualism, that is economic advancement of African Americans as a prereguisite to political equality.

* * *

Ignorant and inexperienced, it is not strange that in the first years of our new life we began at the top instead of at the bottom; that a seat in Congress or the state legislature was more sought than real estate or industrial skill; that the political convention or stump speaking had more attractions than starting a dairy farm or truck garden.

A ship lost at sea for many days suddenly sighted a friendly vessel. From the mast of the unfortunate vessel was seen a signal, "Water, water; we die of thirst!" The answer from the friendly vessel, at once came back, "Cast down your bucket where you are." . . . The captain of the distressed vessel, at last heeding the injunction, cast down his bucket, and it came up full of fresh, sparkling water. . . . To those of my race who underestimate the importance of cultivating friendly relations with the southern white man, who is their next-door neighbor, I would say: "Cast down your bucket where you are"—cast it down in making friends in every manly way of the people of all races by whom we are surrounded.

Cast it down in agriculture, mechanics, in commerce, in domestic service, and in the professions. . . . Our greatest danger is that in the great leap from slavery to freedom we may overlook the fact that the masses of us are to live by the productions of our hands, and fail to keep in mind that we shall prosper in proportion as we learn to dignify and glorify common labour, and put brains and skill into the common occupations of life. . . . No race can prosper till it learns that there is as much dignity in tilling a field as in writing a poem. It is at the bottom of life we must begin, and not at the top.

To those of the white race who look to the incoming of those of foreign birth and strange tongue and habits for the prosperity of the South, were I permitted I would repeat what I say to my own race, "Cast down your bucket where you are." Cast it down among the eight millions of Negroes whose habits you know, whose fidelity and love you have tested in days when to have proved treacherous meant the ruin of your firesides. Cast down your bucket among these people who have, without strikes and labour wars, tilled your fields, cleared your forests, built your railroads and cities, and brought forth treasures from the bowels of the earth. . . . Casting down your bucket among my people . . . you will find that they will buy your surplus land, make blossom the waste places in your fields, and run your factories. While doing this, you can be sure in the future, as in the past, that you and your families will be surrounded by the most patient, faithful, law-abiding, and unresentful people that the world has seen. . . . In all things that are purely social we can be as separate as the fingers, yet one as the hand in all things essential to mutual progress. . . .

The wisest among my race understand that the agitation of questions of social equality is the extremest folly, and that progress in the enjoyment of all the privileges that will come to us must be the result of severe and constant struggle rather than of artificial forcing. No race that has anything to contribute to the markets of the world is long in any degree ostracized. It is important and right that all privileges of the law be ours, but it is vastly more important that we be prepared for the exercise of these privileges. The opportunity to earn a dollar in a factory just now is worth infinitely more than the opportunity to spend a dollar in an opera-house.

Source: Booker T. Washington, "Atlanta Exposition Address" (1895), in R. Twombly, *Blacks in White America since 1865* (New York: McKay, 1971).

DOCUMENT 44: An Episcopal Priest Challenges Enforcement of the Fourteenth Amendment, 1905

Edgar Gardner Murphy was an Episcopal priest imbued with the social gospel, a Protestant movement to alleviate the harsh conditions of modern life. His ideas paralleled those of Booker T. Washington in that he advocated civil rights for African Americans who demonstrated the qualities of character to earn them rights equivalent to those of a white man. In a speech at Tuskegee Institute, he summarized his thoughts on African American equality. To the students, he cautioned "that the Declaration of Independence was at first a prophesy and the Emancipation Proclamation represented but a liberty in a document." Murphy was a southern liberal who feared the social consequences of applying the Fourteenth Amendment in securing African American rights to vote in the South.

Murphy was an 1889 graduate of the University of the South in Swanee, Tennessee. He would not appreciate the merits of W.E.B. Du Bois's arguments of natural rights accorded to African Americans. A southerner with influence in religion and social affairs, Murphy's ideas were shared by many, both the South and the North. In this Madison Square Garden speech, he particularly addressed the Fourteenth Amendment and its enforcement by the national government. His outlook was consistent with the northern retreat from enforcing civil rights in southern states.

* * *

To the mind of the typical citizen of the North, the enforcement of the terms of the second section of the Fourteenth Amendment to the Constitution would represent only an obvious element in an American policy of fair-play.

Interpreting the popular understanding of its language, it is evident that the Amendment does not bestow upon the negro the right to vote. It does not prohibit the restriction of suffrage. It does not refer to the negro, as the negro, at all. It permits restriction. It assumes that the States of the Union may, at their pleasure, deny the suffrage to men, whether white or black, of any description or class. It provides, however, that, when suffrage is arbitrarily restricted, representation shall be restricted also. It declares that no number of the male population shall be "counted out" by the State in making up the body of its electorate and at the same time "counted in" by the State in securing its representation in Congress and in the Electoral College. . . .

The general intention of such a provision is obvious enough. The black man was but the immediate occasion of its passage. . . . As first framed, and as first adopted in the House of Representatives, it had specific reference to his political status. Reduction of representation was to be the penalty for any suffrage restriction based upon color. But as the debate proceeded, all direct reference to color was omitted. Restriction itself, no matter what the race or class proscribed, was made the occasion of the penalty. The law might, as a matter of fact, chiefly affect the Southern States; but it was also intended to affect, in principle, every State in which there should be any denial of the ballot to any class or fraction of the voters. A State is therefore free under this Amendment to reserve the ballot to the few—finally to exclude any element of the voting population—but if it do so it must suffer, proportionately, a loss of congressional and political power.

Such an adjustment of the problem of suffrage involves, more over, a compact—an equitable distribution of influence—between individuals as well as between States. . . . But there is a consideration more serious still. The argument in favor of enforcing the terms of the Amendment is in reality an argument not only for an equitable distribution of political power, but also for the vitality of the Constitution. A dead limb upon the tree of the Constitution is not good for the tree. . . . Public policy demands the fulfilment of the letter of the Constitution, unless it can be clearly shown—under the canons of a public policy broader and truer still—that the life of the Constitution is necessarily freer and larger than its letter.

. . .

So far as political injustice to the negro exists at the South, it exists at this point rather than at any other. Much has been said and written about the "grandfather clause" in the amended Constitutions of certain of our States. Under this clause no right of the qualified negro is denied. Under it the deficient white man is admitted. Inasmuch, however, as the white man who applies for registration under this clause makes implicit confession of his inability to register under other clauses, and inasmuch as the men pleading of the right to vote on the sole ground of descent is an admission of illiteracy or penury, very few white men have ever been willing to claim the ballot under this exemption. No class of people anywhere will ever make much use of an exemption which is an advertisement of deficiency.

The "grandfather clause" has been, therefore, of little practical significance except as a subject of controversy. As, even in its indirect operation, it excluded no negro who could read and write, it worked injustice
to no class of colored people entitled to any special political consideration. Educated, responsible, self-respecting negro men, have, in certain
cases, been unjustly excluded; but the "grandfather clause" has not been
the instrument of discrimination. That instrument has been found in the
discretionary powers lodged in the boards of registrars, by which worthy
negro men, fairly meeting every test of suffrage, have been excluded
from registration because they could not answer some mystifying question or satisfy some arbitrary and super-subtle exaction of the law. It is
idle for writers at the South to deny that such cases exist. It is equally
idle for writers at the North to assume that the whole South is responsible for them, or to forget that tens of thousands of negro men have
already been fairly registered at the South under our amended Constitutions.

Does the Fourteenth Amendment, however, offer a remedy for such
injustice as exists? If injustice exist anywhere, it is well that a remedy
should be found. It is not to the advantage of the State that the sense of
political injury should operate within any of its social forces. . . .

If the powers and penalties of the Federal Constitution may be employed to meet faults of administration within the borders of the several
States, faults in the administration of State laws, at what point can we
ever place the cessation of federal cognizance and control? Is it not obvious that, while individual wrongs should be righted and administrative evils corrected, the primary remedy lies within the Courts of the
State? To these the individual voter has constant access. . . .

Inasmuch as the courts have not hesitated to find in favor of a worthy
negro plaintiff, the machinery of justice within the State has been shown
to be legally adequate for the correction of administrative abuses. I say
"legally" adequate. Morally and practically the process of appeal is naturally difficult. For such moral and practical difficulties there are only
moral and practical remedies, the remedies of public opinion, of a wiser
and juster civic mind. Upon these remedies the legal remedies must at
last depend for efficacy and completeness. To declare that the Federal
Government must govern wherever the State does not govern perfectly,
and to assume that an administrative evil of certain officials within the
State is to challenge congressional action and is to be the subject of a
constitutional penalty, would be to make havoc with the elementary
compact between our national and our local Governments. If it be shown
that the State by its own legislative action has established an unequal
law, the law would be *prima facie* evidence of wrong. But where the evil
is merely an evil of administration, a just official may correct at one
registration the error committed by an unjust official at the last; the

whole electorate is constantly in a state of change, one class may be favored in one locality and another class favored in another; in one year the vote may be large, the next year it may be small; the situation is never one for mathematical determination; and yet the very essence of the second section of the Amendment is its assumption of mathematical sufficiency.

If, as the federal argument would imply, the inadequate operation of the local conscience must challenge the intervention of the federal authority, it is hardly to be expected that the enforcement of the Amendment will essentially enlarge the popular temper of the South. . . .

It is questionable, however, if the suffrage is precisely the point at which the aid or intervention of the Nation can ever be made effective. That suffrage is essentially a local concern of the individual State is implicit in our whole constitutional system. So long as the primal basis of suffrage legislation lies within the State—a basis which cannot be destroyed at the South without being destroyed at the North—the State will always be able to meet any national enactment by some device of local administration. There is no way in which the Nation can guarantee the processes of local administration except by itself assuming the burden of such administration. The Nation will not be able to coerce the local will, unless it break down the whole system of local self-government and substitute the military for the civil power.

The attempt, however, to establish any principle of true democracy by a process of penalties is likely to be futile; it is not unlikely to be self-destructive. . . .

The Federal Government may be solicitous as to his vote, but the negro needs the daily and neighborly solicitude of those who offer opportunities of labor, possibilities of bread. The North, especially the negro of the North, may wish to strike at the South, but the Southern negro, knowing that he must live with the Southern white man, rightly feels no cowardice in the confession that a privilege accorded voluntarily by the South is worth more than any conceivable privilege that might be imposed externally by the North. . . .

Compromise with injustice means the compromise of our own welfare. Wrong done in the name of our institutions is a wrong to our institutions rather than to its victims. . . .

I profoundly disbelieve in any social admixture or amalgamation of the races, but I confess that, in a certain high civic sense, I am glad that I can hold in honor the negro man who after only forty years of freedom is able fairly to stand upon his feet before the white man's law and take the white man's test. . . .

To increase their numbers, to knit their loyalty to our institutions, to confirm their liberties, to enlarge the opportunities of the worthy, the industrious, the peaceable among them; to restore between these and our white population the confidence of the past—this may well rank among the honorable and serious interests of church and school and press, of all our adequate leadership.

If I have written, therefore, in opposition to the enforcement of the popular conception of the Fourteenth Amendment, I have done so because I believe the truth and purport of this section of the Constitution lie deeper than its proposals of coercion. If its essential burden be "the equality of men before the law," coercion might delay but could not advance the free and permanent acceptance of this burden at the South. To the weight and meaning of it our civilization is responding. The Amendment is weak where it appeals to force, strong where it appeals to truth. The deeper mind of the South, in appealing from its penalties to its principles and its anticipations, is not at war with life.

Source: Edgar Gardner Murphy, "Shall the Fourteenth Amendment Be Enforced?" *North American Review* (January 1905): 109–133.

DOCUMENT 45: Theodore Roosevelt on Lincoln and the Race Problem, February 13, 1905

Theodore Roosevelt, known affectionately as TR, became president when William McKinley was assassinated in 1901. TR was an ardent nationalist and neo-Hamiltonian who favored an active government in economic affairs. While he called for national unity and an avoidance of disagreement between northern and southern states, his nationalism called for a gradualist policy when it came to rights for African Americans. TR spoke glowingly of the need for "Northerners and Southerners, Easterners and Westerners" to "prove . . . fealty to the Nation's post." In this address to members of the Republican Club of New York City, he called for protection of the rights of the "backward race" while maintaining those of the "forward race."

* * *

IN HIS second inaugural, in a speech which I will be read as long as the memory of this Nation endures, Abraham Lincoln closed by saying: "With malice toward none; with charity for all; with firmness in the right, as God gives us to see the right, let us strive on to finish the work we are in; to do all which may achieve and cherish a just and lasting peace among ourselves, and with all nations."

. . .

This is the spirit in which mighty Lincoln sought to bind up the Nation's wounds when its soul was yet seething with fierce hatreds, with wrath, with rancor, with all the evil and dreadful passions provoked by civil war. . . .

Lincoln, himself a man of Southern birth, did not hesitate to appeal to the sword when he became satisfied that in no other way could the Union be saved, for high though he put peace he put righteousness still higher. He warred for the Union; he warred to free the slave and when he warred he warred in earnest, for it is a sign of weakness to be half-hearted when blows must be struck. But he felt only love, a love as deep as the tenderness of his great and sad heart, for all his countrymen alike in the North and in the South, and he longed above everything for the day when they should once more be knit together in the unbreakable bonds of eternal friendship.

We of to-day, in dealing with all our fellow-citizens, white or colored, North or South should strive to show just the qualities that Lincoln showed—his steadfastness in striving after the right and his infinite patience and forbearance with those who saw that right less clearly than he did; his earnest endeavor to do what was best, and yet his readiness to accept the best that was practicable when the ideal best was unattainable; his unceasing effort to cure what was evil, coupled with his refusal to make a bad situation worse by any ill-judged or ill-timed effort to make it better.

. . .

The problem is so to adjust the relations between two races of different ethnic type that the rights of neither be abridged nor jeoparded; that the backward race be trained so that it may enter into the possession of true freedom while the forward race is enabled to preserve unharmed the high civilization wrought out by its forefathers.

. . .

Let us be steadfast for the right; but let us err on the side of generosity rather than on the side of vindictiveness toward those who differ from us as to the method of attaining the right. Let us never forget our duty to help in uplifting the lowly, to shield from wrong the humble.

. . .

The Southern States face difficult problems; and so do the Northern States. Some of the problems are the same for the entire country. Others exist in greater intensity in one section, and yet others exist in greater intensity in another section. But in the end they will all be solved; for fundamentally our people are the same throughout this land; the same in the qualities of heart and brain and hand which have made this Republic what it is in the great today; which will make it what it is to be in the infinitely greater tomorrow. I admire and respect and believe in and have faith in the men and women of the South as I admire and respect and believe in and have faith in the men and women of the

North. All of us alike, Northerners and Southerners, Easterners and Westerners, can best prove our fealty to the Nation's post by the way in which we do the Nation's work in the present; for only thus can we be sure that our children's children shall inherit Abraham Lincoln's single-hearted devotion to the great unchanging creed that "righteousness exalteth a nation."

Source: http://douglass.speech.nwu.edu/roos_a78.htm.

DOCUMENT 46: Elihu Root Calls for the Preservation of Local Self-Government of the States, December 12, 1906

Elihu Root was secretary of state under Theodore Roosevelt when he made this speech before the Pennsylvania Society in New York. Root, probably the nation's top corporate lawyer during the era of the robber barons, understood how the new U.S. economic power shaped the nation's overseas needs. Root was a leading figure among "Old Guard" Republicans, who represented the traditional views of the nineteenth century Republican party. He was a statesman, jurist, and experienced diplomat who addressed the Pennsylvania Society on preserving the role of the states in an era when the national government gained prominence in constitutional government.

* * *

What is to be the future of the states of the union under our dual sytem of constitutional government?

The conditions under which the clauses of the Constitution distributing powers to the national and state governments are now and henceforth to be applied, are widely different from the conditions which were or could have been within the contemplation of the framers of the Constitution, and widely different from those which obtained during the early years of the republic. When the authors of *The Federalist* argued and expounded the reasons for union and utility of the provisions contained in the Constitution, each separate colony transformed into a state was complete in itself and sufficient to itself, except as to a few exceedingly simple external relations of state to state and to foreign nations; from the origin of production to the final consumption of the product, from the birth of a citizen to his death, the business, the social and the political life of each separate community began and ended for the most part within the limits of the state itself. . . . The fear of the fathers of the republic was that these separate and self-sufficient communities would fall apart, that the union would resolve into its constituent elements, or that, as it grew in population and area, it would split up into a number of separate confederacies. Few of the men of 1787 would have deemed it possible that the union they were forming could be maintained among eighty-five millions of people, spread over the vast expanse from the Atlantic to the Pacific and from the Lakes to the Gulf.

Three principle causes have made this possible.

One cause has been the growth of a national sentiment. . . . The Civil War settled the supremacy of the nation throughout the territory of the union, and its sacrifices sanctified and made enduring that national sentiment. . . .

The second great influence has been the knitting together in ties of common interest, of the people forming the once separate communities through the working of free trade among the states. Never was a concession dictated by enlightened judgment for the common benefit, more richly repaid than that by which the states surrendered in the Federal Constitution the right to lay imposts or duties on imports or exports without the consent of the Congress. . . .

The third great cause of change is the marvelous development of facilities for travel and communication produced by the inventions and discoveries of the past century. . . . Our whole life has swung away from the old state centers and is crystallizing about national centers. . . .

Such changes in the life of the people cannot fail to produce corresponding political changes. Some of those changes can be plainly seen now in progress. It is plainly to be seen that the people of the country are coming to the conclusion that in certain important respects the local laws of the separate states, which were adequate for the due and just regulation and control of the business which was transacted and the activity which began and ended within the limits of the several states, are inadequate for the due and just control of the business and activities which extend throughout all the states, and that such power of regulation and control is gradually passing into the hands of the national government. . . . [There] are [many] examples of the purpose of the people of the United States to do through the agency of the national government the things which the separate state governments formerly did adequately but no longer do adequately. The end is not yet. The process that interweaves the life and action of the people in every section of our country with the people in every other section, continues and will continue with increasing force and effect; we are urging forward in a development of business and social life which tends more and more to the obliteration of state lines and the decrease of state power as compared with national power. . . .

With these changes and tendencies, in what way can the power of the states be preserved?

. . . [T]here is but one way in which the states of the union can maintain their power and authority under the conditions which are now before us, and that is by an awakening on the part of the states to a realization of their own duties to the country at large. Under the conditions which now exist, no state can live unto itself alone, and regulate its affairs with sole reference to its own treasury, its own convenience, its own special interests. Every state is bound to frame its legislation and its administration with reference not only to its own special affairs, but with reference to the effect upon all its sister states. . . . The intervention of the national government in many matters which it has recently undertaken would have been wholly unnecessary if the states themselves had been alive to their duty toward the general body of the country.

It is useless for the advocates of states rights to inveigh against the supremacy of the constitutional laws of the United States or against the extension of national authority in the fields of necessary control where the states themselves fail in the performance of their duty. The instinct for self-government among the people of the United States is too strong to permit them long to respect any one's right to exercise a power which he fails to exercise. The governmental control which they deem just and necessary they will have. It may be that such control would better be exercised in particular instances by the governments of the states, but the people will have the control they need, either from the states or from the national government; and if the states fail to furnish it in due measure, sooner or later constructions of the Constitution will be found to vest the power where it will be exercised—in the national government. The true and only way to preserve state authority is to be found in the awakened conscience of the states, their broadened views and higher standard of responsibility to the general public; in effective legislation by the states, in conformity to the general moral sense of the country; and in the vigorous exercise for the general public good of that state authority which is to be preserved.

Source: Lamar T. Beman, ed., *Selected Articles on States Rights* (New York: H. W. Wilson Company, 1926), pp. 61–68.

DOCUMENT 47: Wilson Rejects the Old Ideal of Limited Government, October 30, 1909

Throughout the nineteenth century the Federalist, Whig, and Republican parties assumed the mantle of the party of the nation. The Democratic party, as organized by Thomas Jefferson, James Madison, Andrew Jackson, and Martin Van Buren, had a role of opposition and defined itself in terms of the party representing states and the local government. From 1860 until 1912, the Republican party controlled the presidency except for two nonconsecutive elections. In 1912, Woodrow Wilson and the Democrats captured the White House. They moved their philosophy toward defining the party as representing national interests and one that would take aggressive actions in the economy. This positive liberalism set the tone for the twentieth century. Even before winning the presidency, Woodrow Wilson took a position favoring an active and energetic national government. This document reported his ideas about the role of the national government in the federal system.

* * *

The Democratic Party is now facing an unusual opportunity and a very great duty. . . .

Take the old ideal of "as little government as possible." The indisputable fact is that the Federal Government has in recent years been launched into many fields of activity even the existence of which previous generations did not foresee. I for one am very jealous of the separate powers and authority of the individual States of the Union. But it is no longer possible with the modern combinations of industry and transportation to discriminate the interests of the States as they could once be discriminated. Interests once local and separate have become unified and National. They must be treated by the National Government.

Stated in general terms, our principles should be: Government not for the sake of success at whatever cost and the multiplication of material resources by whatever process, but for the sake of discriminating justice and the wholesome development as well as regulation of the national life.

Source: "Wilson Points Way to New Democracy: Old Ideal of 'as Little Government as Possible' Outlived," *New York Times*, October 30, 1909, quoted in William E. Leuchtenburg and Gene Brown, eds., *The Great Contemporary Issues: Political Parties* (New York: Arno Press, 1977), p. 57.

DOCUMENT 48: Woodrow Wilson's New Freedom Changes the Old Order, 1913

The old argument between Federalists and Antifederalists and the Federalist party and the Democratic-Republican party was rekindled at the beginning of the twentieth century around the issue of the national government's involvement in the economy. Progressives such as *New Republic* editor Herbert Croly advocated an aggressive role for the national government to ensure American prosperity and to afford opportunities for business in the modern economy.

Throughout the twentieth century politicians and citizens have debated the role of government in regulating economic affairs. In this document, President Woodrow Wilson echoed the ideas of progressive intellectuals in advocating government policies to improve economic conditions. "New Freedom" would be the name and direction of positive liberal government.

* * *

There is a great deal that needs reconstruction in the United States. I should like to take a census of the businessmen,—I mean the rank and file of the businessmen,—as to whether they think that business conditions in this country, or rather whether the organization of business in this country, is satisfactory or not. I know what they would say if they dared. If they could vote secretly they would vote overwhelmingly that the present organization of business was meant for the big fellows and was not meant for the little fellows; that it was meant for those who are at the top and was meant to exclude those who are at the bottom; that it was meant to shut out beginners, to prevent new entries in the race, to prevent the building up of competitive enterprises that would interfere with the monopolies which the great trusts have built up.

What this country needs above everything else is a body of laws which will look after the men who are on the make rather than the men who are already made. . . .

No country can afford to have its prosperity originated by a small controlling class. The treasury of America does not lie in the brains of the small body of men now in control of the great enterprises that have been concentrated under the direction of a very small number of persons. The treasury of America lies in those ambitions, those energies, that cannot be restricted to a special favored class. It depends upon the inventions of unknown men, upon the ambitions of unknown men. Every country is renewed out of the ranks of the unknown, not out of the ranks of those already famous and powerful and in control.

There has come over the land that un-American set of conditions which enables a small number of men who control the government to get favors from the government. . . .

We used to think in the old-fashioned days when life was very simple that all that government had to do was to put on a policeman's uniform, and say, "Now don't anybody hurt anybody else." We used to say that the ideal of government was for every man to be left alone and not interfered with, except when he interfered with somebody else; and that the best government was the government that did as little governing as possible. That was the idea that obtained in Jefferson's time. But we are coming now to realize that life is so complicated that we are not dealing with the old conditions, and that the law has to step in and create new conditions under which we may live, the conditions which will make it tolerable for us to live.

Source: Woodrow Wilson, *The New Freedom: A Call for the Emancipation of the Generous Energies of a People* (Garden City, N.Y.: Doubleday, Page & Company, 1913), pp. 16–20.

DOCUMENT 49: Kate Gordon's Letter to the Governors of the Southern States, 1913

Kate Gordon was a southern states' rights suffragist who epitomized an extreme position in the suffragist movement. While working diligently for women's right to vote, she confined her efforts to obtaining that right at the state level. Ever fearful that a national amendment would include support for suffrage of African American males and females, a right that was curtailed by Jim Crow laws, Gordon vehemently sought states' rights as the only way to forward her cause. Her racism dominated her desire to obtain suffrage for women from the state rather than the national government.

Gordon became the president of Southern States Woman Suffrage Conference. She and her colleagues requested the support of southern legislators by pronouncing their consistent loyalty to states' rights while posing the threat of the federal amendment over the heads of politicians. This document is a portion of a letter Gordon wrote to southern governors.

* * *

We are united in the belief that suffrage is a State right, and that the power to define a States' electorate should remain the exclusive right of the State. However, we recognize that woman suffrage is no longer a theory to be debated but a condition to be met. The inevitable "votes for women" is a world movement, and unless the South squarely faces the issue and takes steps to preserve the State right, the force of public opinion will make it mandatory through a National Constitutional Amendment. . . .

While as Southerners, we wish to see the power of the State retained, yet as women we are equally determined to secure, as of paramount importance, the right which is the birthright of an American citizen. We, therefore, appeal to you gentlemen vested with the power to so largely shape conditions, to confer with us and influence public opinion to adopt woman suffrage through State action. Failing to accomplish this, the onus of responsibility will rest upon the men of the South, if Southern women are forced to support a National Amendment, weighted with the same objections as the Fifteenth Amendment.

Source: Reprinted in Anna Howard Shaw, "Woman's Suffrage: Suffrage in the 'Solid South,'" from *Trend*, clipping in the Catharine Waugh McCulloch Papers, Schlesinger Library, Radcliffe College, Cambridge, Massachusetts, as quoted in Marjorie Spruill Wheeler, *New Women of the New South: The Leaders of the Woman Suffrage Movement in the Southern States* (New York: Oxford University Press, 1993), pp. 140–141.

DOCUMENT 50: Petition from Women Voters, Anti-Suffrage Party of New York, 1917

In contrast to Elizabeth Cady Stanton, Susan B. Anthony, and Jane Addams's call for women to take an active role in American democratic society, including the right to vote, other groups of women and men organized in opposition to extending the right of franchise to women. The following document petitioned the U.S. Senate, urging the senators to take no action on the suffrage issue while America was engaged in World War I. The Anti-Suffragists in this instance were appealing to the national government to prevent the passage of an amendment to the Constitution extending the franchise to women.

* * *

Whereas, This country is now engaged in the greatest war in history, and

Whereas, The advocates of the Federal Amendment, though urging it as a war measure, announce, through their president, Mrs. Catt, that its passage "means a simultaneous campaign in 48 states. It demands organization in every precinct, activity, agitation, education in every corner. Nothing less than this nation-wide, vigilant, unceasing campaign will win ratification," therefore be it

Resolved, That our country in this hour of peril should be spared the harassing of its public men and the distracting of its people from work for the war, and further

Resolved, That the United States Senate be respectfully urged to pass no
    measure involving such a radical change in our government while
    the attention of the patriotic portion of the American people is con-
    centrated on the all-important task of winning the war, and during
    the absence of over a million men abroad.
Source: http://www.nara.gov/education/teaching/woman/doc9p1.gif.

DOCUMENT 51: State of Tennessee Approves Nineteenth Amendment, August 1920

The amendment process to the U.S. Constitution provided an opportunity for three-fourths of the states, either in special conventions
or in their legislatures, to approve of proposed amendments to the Constitution. The passage of the Nineteenth Amendment (Tennessee was
the last state needed to ratify the amendment) was the culmination of
efforts that had begun in the early nineteenth century to secure
women's suffrage. Furthermore, women's rights movements were intertwined with efforts to ensure the rights of other minority groups.
When the rights of African Americans resurfaced in the 1940s, the
foundation for debate was enriched by arguments developed out of the
women's suffrage movement.

* * *

EXECUTIVE CHAMBER, CAPITOL, NASHVILLE
STATE OF TENNESSEE

I, A.H. Roberts, by virtue of the authority vested in me as Governor
of the State of Tennessee, and also the authority conferred upon me
therein, do certify to the President of the United States, to the Secretary
of State of the United States at Washington, District of Columbia, to the
President of the Senate of the United States, and to the Speaker of the
House of Representatives of the United States, that the attached paper is
true and perfect copy of Senate Joint Resolution Number 1, ratifying an
amendment to the Constitution of the United States, declaring that the
rights of the citizens of the United States to vote shall not be denied or
bridged by the United States or by any state on account of sex, and that
the Congress shall have power to enforce said article by appropriate
legislation, as setout in said resolution; and that same was passed and
adopted by the first extra session of the Sixty-First General Assembly of
the State of Tennessee, constitutionally called to meet and convened at
the Capitol, in the city of Nashville on August 9, 1920, thereby ratifying

said proposed Nineteenth Amendment to the said constitution of the United States of America, in manner and form appearing on the Journals of the two houses of the General Assembly of the State of Tennessee, true, full and correct transcript of all entries pertaining to which said Resolution Number 1, are attached hereto and made part hereof.

In Witness Whereof, I have hereunto signed my name as Governor of the State of Tennessee, and have affixed hereto the Great Seal of the State of Tennessee, at the Capitol, in the city of Nashville, Tennessee, on this the twenty-fourth day of August, 1920, at 10:17 a.m. [notation]

Signed: A.H. Roberts

Source: http://www.nara.gov/education/teaching/woman/ldocl.

DOCUMENT 52: President Calvin Coolidge on the Responsibilities of the States, May 30, 1925

President Calvin Coolidge was born in Plymouth, Vermont, and participated in the politics of Massachusetts, where he was governor from 1919 to 1920. In the 1920 election he was the vice-presidential running mate of Warren G. Harding (Republican party). In 1923, Coolidge became president on the death of Harding. He was elected president in the 1924 election. Coolidge strictly adhered to laissez-faire economic philosophy. His sedate decorum, pithy utterances, and taciturn nature led to his nickname, "Silent Cal." The following selection is from President Coolidge's Memorial Day Address at Arlington National Cemetery.

* * *

. . . Our constitutional history started with the states retaining all powers of sovereignty unimpaired, save those conferred upon the national government. The evolution of the constitutional system has consisted largely in determining the line of demarcation between state and national authority. The cases involved are many and complicated, but there is a fairly good popular understanding of this continuing struggle between these contending sovereignties. Because of better communication and transportation, the constant tendency has been to more and more social and economic unification. The present continent-wide union of forty-eight states is much closer than was the original group of thirteen states.

This increasing unification has well-nigh obliterated state lines so far as concerns many relations of life. Yet in a country of such enormous expanse, there must always be certain regional differences in social out-look and economic thought. The most familiar illustration of this is found in the history of slavery. . . .

Though the [civil] war ended forever the possibility of disunion, there still remain problems between state and Federal authority. There are divisions of interest, perhaps more apparent than real, among geograph-ical sections or social groups. . . . Obviously, these differences give rise to many problems in government, which must always be recognized. . . .
Source: Lamar T. Beman, *Selected Articles on States Rights* (New York: H. W. Wil-son Company, 1926), pp. 68–69.

DOCUMENT 53: President Calvin Coolidge's Fourth Annual State of the Union Message, December 7, 1926

Calvin Coolidge delivered six State of the Union messages to Con-gress while president. With an adherence to a laissez-faire philosophy, Coolidge's Fourth Annual message addressed the issue of states' rights and federalism.

* * *

Members of the Congress:
In reporting to the Congress the state of the Union, I find it impossible to characterize it other than one of general peace and prosperity. . . .
. . .

FEDERAL REGULATION

I am in favor of reducing, rather than expanding, Government bureaus which seek to regulate and control the business activities of the people. Everyone is aware that abuses exist and will exist so long as we are limited by human imperfections. Unfortunately, human nature can not be changed by an act of the legislature. When practically the sole remedy for many evils lies in the necessity of the people looking out for them-selves and reforming their own abuses, they will find that they are re-lying on a false security if the Government assumes to hold out the promise that it is looking out for them and providing reforms for them. The principle is preeminently applicable to the National Government. It is too much assumed that because an abuse exists it is the business of the National Government to provide a remedy. The presumption should be that it is the business of local and State governments. Such national action results in encroaching upon the salutary independence of the States and by undertaking to supersede their natural authority fills the land with bureaus and departments which are undertaking to do what it is impossible for them to accomplish and brings our whole system of government into disrespect and disfavor. We ought to maintain high standards. We ought to punish wrongdoing. Society has not only the privilege but the absolute duty of protecting itself and its individuals. But we can not accomplish this end by adopting a wrong method. Permanent success lies in local, rather than national action. Unless the locality rises to its own requirements, there is an almost irresistible impulse for the National Government to intervene. The States and the Nation should both realize that such action is to be adopted only as a last resort.

Source: Fred L. Israel, ed., *The State of the Union Messages of the Presidents, 1790–1966* (New York: Chelsea House, 1967), 3:2690, 2701–2702.

DOCUMENT 54: Herbert C. Hoover's Fourth Annual State of the Union Message, December 6, 1932

Before he became president, Herbert Hoover had served as chairman of the American Relief Committee in London, chairman of the Commission for Relief in Belgium, and U.S. food administrator during World War I. Under both Presidents Harding and Coolidge, Herbert Hoover displayed his talents as secretary of commerce. His one term as president came when the Great Depression began. In 1932, he delivered to the Congress his fourth and last State of the Union message, part of which addressed the relationship between state and national governments.

* * *

To the Senate and House of Representatives:

In accord with my constitutional duty, I transmit herewith to the Congress information upon the state of the Union together with recommendation of measures for consideration.

Our country is at peace. Our national defense has been maintained at a high state of effectiveness. . . .

In the face of widespread hardship our people have demonstrated daily a magnificent sense of humanity, of individual and community responsibility for the welfare of the less fortunate. They have grown in their conceptions and organization for cooperative action for the common welfare.

In the provision against distress during this winter, the great private agencies of the country have been mobilized again; the generosity of our people has again come into evidence to a degree in which all America may take pride. Likewise the local authorities and the States are engaged everywhere in supplemental measures of relief. The provisions made for loans from the Reconstruction Finance Corporation, to States that have exhausted their own resources, guarantee that there should be no hunger or suffering from cold in the country. The large majority of States are showing a sturdy cooperation in the spirit of the Federal aid.

. . .

It seems to me appropriate upon this occasion to make certain general observations upon the principles which must dominate the solution of problems now pressing upon the Nation. Legislation in response to national needs will be effective only if every such act conforms to a complete philosophy of the people's purposes and destiny. Ours is a distinctive government with a unique history and background, consciously dedicated to specific ideals of liberty and to a faith in the inviolable sanctity of the individual human spirit. Furthermore, the continued existence and adequate functioning of our government in preservation of ordered liberty and stimulation of progress depends upon the maintenance of State, local, institutional, and individual sense of responsibility. We have builded a system of individualism peculiarly our own which must not be forgotten in any governmental acts, for from it have grown greater accomplishments than those of any other nation.

On the social and economic sides, the background of our American system and the motivation of progress is essentially that we should allow free play of social and economic forces as far as will not limit equality of opportunity and as will at the same time stimulate the initiative and enterprise of our people. In the maintenance of this balance the Federal Government can permit of no privilege to any person or group. It should act as a regulatory agent and not as a participant in economic and social life. The moment the Government participates, it becomes a competitor with the people. As a competitor it becomes at once a tyranny in whatever direction it may touch. We have around us numerous such experiences, no one of which can be found to have justified itself except in cases where the people as a whole have met forces beyond their control, such as those of the Great War and the great depression, where the full powers of the Federal Government must be exerted to protect the people. But even these must be limited to an emergency sense and must be promptly ended when these dangers are overcome. . . .

Source: Fred L. Israel, ed., *The State of the Union Messages of the Presidents, 1790–1966* (New York: Chelsea House, 1967), 3:2795, 2803.

DOCUMENT 55: FDR's First Inaugural Address, March 4, 1933

Franklin D. Roosevelt was elected to the presidency during the depression that had begun in the 1930s and would persist until World
War II. The positive liberalism, or the belief that federal policies and
actions could serve as the mechanism to alleviate social and economic
problems, of Woodrow Wilson was escalated by the Great Depression.
FDR made sure that the system of capitalism was protected through
initiatives of the national government, many of which had begun during the presidency of Herbert Hoover. Roosevelt's expansion of the
national government's role was vague in this inaugural address. The
call to arms was left unclear regarding the precise responsibility the
national government would assume. What FDR did make clear, however, was a fervent conviction that the national government required
broad executive powers to meet the national emergency.

* * *

I am certain that my fellow Americans expect that on my induction
into the Presidency I will address them with a candor and a decision
which the present situation of our Nation impels. This is preeminently
the time to speak the truth, the whole truth, frankly and boldly. Nor
need we shrink from honestly facing conditions in our country today.
This great Nation will endure as it has endured, will revive and will
prosper. So, first of all, let me assert my firm belief that the only thing
we have to fear is fear itself—nameless, unreasoning, unjustified terror
which paralyzes needed efforts to convert retreat into advance. In every
dark hour of our national life a leadership of frankness and vigor has
met with that understanding and support of the people themselves
which is essential to victory. I am convinced that you will again give
that support to leadership in these critical days.
   . . .
Restoration calls, however, not for changes in ethics alone. This Nation
asks for action, and action now.
   Our greatest primary task is to put people to work. This is no unsolv-
able problem if we face it wisely and courageously. It can be accomplished in part by direct recruiting by the Government itself, treating the
task as we would treat the emergency of a war, but at the same time,
through this employment, accomplishing greatly needed projects to stimulate and reorganize the use of our natural resources.
   Hand in hand with this we must frankly recognize the overbalance of

population in our industrial centers and, by engaging on a national scale in a redistribution, endeavor to provide a better use of the land for those best fitted for the land. The task can be helped by definite efforts to raise the values of agricultural products and with this the power to purchase the output of our cities. It can be helped by preventing realistically the tragedy of the growing loss through foreclosure of our small homes and our farms. It can be helped by insistence that the Federal, State, and local governments act forthwith on the demand that their cost be drastically reduced. It can be helped by the unifying of relief activities which today are often scattered, uneconomical, and unequal. It can be helped by national planning for and supervision of all forms of transportation and of communications and other utilities which have a definitely public character. There are many ways in which it can be helped, but it can never be helped merely by talking about it. We must act and act quickly.

Finally, in our progress toward a resumption of work we require two safeguards against a return of the evils of the old order; there must be a strict supervision of all banking and credits and investments; there must be an end to speculation with other people's money, and there must be provision for an adequate but sound currency.

There are the lines of attack. I shall presently urge upon a new Congress in special session detailed measures for their fulfillment, and I shall seek the immediate assistance of the several States.

Through this program of action we address ourselves to putting our own national house in order and making income balance outgo. Our international trade relations, though vastly important, are in point of time and necessity secondary to the establishment of a sound national economy. I favor as a practical policy the putting of first things first. I shall spare no effort to restore world trade by international economic readjustment, but the emergency at home cannot wait on that accomplishment.

. . .

If I read the temper of our people correctly, we now realize as we have never realized before our interdependence on each other; that we can not merely take but we must give as well; that if we are to go forward, we must move as a trained and loyal army willing to sacrifice for the good of a common discipline, because without such discipline no progress is made, no leadership becomes effective. We are, I know, ready and willing to submit our lives and property to such discipline, because it makes possible a leadership which aims at a larger good. This I propose to offer, pledging that the larger purposes will bind upon us all as a sacred obligation with a unity of duty hitherto evoked only in time of armed strife.

With this pledge taken, I assume unhesitatingly the leadership of this great army of our people dedicated to a disciplined attack upon our common problems.

Action in this image and to this end is feasible under the form of government which we have inherited from our ancestors. Our Constitution is so simple and practical that it is possible always to meet extraordinary needs by changes in emphasis and arrangement without loss of essential form. That is why our constitutional system has proved itself the most superbly enduring political mechanism the modern world has produced. It has met every stress of vast expansion of territory, of foreign wars, of bitter internal strife, of world relations.

It is to be hoped that the normal balance of executive and legislative authority may be wholly adequate to meet the unprecedented task before us. But it may be that an unprecedented demand and need for undelayed action may call for temporary departure from that normal balance of public procedure.

I am prepared under my constitutional duty to recommend the measures that a stricken nation in the midst of a stricken world may require. These measures, or such other measures as the Congress may build out of its experience and wisdom, I shall seek, within my constitutional authority, to bring to speedy adoption.

But in the event that the Congress shall fail to take one of these two courses, and in the event that the national emergency is still critical, I shall not evade the clear course of duty that will then confront me. I shall ask the Congress for the one remaining instrument to meet the crisis—broad Executive power to wage a war against the emergency, as great as the power that would be given to me if we were in fact invaded by a foreign foe. . . .

We face the arduous days that lie before us in the warm courage of the national unity; with the clear consciousness of seeking old and precious moral values; with the clean satisfaction that comes from the stem performance of duty by old and young alike. We aim at the assurance of a rounded and permanent national life.

We do not distrust the future of essential democracy. The people of the United States have not failed. In their need they have registered a mandate that they want direct, vigorous action. They have asked for discipline and direction under leadership. They have made me the present instrument of their wishes. In the spirit of the gift I take it.

In this dedication of a Nation we humbly ask the blessing of God. May He protect each and every one of us. May He guide me in the days to come.

Source: http://douglass.speech.nwu.edu/roos_a76.htm.

V

States' Rights and American Federalism from the New Deal to the Present, 1940–1999

In 1938, Gunnar Myrdal, a social economist and economic adviser to the Swedish government, arrived in the United States at the invitation of the trustees of the Carnegie Corporation to direct "a comprehensive study of the Negro in the United States." He focused his extended four-year visit on the issue of race relations in the United States. In particular, he was interested in the failure of Americans to apply the principles of founding documents to African Americans. In part, Myrdal's ideas offered a foundation for national involvement to provide equality for African Americans.

Myrdal expressed his criticisms in his 1944 book, *An American Dilemma*.[1] His important book was highly controversial, for it appeared during World War II and at a time when strict de jure and de facto racial segregation was widespread in the United States. Myrdal provided an argument for the civil rights movement from the 1940s to the present. African Americans and whites working in organizations such as the National Association for the Advancement of Colored People (NAACP) took action against racial inequalities by turning to the national government for support. The administration of President Harry Truman recognized the existence of social, economic, and political inequities and initiated federal action beginning with the desegregation of the military by executive order.

THE NEW DEAL AND FAIR DEAL

During the presidencies of Franklin Roosevelt and Harry Truman, international and domestic challenges transformed American society. World War II and the Korean conflict established the United States as a world power that recognized its responsibilities in international politics. The depression of the 1920s and 1930s created challenges to the political and economic order of the United States. The farm crisis, the dust bowl crisis, and unemployment in the 1930s were national in scope and required the financial resources that only the national government possessed. Problems of ecology, the mass migration of plains farmers to California, and the movement of rural peoples into cities throughout the United States created unprecedented problems that necessitated large-scale federal action. The federal government became more actively involved in issues concerning civil rights and personal liberties. The presidency of Harry S. Truman, a southerner and veteran of Missouri politics, sought to compensate Japanese Americans who lost their freedom and property when they were placed in internment camps (see Document 57). Truman was repulsed by the lynchings of African American military veterans that occurred in the 1940s in southern states and initiated the U.S. Commission on Civil Rights to guarantee individual liberties and equal protection under the laws.

The civil rights movement of the 1940s, 1950s, and 1960s sought to extend the ideals of the American creed to include African Americans as well as to finish the work begun with Reconstruction legislation. The Supreme Court, in a series of rulings beginning in the 1940s, reversed its previous position to sustain the actions of the national government to protect African Americans. It upheld civil rights legislation, including the use of force. The 1954 decision in *Brown v. Board of Education of Topeka* (see Document 62) was a monumental breakthrough. The Civil Rights Acts of 1957, 1964, and 1968, the Voting Rights Act of 1965, and the programs of Lyndon Johnson's Great Society also demonstrated the alignment of the various branches of the national government's commitment to secure the civil rights of African Americans.

THE ASSERTION OF STATES RIGHTS

Truman's executive order establishing the Commission on Civil Rights resurrected the states' rights argument held by the South. In the 1948 presidential campaign Democratic delegates who would form the States' Rights party (also Known as the Dixiecrats), led by Strom

Thurmond of South Carolina (see Document 58), walked out of the Democratic National Convention in protest against the Truman administration's civil rights plank. In the 1950s and 1960s southerners rallied under the banner of states' rights (see Document 63). They resurrected the idea that the national government was a compact among the states in protest to the *Brown* decision, which called on education to serve as a primary means nationally to integrate society and create greater equality of opportunity.

President Dwight D. Eisenhower, winning both the 1952 and 1956 presidential elections, struggled over what to do concerning civil rights. Eisenhower's style of presidential activism has aptly been described as "hidden-hand leadership."[2] (See Document 61.) He did not publicize his active involvement in policymaking, especially his desire to moderate domestic policy change, preferring istead to "conceal his activities from all nonassociates." His goal was to convince others to follow his lead so as to defuse issues rather than to publicize dramatically a cause that would produce hostile confrontation. Eisenhower was active and worked arduously to shape the direction of public policy. He also controlled strong-willed advisers such as John Foster Dulles and Ezra Taft Benson. Often he let them serve as "point men" to satisfy the right wing of the Republican party.

Although Eisenhower avoided being linked with overt political operations, preferring to be above political machinations, he did influence congressional leaders by calling on intermediaries to use their political influence and thus serve subtly as conduits to manage relations with leaders of Congress. He was, for example, able to discreetly manipulate the Senate Democratic leader, Lyndon Baines Johnson, through Federal Reserve Board Member Robert Anderson. He also used Senate Republican leader Everett McKinley Dirksen of Illinois on numerous issues, including the eventual condemnation of Senator Joseph McCarthy. Historians Edward L. Schapsmeier and Frederick H. Schapsmeier have noted that Eisenhower could lead authoritatively "without appearing to be abrasively imperious."[3]

Eisenhower no doubt acquired his leadership style from his years of experience as a military leader. Ike had point men who took the heat for ideas that needed to be presented to the public. He did this because if the ideas were unacceptable or would tarnish his reputation, he could back off. His hidden-hand style allowed him to conceal his involvement. This he did as the civil rights issue grew in intensity in the 1950s.

Eisenhower regarded desegregation as an impediment to harmony and civil rights as a most divisive issue. The president sought "a path through the thorny field of civil rights that nearly all sections of the country could agree on." Eisenhower held a firm conviction that federal "legislation alone" would not "institute morality." He confided that "coercion" would not "cure all civil rights problems."[4] Nevertheless he began his presidency with a commitment to civil rights. In his State of the Union message, he pledged to use the power of the presidency to end segregation in the District of Columbia, the armed forces, and the federal bureaucracy (see Document 60). He immediately ran into trouble with southern administrators of federal schools, hospitals, and navy yards. When federal administrators refused to follow the president's request, Congressman Adam Clayton Powell, Jr., chided Ike for failing to enforce his State of the Union message. Powell, an African American and Democrat from New York, caused Ike to act more decisively. In response, Ike demanded that the navy end its practice of following "local customs" concerning racial policies among its civilian employees who were working in the South. Eisenhower might have taken more overt and public action to enforce his order. Instead, he exchanged private letters with the governor of South Carolina, James F. Byrnes. This action concealed his activities concerning civil rights from the public but sought to promote change (see Document 61).

Byrnes had been an adviser to FDR and served as secretary of state for Harry S. Truman, but in 1952, he supported Eisenhower for president because the Democratic candidate, Adlai Stevenson, had advocated a permanent federal fair employment practices commission law similar to Truman's Committee on Government Contract Compliance. Byrnes disliked Eisenhower's Committee on Government Contracts, which would establish compliance procedures designed to end discrimination. Byrnes advised Eisenhower to use the legislative process instead of executive orders to achieve his purposes. He urged, "I only hope you do not seek to accomplish by executive fiat objectives that the Congress has considered and rejected." The South Carolina governor vehemently denied the existence of discrimination at the Charleston Naval Shipyard and refused to acknowledge separate restaurants, rest rooms, and drinking fountains for African American and white civilian employees. He did concede that the NAACP had protested against "a distinction between the races in certain facilities, namely, rest rooms, cafeterias and drinking fountains."

Ike's letter emphasized to Byrnes (who held racist convictions) that he regarded the governor as a friend. In an original draft of the letter, Ike let Byrnes know that he was personally sensitive to the traditions and feelings of the South concerning race, but after careful thought he decided not to endorse Byrnes's attitudes. To do so, might have led to "potential trouble" if word were leaked to the press. What he did write to Byrnes was a firm statement about enforcing federal law. Ike believed it was his constitutional requirement to do so as president (see

Documents 60 and 61). Byrnes responded to Ike's 1953 executive order calling for racial integration in southern federal facilities, noting that "there will be differences of opinion as to the wisdom of your action." He saw Ike's policy as new and as a move that "not even President Truman deemed necessary at such installations, but everyone will realize and must admit the power of the Federal Government." Byrnes distinguished the situation at the navy shipyard, where "no man is compelled to work," from the "public school situation." He would comply with "wholehearted cooperation" to help if trouble erupted outside the naval shipyard. He concluded, "Because of the cordial phrasing of your letter, I have unburdened myself freely. . . . I would not be true to myself or to my friendship for you to dissemble my apprehension."

Eisenhower had been able to defuse the civil rights issue in the case of federal jurisdiction in federal facilities. During his first three years as president, desegregation occurred in Washington, D.C., veterans' hospitals, and naval shipyards.[5] Beyond these years, however, Eisenhower found it more difficult to act. The president preferred state action on civil rights issues and did not believe federal laws would be effective. During the remainder of his presidency, Congress passed the Civil Rights Acts of 1957 and 1960, respectively, the first civil rights acts since 1867. The Civil Rights Act of 1957 led to a crisis in Arkansas, when Governor Orval Faubus called out the National Guard to prevent nine African American students from entering Central High School in Little Rock. Eisenhower was forced to respond by sending paratroopers and placing the Arkansas National Guard under federal control.

During the 1960s, the administrations of John F. Kennedy and, particularly, Lyndon Baines Johnson acted more overtly in protecting the civil rights of African Americans (see Document 64). JFK made dramatic gestures of verbal support to civil rights leaders, but never acted decisively to achieve congressional action. After Kennedy's death, LBJ pushed through and signed the Civil Rights Act of 1964. Republican senator Everett McKinley Dirksen of Illinois skillfully midwifed GOP votes in support of the civil rights legislation and in so doing broke the southern filibuster.[6]

The civil rights movement of the 1960s stressed the problems of urban blacks. Approximately 70 percent of African Americans lived in metropolitan areas. Nonviolent tactics that had successfully worked in the rural South were less effective in northern cities. Violence erupted throughout the North and in Los Angeles, and "Black Power" became a rallying cry. The Student Nonviolent Coordinating Committee (SNCC), composed of African Americans and whites, worked with Martin Luther King's Southern Christian Leadership Conference (SCLC).

King's nonviolent strategy became estranged from SNCC by 1966. So too did African Americans and whites in SNCC as Stokely Carmichael directed SNCC toward a separatist philosophy.

By the late 1960s and early 1970s questions had arisen regarding the lengths to which federal education policies could go to equalize opportunities for individuals. Southern governors such as Alabama's George Wallace questioned the resolve of the federal government in guaranteeing African American rights (see Document 67). The 1978 *Bakke* decision countermanded the policy of the University of California at Davis, which considered race and other minority status as factors in the admission of medical students to state universities. Allan Bakke, a thirty-three year old white man with a mechanical engineering degree from the University of Minnesota and a master's degree from Stanford charged "reverse discrimination" when he was denied entrance to the Davis medical school even though his test scores were higher by far than sixteen African Americans admitted under a special program. The *Bakke* decision (5-4) lessened the factor of race as a quota condition for admission to institutions of higher learning. Although the decision did not negate the *Brown* decision of 1954, it challenged the use of racial and ethnic origins in offering preferential treatment to individuals in admission to schools.

The position of states in the federal system also came under question concerning the issue of commerce and economic policies. Since the New Deal, Keynesian economics had justified deficit spending. Deficits, according to British economist John Maynard Keynes, were allowable during depressions because they served as pump-priming mechanisms. What was often forgotten, however, was Keynes's advice to balance budgets and accumulate surpluses during periods of economic prosperity. From the era of FDR on, only. Eisenhower's administration consistently practiced Keynesian fiscal policy. By 1965, while Lyndon Johnson was president, the unbalanced budgets and higher taxes (as well as inflation) worried more fiscally conservative policymakers. For example, the 89th Congress of 1965 competed with the 73rd Congress of the New Deal period in churning out social and economic legislation. Some of the legislation was desperately needed to address economic inequities in American society. The Great Society legislation, however, disturbed those Americans who saw such laws and statutes as detrimental to fundamental values and traditions. The Great Society enlarged the size of the federal bureaucracy and increased governmental centralization, at the expense of the states.

Furthermore, the activism of the U.S. Supreme Court reverberated under the leadership of Chief Justice Earl Warren. The chief justice, a former governor of California, had been a 1953 appointee of President Eisenhower. The Warren Court made the bold and important decision in *Brown v. Board of Education of Topeka* (1954) to overturn *Plessy v. Ferguson* (1896). But Warren's dominant majority was too activist in their legal philosophy from the perspective of conservatives. The Warren Court's judicial activism also acted on state authority.

The Warren Court's activism expressed itself on two special issues: church and state relations and reapportioning representation of state legislatures. In regard to church-state relations, the Court issued a decision in *Engle v. Vitale* (1962) that the regents' prayer, a prescribed prayer, of the state of New York was unconstitutional. The Court decided that separation of church and state, under the First Amendment, prohibited the recitation of prayer in public schools. The Court ignored the "free exercise" clause in the First Amendment and instead focused on the phrase "make no law." Using the Fourteenth Amendment, the Court then applied the prohibition about establishing a religion to the various states.

The Warren Court also exercised its authority over the issue of reapportioning state legislatures. Prior to the Warren Court, the Supreme Court had maintained that issues of legislative malapportionment (or gerrymandering) were political, not judicial, questions. Throughout most of the twentieth century, the U.S. population had increasingly become urban. The 1920 census indicated this shift from a rural to an urban society. At issue was this question: How much were urban concerns considered in the representation of state legislatures? Rural legislators in the states did not want to lose their seats, and after 1920 they were less willing to reapportion.

In *Colegrove v. Green* (1946), the Supreme Court determined that legislative malapportionment was not a justiciable question. Then in 1962, the Warren Court overturned *Colegrove v. Green* by its decision in *Baker v. Carr.* It announced that apportionment was indeed a justiciable question on the grounds of the Fourteenth Amendment's equal protection clause. Yet *Baker v. Carr* was not a plan of action. Rather, it was an articulation of a constitutional principle opposed to unequal representation on voting power. In 1964, the Warren Court took a further step in its judicial activism. In *Reynolds v. Sims,* it required states to base their apportionment of seats on population and thus affected state senates in bicameral legislatures.

The Supreme Court exercised its judicial power by entering state politics and now could involve itself in the right of states to determine the composition of its constituents. During the 1960s, the United States began to think of itself less as a union of sovereign states and more as a union of individuals. *Reynolds v. Sims,* requiring "one person, one vote" in the creation of legislative districts, fostered this change. Members of Congress now were compelled to look to national interest groups rather than state political parties for political support.[7] Beginning with the presidency of Richard Nixon, a reaction of New Federalism attempted to counter the era of big government, which had its climax under Lyndon Baines Johnson and the Great Society. New Federalism shifted more power to the states concerning the spending of tax money. The challenge to a centralized government became apparent in the Supreme Court as well. In 1971, during the presidency of Richard Nixon, Justice Hugo L. Black raised an issue that has persisted to the present day. Justice Black, who was appointed to the Supreme Court by FDR in 1937 as a liberal southerner, described "Our Federalism" in *Younger v. Harris.* He explained that federalism involved

a proper respect for state functions, a recognition of the fact that the entire country is made up of a Union of separate governments, and a continuance of the belief that the National Government will fare best if the States and their institutions are left to perform their separate functions in their separate ways.[8]

Concerning commerce in the 1970s, the Supreme Court limited the regulatory powers of the national government and gave greater credence to states' rights arguments. States were concerned about state sovereignty because the power of the national government had grown immensely over the preceding fifty years.

The presidency of Ronald Reagan also reinvigorated states' rights theory. Reagan campaigned in 1980 on an anti–big government platform of New Federalism that proved popular enough to win him the presidency. His victory in the presidential election against incumbent Jimmy Carter was a harbinger of a new conservative Republican majority coalition. The 1980 election showed that the traditional liberal agenda was a victim of its past successes and its exhaustion. The old New Deal–Fair Deal majority coalition had disappeared. Liberalism had lost much of its constituency. In his First Inaugural Address, Reagan proclaimed that "the Federal government did not create the states; the states created the Federal government" (see Document 68).[9] Whether right or wrong, Reagan set the tone for a revitalization of the role of states in our federal system. As illustrated in the Supreme Court decisions of *Garcia v. San Antonio Metropolitan Transit Authority, United States v. Lopez, Seminole Tribe v. Florida, Printz v. United States,* and *Alden v. Maine* (see Documents 71 and 72) in the 1980s and 1990s, made during the presidencies of Ronald Reagan, George Bush, and William Clinton, the issue of states' rights has not subsided.

Federalism remained a major issue in the mid-1990s (see Document 69). By the 1996 elections, presidential candidates, congressional leaders, and governors proposed measures to shift responsibility from the national government to state and local governments. The year 1996 was identified as the so-called "Devolution Revolution" as some power, such as budget balances and social welfare, was transferred from the federal government to the states. By 1997 the development of the "New Federal Order" meant less intrusion by the federal government into the affairs of state governments (see Document 70). At the same time, it increased the responsibilities of states, including financial support for public policies. The shift of power from national to state governments was a means to effect particular identities and underscore local value commitments.

Federalism has been more than the dispassionate distribution of authority. It returns to the fundamental beliefs of the relationship of the institutions and governmental organizations, which represent the individual.

NOTES

1. Gunnar Myrdal, *An American Dilemma: The Negro Problem and Modern Democracy* (New York: Harper, 1944).

2. Fred I. Greenstein, *The Hidden-Hand Presidency: Eisenhower as Leader* (New York: Basic Books, 1982), pp. 58–65.

3. Edward L. Schapsmeier and Frederick H. Schapsmeier, *Dirksen of Illinois: Senatorial Statesman* (Urbana: University of Illinois Press, 1985), p. 92.

4. Dwight D. Eisenhower, *Waging Peace: 1956–1961* (Garden City, N.Y.: Doubleday, 1965), p. 149.

5. *The Papers of Dwight David Eisenhower*, ed. Louis Galambos and Duan Van EE, XIV, *The Presidency: The Middle Way* (Baltimore: Johns Hopkins Press, 1996), pp. 472–473.

6. Schapsmeier and Schapsmeier, *Dirksen of Illinois*, pp. 155–160.

7. John Kincaid, "The Devolution Tortoise and the Centralization Hare," *New England Economic Review* (May–June 1998): 34–35.

8. *Younger v. Harris*, 401 U.S. 37, at 44 (1971).

9. "President Reagan's First Inaugural Address, January 20, 1981," *Binghamton Review*, http://www.netstep.net/review/rr1stia.html.

DOCUMENT 56: Governor Fielding Wright of Mississippi, Statement to Democratic Party Leaders, January 1948

Fielding Wright, governor of Mississippi, responded vehemently to President Truman's Commission on Civil Rights. His argument hearkened back to the states' rights position of the nineteenth century as he described the Constitution as "the great instrument creating this Government which makes of us a union of sovereign states." The civil rights legislation, he charged, "flagrantly invades the sovereign rights of individual states." Cloaking the race issue, he continued, "It undertakes to destroy our proper privilege of solving our own individual problems in the light of all our circumstances."

Wright threatened secession. This time the South would temporarily secede from the Democratic party in the 1948 election. Wright ran as vice president on the States' Rights (Dixiecrat) party ticket in 1948, with Governor J. Strom Thurmond as the presidential candidate. The document that follows was an assertion of states' rights and a preview of positions white southerners would assume surrounding civil rights legislation. Wright's comments were both forward looking and backward looking. His statement looked back to the compact theory of government that had described the origins of the national government during ratification of the Constitution. His threats to the Democratic party were a forecast of schisms between northern and southern Democrats and eventual shift toward the Republican party in 1968 and subsequent years.

* * *

Facing the future, as your chief executive, I would be remiss in my responsibilities if your attention were not directed to the fact that we are living in unsettled, uncertain, and even perilous times. One need not be a diplomat nor a student of international affairs to see the many danger flags flying throughout the world in the field of international relations as democracy clashes with communism in a struggle which will determine whether or not these two ideologies can live together in cooperation or if we must once again maintain our heritage and our freedom in the cold and cruel crucible of war. Nor need one be an economic prophet to realize that the inflation running rampant in this country today—if allowed to continue its mad flight unchecked—will eventually, and in the not-too-distant future, lead us into the depths of another great depression.

But, serious as these problems may be, they can be met and solved if approached in the spirit of common sense, honesty, and unselfishness which has characterized our efforts in so many difficult and trying times in the past.

And as we search for the answers to these problems, there is yet another most serious conflict being thrust upon the people of Mississippi and our beloved Southland; thrust upon us in the Congress of the United States and through press and radio services throughout the country. That is the campaign of abuse and misrepresentation being levelled against our section by those who seek to tear down and disrupt our institutions and our way of life. They are using as their tools such infamous proposals as FEPC [Fair Employment Practices Committee], antilynching legislation, anti-poll-tax bills, and now the antisegregation proposals.

The charge of dereliction of duty could be hurled at me by the citizens of this State were I to fail to direct your thoughts to the vicious effect of the proposals of the committee appointed by the President of the United States to study and make recommendations under the guise of preservation of civil liberties. Those of you who read and studied the [FEPC] report recognize in it a further, and I might say, the most dangerous step, toward the destruction of those traditions and customs so vital to our way of life, particularly in our Southland.

These measures and the proposals of this committee are deliberately aimed to wreck the South and our institutions. But they are far more sinister than being mere pieces of antisouthern legislation and recommendations, for hidden under their misleading titles and guarded phraseology are elements so completely foreign to our American way of living and thinking that they will, if enacted, eventually destroy this Nation and all of the freedoms which we have long cherished and maintained.

The advocates of today's antisouthern legislation disregard the great instrument creating this Government which makes of us a union of sovereign States. This Nation, of which we are so justly proud, has grown great amid our very many differences of ideas. Each of our 48 States has made singular and specific contributions to the national whole because while they are different the people had the individual leeway to decide their own best methods for solving their local problems. Individuals in this Nation have achieved the heights because they had the right to use their own personal talents, and no man was standardized or limited to any given level of attainment or service to or among his fellows.

With this record of achievement which has made our country the greatest in the world—with our structure of republican government which has enabled our sovereign States to live together in relative harmony and progress and which has brought to all our people a standard of living never before achieved in human history—I cannot understand why there are those in this land today and in the Congress of the United States who would begin its disintegration by such types of nefarious legislation as I have previously mentioned. The [civil rights] legislation to which I have referred flagrantly invades the sovereign rights of the individual States. It undertakes to destroy our proper privilege of solving our own individual problems in the light of all our circumstances.

Aside from this fundamental right, such legislation violates the very experience of man, namely, that the problems of human relationships are so varied and diverse that we can never begin to solve all of them by laws. They can only be answered by education and continuing progress in the light of truth as God may give us wisdom to see and embrace the truth. And they can only be solved by the people who understand and know and are familiar with the problem.

Here in Mississippi and the South may be found the greatest example in human history of harmonious relationships ever recorded as existing between two so different and distinct races as the white and the Negro, living so closely together and in such nearly equal numbers. The uninterrupted progress which has been made will be continued in an orderly, effective manner if both races are left alone by those unfamiliar with the true situation. This problem is being solved by Mississippians and by southerners in a wholesome and constructive manner. We know that human relationship cannot be equalized and balanced by legislation, unless through such legislation the power of the State is exercised to force all men into a pattern—a rigid pattern which would operate to destroy the freedoms of all and cut off our march of progress.

We believe that the people of each of the 48 States—north, south, east, and west—are the most capable of judging their own respective local needs and meeting them. We know that this was the program set up by our founding fathers and guaranteed in our Constitution.

In Mississippi, and I think in the other States known as the South, we feel that our rights are being threatened by enemies of the South who are in fact also enemies of the Nation. We are convinced that in upholding our position in this current struggle, we are in fact maintaining the interest of all the American people and each of the 48 States. Yes, we are confident that we are by our position upholding the rights of the members of all races and sections.

As a lifelong Democrat, as a descendant of Democrats, as the Governor of this Nation's most Democratic State, I would regret to see the day come when Mississippi or the South should break with the Democratic Party in a national election. But vital principles and eternal truths transcend party lines, and the day is now at hand when determined action must be taken.

We have repeatedly seen the proposal of various measures in the Congress which were not for the best interests of the Nation but definitely designed to appeal to certain voting groups holding the balance of power in other States. We of the South will no longer tolerate being the target for this type of legislation which would not only destroy our way of life, but which, if enacted, would eventually destroy the United States. The time has come for the militant people of the South and the Nation, who have never shirked any patriotic responsibility, to band together for the preservation of true Americanism. United in our cause, we serve not only ourselves and our neighbors, but all of our fellow citizens throughout the Nation.

As we face this particular task I invite the patience, calm deliberation, counsel, and cooperation of all men of good will and true Americanism, wherever they may be. We are Democrats; we have been loyal to the Democratic Party at all times, in its periods of success as well as in the dark days of despair. We voted the Democratic ticket when no other section stayed with the banner. We have never shirked, nor have we ever faltered in our loyalty to our party. There are some who subscribe to the belief that due to this record of faithful service we are taken for granted and are not deemed worthy of consideration in formulating party policy and platforms. A continuation of the harassing and unfair legislation to which I have referred will compel all of us to such a conclusion.

This is a new day in State and national politics and circumstances may make necessary a new, and, we hope, a temporary approach to national politics by our State and Southland. We have always remained true to the traditions of our party and will continue to do so, but when the national leaders attempt to change those principles for which the party stands, we intend to fight for its preservation with all means at our hands. We must make our national leaders fully realize we mean precisely what we say, and we must, if necessary, implement our words with positive action. We warn them now, to take heed. Drastic though our methods may be, and as far reaching as the results may prove, we are certain that the ultimate consequence will fully justify any temporary set-back that may follow our action.

Source: Arthur M. Schlesinger, ed., *History of U.S. Political Parties* (New York: Chelsea House, 1973), 4:3399–3401.

DOCUMENT 57: The Civil Rights Message of Harry S Truman to the U.S. Congress, February 2, 1948

Harry S. Truman demonstrated his strength as a national leader when in 1948 he challenged the legislative branch of the national government to authorize a permanent Commission on Civil Rights. In addition he called on the Congress to establish a Joint Congressional Committee on Civil Rights and to create a Civil Rights Division in the Justice Department. Truman's proposal was a bold national action that established an agenda for civil rights for the remainder of the twentieth century. These executive actions risked a split in Truman's own political party and jeopardized his candidacy for a second term as president. While a policy of gradualism among African American and white leaders had predominated in the twentieth century, Truman attempted to invigorate more rapid change.

* * *

To the Congress of the United States:

In the state of the Union message on Jan. 7, 1948, I spoke of five great goals toward which we should strive in our constant effort to strengthen our democracy and improve the welfare of our people. The first of these is to secure fully our essential human rights. I am now presenting to the Congress my recommendations for legislation to carry us forward toward that goal.

This nation was founded by men and women who sought these shores that they might enjoy greater freedom and greater opportunity than they had known before. The founders of the United States proclaimed to the world the American belief that all men are created equal, and that Governments are instituted to secure the inalienable rights with which all men are endowed. In the Declaration of Independence and the Constitution of the United States, they eloquently expressed the aspirations of all mankind for equality and freedom.

These ideals inspired the peoples of other lands and their practical fulfillment made the United States the hope of the oppressed everywhere. . . .

With those who preceded them, they have helped to fashion and strengthen our American faith—a faith that can be simply stated:

We believe that all men are created equal and that they have the right to equal justice under law.

We believe that all men have the right to freedom of thought and of expression and the right to worship as they please.

We believe that all men are entitled to equal opportunities for jobs, for homes, for good health and for education.

We believe that all men should have a voice in their government and that government should protect, not usurp, the rights of the people.

These are the basic civil rights which are the source and the support of our democracy. . . .

Unfortunately, there still are examples—flagrant examples—of discrimination which are utterly contrary to our ideals. Not all groups of our population are free from the fear of violence. Not all groups are free to live and work where they please or to improve their conditions of life by their own efforts. Not all groups enjoy the full privileges of citizenship and participation in the government under which they live.

We cannot be satisfied until all our people have equal opportunities for jobs, for homes, for education, for health and for political expression, and until all our people have equal protection under the law. . . .

The protection of civil rights begins with the mutual respect for the rights of others which all of us should practice in our daily lives. Through organizations in every community in all parts of the country—

we must continue to develop practical, workable arrangements for achieving greater tolerance and brotherhood.

The protection of civil rights is the duty of every government which derives its powers from the consent of the people. This is equally true of local, state and national governments. There is much that the states can and should do at this time to extend their protection of civil rights. Wherever the law enforcement measures of State and local governments are inadequate to discharge this primary function of government, these measures should be strengthened and improved.

The Federal Government has a clear duty to see that constitutional guarantees of individual liberties and of equal protection under the laws are not denied or abridged anywhere in our Union. That duty is shared by all three branches of the Government, but it can be fulfilled only if the Congress enacts modern, comprehensive civil rights laws, adequate to the needs of the day, and demonstrating our continuing faith in the free way of life.

I recommend, therefore, that the Congress enact legislation at this session directed toward the following specific objectives:

1. Establishing a permanent Commission on Civil Rights, a Joint Congressional Committee on Civil Rights, and a Civil Rights Division in the Department of Justice.

2. Strengthening existing civil rights statutes.

3. Providing Federal protection against lynching.

4. Protecting more adequately the right to vote.

5. Establishing a Fair Employment Practice Commission to prevent unfair discrimination in employment.

6. Prohibiting discrimination in interstate transportation facilities.

7. Providing home rule and suffrage in Presidential elections for the residents of the District of Columbia.

8. Providing statehood for Hawaii and Alaska and a greater measure of self-government for our island possessions.

9. Equalizing the opportunities for residents of the United States to become naturalized citizens.

10. Settling the evacuation claims of Japanese-Americans.

As a first step, we must strengthen the organization of the Federal Government in order to enforce civil rights legislation more adequately and to watch over the state of our traditional liberties.

I recommend that the Congress establish a permanent Commission on Civil Rights, reporting to the President. The Commission should continuously review our civil rights policies and practices, study specific problems and make recommendations to the President at frequent intervals.

It should work with other agencies of the Federal Government, with state and local governments and with private organizations.

I also suggest that the Congress establish a Joint Congressional Committee on Civil Rights. This committee should make a continuing study of legislative matters relating to civil rights and should consider means of improving respect for and enforcement of those rights.

These two bodies together should keep all of us continuously aware of the condition of civil rights in the United States and keep us alert to opportunities to improve their protection. . . .

A specific Federal measure is needed to deal with the crime of lynching—against which I cannot speak too strongly.

It is a principle of our democracy, written into our Constitution, that every person accused of an offense against the law shall have a fair, orderly trial in an impartial court. We have made great progress towards this end, but I regret to say that lynching has not yet finally disappeared from our land. So long as one person walks in fear of lynching, we shall not have achieved equal justice under law.

I call upon the Congress to take decisive action against this crime.

Under the Constitution, the right of all properly qualified citizens to vote is beyond question. . . .

We need stronger statutory protection of the right to vote. . . .

Requirements for the payment of poll taxes also interfere with the right to vote. . . .

We in the United States believe that all men are entitled to equality of opportunity. Racial, religious and other invidious forms of discrimination deprive the individual of an equal chance to develop and utilize his talents and to enjoy the rewards of his efforts.

Once more I repeat my request that Congress enact fair employment practice legislation prohibiting discrimination in employment based on race, color, religion or national origin. The legislation should create a Fair Employment Practice Commission with authority to prevent discrimination by employers and labor unions, trade and professional associations and Government agencies and employment bureaus.

I am in full accord with the principle of local self-government for residents of the District of Columbia. In addition, I believe that the Constitution should be amended to extend suffrage in Presidential elections to the residents of the district.

The District of Columbia should be a true symbol of American freedom and democracy for our own people and for the people of the world. It is my earnest hope that the Congress will promptly give the citizens of the District of Columbia their own local, elective government.

They themselves can then deal with the inequalities arising from segregation in the schools and other public facilities and from racial barriers to places of public accommodation which now exist for one-third of the district's population.

The present political status of our territories and possessions impairs the enjoyment of civil rights by their resident.

I have in the past recommended legislation granting statehood to Alaska and Hawaii, and organic acts for Guam and American Samoa, including a grant of citizenship to the people of these Pacific islands. I repeat these recommendations.

Furthermore, the residents of the Virgin Islands should be granted an increasing measure of self-government and the people of Puerto Rico should be allowed to choose their form of government and their ultimate status with respect to the United States.

All properly qualified legal residents of the United States should be allowed to become citizens without regard to race, color, religion or national origin.

The Congress has recently removed the bars which formerly prevented persons from China, India and the Philippines from becoming naturalized citizens. I urge the Congress to remove the remaining racial or nationality barriers which stand in the way of citizenship for some residents of our country.

During the last war more than 100,000 Japanese-Americans were evacuated from their homes in the Pacific States solely because of their racial origin. Many of these people suffered property and business losses as a result of this forced evacuation and through no fault of their own.

The Congress has before the legislation establishing a procedure by which claims based upon these losses can be promptly considered and settled. I trust that favorable action on this legislation will soon be taken.

The legislation I have recommended for enactment by the Congress at the present session is a minimum program if the Federal Government is to fulfill its obligation of insuring the Constitutional guarantees of individual liberties and of equal protection under the law.

Under the authority of existing law, the Executive Branch is taking every possible action to improve the enforcement of the Civil Rights Statutes and to eliminate discrimination in Federal employment, in providing Federal services and facilities, and in the Armed Forces. . . .

It is the settled policy of the United States Government that there shall be no discrimination in Federal employment or in providing Federal service and facilities. Steady progress has been made toward this objective in recent years. I shall shortly issue an Executive Order containing a comprehensive restatement of the Federal non-discrimination policy, together with appropriate measures to ensure compliance. . . .

The peoples of the world are faced with the choice of freedom or enslavement, a choice between a form of government which harnesses the State in the service of the individual and a form of government which chains the individual to the needs of the State.

We in the United States are working in company with other nations who share our desire for enduring world peace and who believe with us that, above all else, men must be free. We are striving to build a world family of nations—a world where men may live under governments of their own choosing and under laws of their own making.

As part of that endeavor, the Commission on Human Rights of the United Nations is now engaging in preparing an international bill of human rights by which the nations of the world may bind themselves by international covenant to give effect to basic human rights and fundamental freedoms. We have played a leading role in this undertaking designed to create a world order of law and justice fully protective of the rights and the dignity of the individual.

To be effective in these efforts, we must protect our civil rights so that by providing all our people with the maximum enjoyment of personal freedom and personal opportunity we shall be a stronger nation— stronger in our leadership, stronger in our moral position, stronger in the deeper satisfactions of a united citizenry.

We know that our democracy is not perfect. But we do not know that it offers a fuller, freer, happier life to our people than any totalitarian nation has ever offered.

If we wish to inspire the peoples of the world whose freedom is in jeopardy, if we wish to restore hope to those who have already lost their civil liberties, if we wish to fulfill the promise that is ours, we must correct the remaining imperfections in our practice of democracy.

We know the way. We need only the will.

Harry S Truman

Source: Arthur M. Schlesinger, ed., *History of U.S. Political Parties* (New York: Chelsea House, 1973), 4:3402–3408.

DOCUMENT 58: Governor J. Strom Thurmond of South Carolina Speaks to Southern Governors, February 7, 1948

In a speech to other southern governors meeting in Wakulla Springs, Florida, Strom Thurmond responded forcefully to the changes in southern law and customs initiated by the national government following the proposed civil rights reforms of President Harry Truman. Thurmond argued for gradualism and viewed racial problems as primarily a function of southern poverty. His call for states' rights would preserve such election practices as the poll tax.

Thurmond emerged as a leader of the southern Democratic party known as the Dixiecrats. Following the 1948 election, he and other southerners would rejoin the ranks of the Democratic party. Thurmond would become U.S. senator from South Carolina. In the late 1960s, he would make moves to align himself with the Republican party.

Thurmond has been an ardent spokesperson for states' rights. As a senator he has implemented legislative tactics to protect state and regional views, opposing national acts that would challenge prevailing practices in the South.

* * *

The people of the States represented by the members of this [Southern Governors'] conference here have been shocked by the spectacle of the political parties of this country engaging in competitive bidding for the votes of small pressure groups by attacking the traditions, customs, and institutions of the section in which we live.

Our people have been engaged for many years in a tremendous effort to restore our section to the place in the economy of the Nation which it should rightfully occupy. On the solution of our economic problems depend the education, welfare, and progress of all of our people and we have spared no effort to solve those problems. Economic underprivilege in the South has known no color line; it has fallen heavily on all races alike. The people of the Nation are well aware of the headway which we have already made toward solving the economic problems of our people, and it will be as a result of the solution of our economic problems that our racial problems will disappear.

Despite our sound, constructive, and sure progress, the political leaders of the country have been unwilling to respect our accomplishments and to let us continue with the task. Their political attacks are calculated only to hamper our efforts and actually militate against the welfare of the very people whom they assert they are trying to help. Under the compulsion of petty political considerations, they have seen fit to outrage and insult our people because they think we have no place to which we can turn.

Without sincerity and in utter disregard of the facts, they again propose a so-called antilynching bill. They ignore the fact that the crime of lynching has been virtually stamped out in the South without outside interference. It is a matter of common knowledge that this legislation would be an unconstitutional invasion of the field of government of the several States.

They have again sponsored a so-called anti-poll-tax bill. It is a matter of common knowledge that this type of legislation is an unconstitutional infringement upon the right of the several States to prescribe voting qualifications.

They talk about breaking down the laws which knowledge and experience of many years have proven to be essential to the protection of the racial integrity and purity of the white and the Negro races alike. The superficial objections to these laws arise from economic rather than political causes, and their sudden removal would jeopardize the peace and good order which prevails where the two races live side by side in large numbers. As a nation we have favored the protection of racial autonomy and integrity in other lands, such as Palestine and India, but a different doctrine is sought to be applied here at home.

They advocate a so-called fair employment practice law, which every thinking American citizen, upon reflection, will recognize to be an anti-American invasion of the fundamental conception of free enterprise upon which our economic structure is erected and which made America great. The right of a man to own and operate his own business, in which he has his savings and to which he devotes his labor and his energy, is to be impaired or destroyed by governmental interference under the guise of protecting the right to work. In effect, such a law would render every private business in this Nation a quasi-public one. Employer and employee alike are adversely affected by this type of legislation, and the concepts upon which it is based are appropriate, not to the American way of life but only to the economic and political philosophy of the Communist Party.

We are expected to stand idle and let all of this happen, for the sole purpose of enticing an infinitesimal minority of organized pressure blocs to vote for one or another candidate for the Presidency. It is thought that we have no redress. This assumption ignores the electoral college set up in the Constitution of the United States.

We should approach the situation thus presented with dignity, self-respect and restraint. We should refuse to be stampeded or to indulge in idle oratory. We must consider the mater calmly and deliberately to the end that by joint and common action and decision we may demand and obtain for our people the consideration and respect to which they are entitled. We must no longer permit pressure groups by their adroit activities to establish by propaganda and political maneuvering a nuisance value for themselves in election years which threatens to defeat the political rights of others and endanger the progress which we in the South have made to better the lot and circumstance of all our people.

Therefore, I move, Mr. Chairman, that this conference go on record as deploring all ill-considered proposals which have the effect of dividing our people at a time when national unity is vital to the establishment of peace in this troubled world; and that this conference set a meeting not later than 40 days from this date, at a time and place to be designated by the chairman, for the careful consideration of the problems of the Southern States arising from such proposals; and that the chair do appoint a committee from the membership of this conference to make careful inquiry and investigation into such problems, and their solution by joint and common action, and to report to the conference at that meeting, with their recommendations as to further action which may be taken in the premises.

Source: Arthur M. Schlesinger, ed., *History of U.S. Political Parties* (New York: Chelsea House, 1973), 4:3409–3410.

DOCUMENT 59: States' Rights Platform of 1948, Southern Democratic Convention, Birmingham, Alabama, July 17, 1948

Democrats in the South reacted to President Truman's call for a Commission on Civil Rights with action of their own. They broke away from the Democratic party in a presidential election year, nominated Governor Strom Thurmond of South Carolina as their presidential candidate of the States' Rights Democratic party (known as the Dixiecrats), and wrote a party platform that opposed federal interference in what they considered issues of state sovereignty. The platform, excepted in the following document, referred to the Tenth Amendment and the reserved powers clause as part of their challenge to the federal government's proposal for national civil rights program. States' rights advocates of the late 1940s appealed to the party platform of the Democrats a century earlier. Throughout their statement of position, southern Democrats condemned the authority of federal actions as usurping the rights of the states.

* * *

We affirm that a political party is an instrumentality for effectuating the principles upon which the party is founded. . . .

We believe that racial and religious minorities should be protected in their rights guaranteed by the Constitution, but the bold defiance of the Constitution in selfish appeals to such groups for the sake of political power forges the chains of slavery of such minorities by destroying the only bulwark of protection against tyrannical majorities. . . .

We believe that the protection of the American people against the onward march of totalitarian government requires a faithful observance of article X of the American Bill of Rights which provides that: "The powers not delegated to the United States by the Constitution, nor prohibited by it to the States, are reserved to the States respectively, or to the people.

THE PRINCIPLES OF STATES' RIGHTS

We direct attention to the fact that the first platform of the Democratic Party, adopted in 1840, resolved that: "Congress has no power under the Constitution to interfere with or control the domestic institutions of the several States, and that such States are the sole and proper judges of everything appertaining to their own affairs not prohibited by the Constitution." Such pronouncement is the cornerstone of the Democratic Party.

. . .

The executive department of the Government is promoting the gradual but certain growth of a totalitarian state by domination and control of a politically minded Supreme Court. As examples of the threat to our form of government, the executive department, with the aid of the Supreme Court, has asserted national dominion and control of submerged oil-bearing lands in California, schools in Oklahoma and Missouri, primary elections in Texas, South Carolina, and Louisiana, restrictive covenants in New York and the District of Columbia, and other jurisdictions, as well as religious instruction in Illinois.

PERIL TO BASIC RIGHTS

By asserting paramount Federal rights in these instances, a totalitarian concept has been promulgated which threatens the integrity of the States and the basic rights of their citizens.

We have repeatedly remonstrated with the leaders of the national organization of our party but our petitions, entreaties, and warning have been treated with contempt. The latest response to our entreaties was a Democratic convention in Philadelphia rigged to embarrass and humiliate the South. This alleged Democratic assembly called for a civil-rights law that would eliminate segregation of every kind from all American life, prohibit all forms of discrimination in private employment, in public and private instruction and administration and treatment of students; in the operation of public and private health facilities; in all transportation, and require equal access to all places of public accommodation for persons of all races, colors, creeds, and national origin.

. . .

NEW POLICY

As Democrats who are irrevocably committed to democracy as defined and expounded by Thomas Jefferson, Andrew Jackson, and Woodrow Wilson, and who believe that all necessary steps must be taken for its preservation, we declare to the people of the United States as follows:

1. We believe that the Constitution of the United States is the greatest charter of human liberty ever conceived by the mind of man.

2. We oppose all efforts to invade or destroy the rights vouchsafed by it to every citizen of this Republic.

3. We stand for social and economic justice, which, we believe, can be vouchsafed to all citizens only by a strict adherence to our Constitution and the avoidance of any invasion or destruction of the constitutional rights of the States and individuals. We oppose the totalitarian, centralized, bureaucratic government and the police state called for by the platforms adopted by the Democratic and Republican conventions.

4. We stand for the segregation of the races and the racial integrity of each race; the constitutional right to choose one's associates; to accept private employment without governmental interference, and to earn one's living in any lawful way. We oppose the elimination of segregation, employment by Federal bureaucrats called for by the misnamed civil-rights program. We favor home rule, local self-government, and a minimum interference with individual rights.

5. We oppose and condemn the action of the Democratic Convention in sponsoring a civil-rights program calling for the elimination of segregation, social equality by Federal fiat, regulation of private employment practices, voting, and local law enforcement.

6. We affirm that the effective enforcement of such a program would be utterly destructive of the social, economic, and political life of the southern people, and of other localities in which there may be differences in race, creed, or national origin in appreciable numbers.

7. We stand for the checks and balances provided by the three departments of our Government. We oppose the usurpation of legislative functions by the executive and judicial departments. We unreservedly condemn the effort to establish Nationwide a police state in this Republic that would destroy the last vestige of liberty enjoyed by a citizen.

8. We demand that there be returned to the people, to whom of right they belong, those powers needed for the preservation of human rights and the discharge of our responsibility as Democrats for human welfare. We oppose a denial of those rights by political parties, a barter or sale of those rights by a political convention, as well as any invasion or violation of those rights by the Federal Government.

We call upon all Democrats and upon all other loyal Americans who are opposed to totalitarianism at home and abroad to unite with us in ignominiously defeating Harry S. Truman and Thomas E. Dewey, and every other candidate for public office who would establish a police state in the United States of America.

Source: Arthur M. Schlesinger, ed., *History of U.S. Political Parties* (New York: Chelsea House, 1973), 4:3422–3425.

DOCUMENT 60: Eisenhower's First Annual Message to the Congress on the State of the Union, February 2, 1953

Dwight D. Eisenhower exerted a hidden-hand leadership as president. Cautious when it came to civil rights, Eisenhower questioned the ability of government to legislate morality. In spite of his reservations, his administration is associated with the first civil rights acts, in 1957 and 1960, passed since Reconstruction. In his first annual State of the Union message, Eisenhower revealed his concerns that the southern states might be alienated by federal initiatives. While addressing the desegregation of Washington, D.C., and the armed services, Eisenhower avoided the issue of racial desegregation in public schools. Such an issue was already was under review in the courts and would confront his administration once the Supreme Court ruled on *Brown v. Board of Education* in 1954.

* * *

Our civil and social rights form a central part of the heritage we are striving to defend on all fronts and with all our strength.

I believe with all my heart that our vigilant guarding of these rights is a sacred obligation binding upon every citizen. To be true to one's own freedom is, in essence, to honor and respect the freedom of all others.

A cardinal ideal in this heritage we cherish is the equality of rights of all citizens of every race and color and creed.

We know that discrimination against minorities persists despite our allegiance to this ideal. Such discrimination—confined to no one section of the Nation—is but the outward testimony to the persistence of distrust and of fear in the hearts of men.

This fact makes all the more vital the fighting of these wrongs by each individual, in every station of life, in his very deed.

Much of the answer lies in the power of fact, fully publicized; of persuasion, honestly pressed; and of conscience, justly aroused. These are methods familiar to our way of life, tested and proven otherwise.

I propose to use whatever authority exists in the office of the President to end segregation in the District of Columbia, including the Federal Government, and any segregation in the Armed Forces.

Here in the District of Columbia, serious attention should be given to the proposal to develop and authorize, through legislation, a system to provide an effective voice in local self-government. While consideration of this proceeds, I recommend an immediate increase of two in the number of District Commissioners to broaden representation of all elements of our local population. This will be a first step toward insuring that this Capital provide an honored example to all communities of our Nation.

In this manner, and by the leadership of the office of the President exercised through friendly conferences with those in authority in our States and cities, we expect to make true and rapid progress in civil rights and equality of employment opportunity.

There is one sphere in which civil rights are inevitably involved in Federal legislation. This is the sphere of immigration.

It is a manifest right of our Government to limit the number of immigrants our Nation can absorb. It is also a manifest right of our Government to set reasonable requirements on the character and the numbers of the people who come to share our land and our freedom.

. . .

In another but related area—that of social rights—we see most clearly the new application of old ideas of freedom.

. . .

Our school system demands some prompt, effective help. During each of the last 2 years, more than 1½ million children have swelled the elementary and secondary school population of the country. Generally, the school population is proportionately higher in States with low per capita income. This whole situation calls for careful congressional study and action. I am sure that you share my conviction that the firm conditions of Federal aid must be proved need and proved lack of local income.

One phase of the school problem demands special action. The school population of many districts has been greatly increased by the swift growth of defense activities. These activities have added little or nothing to the tax resources of the communities affected. Legislation aiding construction of schools in these districts expires on June 30. This law should be renewed; and, likewise, the partial payments for current operating expenses for these particular school districts should be made, including the deficiency requirement of the current fiscal year. . . .

Source: Fred L. Israel, ed., *The State of the Union Messages of the Presidents, 1790–1966* (New York: Chelsea House, 1967), 3:3012–3025.

DOCUMENT 61: President Eisenhower Writes South Carolina Governor James F. Byrnes, August 14, 1953

President Dwight D. Eisenhower held a firm conviction that federal "legislation alone" would not "institute morality" and "coercion" would not "cure all civil rights problems." When he began his presidency, however, he had a commitment to civil rights. His State of the Union message pledged the use of presidential power to end segregation in federal jurisdictions. Immediately, Eisenhower ran into trouble with southern administrators of federal schools, hospitals, and navy yards.

Eisenhower might have taken more overt and public action to enforce his order to desegregate. Instead, he exchanged private letters with the governor of South Carolina, James F. Byrnes. This action concealed his activities concerning civil rights from the public, but sought to promote change. In the following selection, Eisenhower emphasized to Byrnes (who held racist convictions) that he regarded the governor as a friend. Although Eisenhower was personally sensitive to the traditions and feelings of the South concerning race, upon careful thought he decided not to endorse Byrnes's attitudes. To do so might have led to "potential trouble" if word leaked to the press. Byrnes responded to Ike's 1953 executive order calling for racial integration in southern facilities by pledging that, because of Ike's "cordial phrasing" in his letter, he would comply with "wholehearted cooperation" to help if trouble erupted outside the naval shipyard.

* * *

To James Francis Byrnes   August 14, 1953

Dear Jimmy: As you know, I have been thinking of the whole field of equality of opportunity. Since our recent lunch together at which we discussed the pending "School Segregation" case, it has scarcely been absent from my mind.

I think it is incumbent upon people who honestly believe in the power of leadership, education, example, and acceptance of clear official responsibility to show constant progress in the direction of complete justice. We who hold office not only must discharge the duties placed upon us by the constitution and by conscience, but also must, by constructive advances, prove to be mistaken those who insist that true reforms can come only through overriding Federal law and Federal police methods.

As I observed to you, I feel that my oath of office, as well as my own convictions, requires me to eliminate discrimination within the definite areas of Federal responsibility. You replied to the effect: You can do no less.

There is one of these areas of Federal responsibility where my efforts run counter to customs in some States. This is the area involved in the non-discrimination clauses in Federal contracts.

In presenting my views to you on this particular matter, I am keeping in mind the whole scope of our conversation. On the basis of that discussion, I am hopeful not only that we may reach fruitful understanding in this matter—but also that, in so doing, it can be shown that progress does not depend on Federal fiat.

This matter of compliance with the law and regulations in governmental contracts is being put into the hands of a Committee which I am appointing. I realize that if one should follow up the words "Federal contract" far enough—on an academic research job—one could get into a lot of secondary and auxiliary activity conceivably causing a confusion that would make any attempt at enforcement most difficult. But I do believe that States should cooperate in, and never impede, the enforcement of Federal regulations *where the Federal Government has clear and exclusive responsibility in the case.*

Assume, for example, that we should have a Federal contract under execution in the Charleston Navy Yard: I feel that if there should be any trouble at the Yard in enforcing the non-discrimination regulations, you as Governor could instantly announce that, since this is clearly a Federal matter, beyond State jurisdiction, compliance should be complete and cheerful.

I sincerely believe that such cooperation would reassure those who seem to feel that the only alternative to stringent Federal action is no action at all.

I am, of course, dedicated to discharging the official responsibilities of my office, just as I am determined to respect the constitutional authority and responsibilities of others. In this particular case, I believe it is incumbent upon us to make constant and distinct progress toward eliminating those things that all of us would class as unjust and unfair. In this category there clearly falls, to my mind, the right to equal consideration in Federal employment, regardless of race or color.

If the above makes sense to you, then I should like you to communicate with your fellow Governors who feel generally as you do in these matters, and to whom you referred when we had our recent conversation.

With warm personal regard, *Sincerely*
[unsigned]

Source: Louis Galambos and Daun Van EE, eds., *The Papers of Dwight David Eisenhower*, Vol. 14: *The Presidency: The Middle Way* (Baltimore: Johns Hopkins Press, 1996), pp. 470–471.

DOCUMENT 62: *Brown v. Board of Education of Topeka* (1954)

During the late 1940s, the Supreme Court made decisions under the leadership of Chief Justice Fred Vinson to desegregate law schools in southern states. In 1954 the Court, with Chief Justice Earl Warren presiding, announced a landmark decision to overturn the separate-but-equal doctrine established in *Plessy v. Ferguson* (1896). The *Brown* decision, which was unanimous, relied heavily on sociological and psychological data supplied by Kenneth Clark, an African American psychologist, and the arguments put forward by Thurgood Marshall, an attorney for the National Association for the Advancement of Colored People.

The *Brown* decision pronounced that separate but equal facilities produced a badge of inferiority among minority students. In a later decision, Brown II (1955), the Court called for desegregation "with all deliberate speed."

Clearly, the national government had imposed actions on the states. Southern states would continue to resist the desegregation of schools and other institutions for several decades. Northern states would also share in this resistance during the 1970s, particularly in urban areas, where residential segregation made court-ordered busing very unpopular.

* * *

MR. CHIEF JUSTICE WARREN delivered the opinion of the Court.

These cases come to us from the States of Kansas, South Carolina, Virginia, and Delaware. They are premised on different facts and different local conditions, but a common legal question justifies their consideration together in this consolidated opinion.

In each of the cases, minors of the Negro race, through their legal representatives, seek the aid of the courts in obtaining admission to the public schools of their community on a nonsegregated basis. In each instance, they have been denied admission to schools attended by white children under laws requiring or permitting segregation according to race. This segregation was alleged to deprive the plaintiffs of the equal protection of the laws under the Fourteenth Amendment. In each of the cases other than the Delaware case, a three-judge federal district court denied relief to the plaintiffs on the so-called "separate but equal" doctrine announced by this Court in Plessy v. Ferguson. . . . Under that doctrine, equality of treatment is accorded when the races are provided substantially equal facilities, even though these facilities be separate. In the Delaware case, the Supreme Court of Delaware adhered to that doctrine, but ordered that the plaintiffs be admitted to the white schools because of their superiority to the Negro schools.

The plaintiffs contend that segregated public schools are not "equal" and cannot be made "equal," and that hence they are deprived of the equal protection of the laws. Because of the obvious importance of the question presented, the Court took jurisdiction. Argument was heard in the 1952 Term, and reargument was heard this Term on certain questions propounded by the Court.

. . .

In the first cases in this Court constructing the Fourteenth Amendment, decided shortly after its adoption, the Court interpreted it as proscribing all state-imposed discriminations against the Negro race. The doctrine of "separate but equal" did not make its appearance in this Court until 1896 in the case of Plessy v. Ferguson, . . . involving not education but transportation. American courts have since labored with the doctrine for over half a century. In this court, there have been six cases involving the "separate but equal" doctrine in the field of public education. In Cumming v. Board of Education of Richmond County, . . . and Gong Lum v. Rice, . . . , the validity of the doctrine itself was not challenged. In more recent cases, all on the graduate school level, inequality was found in that specific benefits enjoyed by white students were denied to Negro students of the same educational qualifications. State of Missouri ex rel. Gaines v. Canada, . . . ; Sipuel v. Board of Regents of University of Oklahoma, . . . ; Sweatt v. Painter, . . . ; McLaurin v. Oklahoma State Regents. . . . In none of these cases was it necessary to re-examine the doctrine to grant relief to the Negro plaintiff. And in Sweatt v. Painter . . . the Court expressly reserved decision on the question whether Plessy v. Ferguson should be held inapplicable to public education.

In the instant cases, that question is directly presented. Here, unlike Sweatt v. Painter, there are findings below that the Negro and white schools involved have been equalized, or are being equalized, with respect to buildings, curricula, qualifications and salaries of teachers, and other "tangible" factors. Our decision, therefore, cannot turn on merely a comparison of these tangible factors in the Negro and white schools involved in each of the cases. We must look instead to the effect of segregation itself on public education.

In approaching this problem, we cannot turn the clock back to 1868 when the Amendment was adopted, or even to 1896 when Plessy v. Ferguson was written. We must consider public education in the light of its full development and its present place in American life throughout the Nation. Only in this way can it be determined if segregation in public schools deprives these plaintiffs of the equal protection of the laws.

Today, education is perhaps the most important function of state and local governments. Compulsory school attendance laws and the great expenditures for education both demonstrate our recognition of the importance of education to our democratic society. It is required in the performance of our most basic public responsibilities, even service in the armed forces. It is the very foundation of good citizenship. Today it is a principal instrument in awakening the child to cultural values, in preparing him for later professional training, and in helping him to adjust normally to his environment. In these days, it is doubtful that any child may reasonably be expected to succeed in life if he is denied the opportunity of an education. Such an opportunity, where the state has undertaken to provide it, is a right which must be made available to all on equal terms.

We come then to the question presented: Does segregation of children in public schools solely on the basis of race, even though the physical facilities and other "tangible" factors may be equal, deprive the children of the minority group of equal educational opportunities? We believe that it does.

In Sweatt v. Painter, . . . , in finding that a segregated law school for Negroes could not provide them equal educational opportunities, this Court relied in large part on "those qualities which are incapable of objective measurement but which make for greatness in a law school." In McLaurin v. Oklahoma State Regents, . . . , the Court, in requiring that a Negro admitted to a white graduate school be treated like all other students, again resorted to intangible considerations: "his ability to study, to engage in discussions and exchange views with other students, and, in general, to learn his profession." Such considerations apply with added force to children in grade and high schools. To separate them from others of similar age and qualifications solely because of their race generates a feeling of inferiority as to their status in the community that may affect their hearts and minds in a way unlikely ever to be undone. The effect of this separation on their educational opportunities was well stated by a finding in the Kansas case by a court which nevertheless felt compelled to rule against the Negro plaintiffs:

Segregation of white and colored children in public schools has a detrimental effect upon the colored children. The impact is greater when it has the sanction of the law; for the policy of separating the races is usually interpreted as denoting the inferiority of the negro group. A sense of inferiority affects the motivation of a child to learn. Segregation with the sanction of law, therefore, has a tendency to [retard] the educational and mental development of Negro children and to deprive them of some of the benefits they would receive in a racial[ly] integrated school system.

Whatever may have been the extent of psychological knowledge at the time of Plessy v. Ferguson, this finding is amply supported by modern authority. Any language in Plessy v. Ferguson contrary to this finding is rejected.

We conclude that in the field of public education the doctrine of "separate but equal" has no place. Separate educational facilities are inherently unequal. Therefore, we hold that the plaintiffs and others similarly situated for whom the actions have been brought are, by reason of the segregation complained of, deprived of the equal protection of the laws guaranteed by the Fourteenth Amendment. This disposition makes unnecessary any discussion whether such segregation also violates the Due Process Clause of the Fourteenth Amendment.

Source: Henry Steele Commager, ed., *Documents of American History*, 7th ed. (New York: Appleton-Century-Crofts, 1963), 2:619–622.

DOCUMENT 63: The Southern Manifesto, 1956

The first response of southerners to the *Brown* decision was deceptively calm. Token integration began in the border states as early as 1954. Then hostility occurred in Virginia and the Deep South as newly formed Citizens' Councils were created to counter integration efforts. Senator Harry Byrd of Virginia provided a rallying cry for southerner segregationists: "Massive resistance." Southern state legislatures enacted pupil assignment laws and created other strategies to interpose their power between the schools and the Supreme Court.

In March 1956, the Southern Manifesto, authored by a group of southern congressmen, announced there had been "a clear abuse of judicial power" with the *Brown* decision, and 101 southern members of Congress endorsed the denouncement of federal encroachment on the states. The Southern Manifesto appealed to previous Supreme Court decisions that had pronounced that the separate-but-equal principle fell under the jurisdiction of the states. Resistance to school segregation along with laws that condoned segregation in public places and accommodations led to civil rights movements and other forms of protest by African Americans.

* * *

We regard the decision of the Supreme Court in the school cases as clear abuse of judicial power. It climaxes a trend in the Federal judiciary under-taking to legislate, in derogation of the authority of Congress, and to encroach upon the reserved rights of the states and the people.

The original Constitution does not mention education. Neither does the Fourteenth Amendment nor any other amendment. The debates preceding the submission of the Fourteenth Amendment clearly show that there was no intent that it should affect the systems of education maintained by the states.

The very Congress which proposed the amendment subsequently provided for segregated schools in the District of Columbia.

When the amendment was adopted in 1868, there were thirty-seven states of the Union. Every one of the twenty-six states that had any substantial racial differences among its people either approved the operation of segregated schools already in existence or subsequently established such schools by action of the same law-making body which considered the Fourteenth Amendment.

As admitted by the Supreme Court in the public school case (*Brown v. Board of Education*), the doctrine of separate but equal schools "apparently originated in *Roberts v. City of Boston* (1849), upholding school segregation against attack as being violative of a state constitutional guarantee of equality." This constitutional doctrine began in the North—not in the South—and it was followed not only in Massachusetts but in Connecticut, New York, Illinois, Indiana, Michigan, Minnesota, New Jersey, Ohio, Pennsylvania and other northern states until they, exercising their rights as states through the constitutional process of local self-government, changed their school systems.

In the case of *Plessy v. Ferguson* in 1896 the Supreme Court expressly declared that under the Fourteenth Amendment no person was denied any of his rights if the states provided separate but equal public facilities. This decision has been followed in many other cases. It is notable that the Supreme Court, speaking through Chief Justice Taft, a former President of the United States, unanimously declared in 1927 in *Lum v. Rice* that the "separate but equal" principle is " . . . within the discretion of the state in regulating its public schools and does not conflict with the Fourteenth Amendment."

This interpretation, restated time and again, became a part of the life of the people of many of the states and confirmed their habits, customs, traditions and way of life. It is founded on elemental humanity and common sense, for parents should not be deprived by Government of the right to direct the lives and education of their own children.

Though there has been no constitutional amendment or act of Congress changing this established legal principle almost a century old, the Supreme Court of the United States, with no legal basis for such action, undertook to exercise their naked judicial power and substituted their personal political and social ideas for the established law of the land.

This unwarranted exercise of power by the court, contrary to the Constitution, is creating chaos and confusion in the states principally affected. It is destroying the amicable relations between the white and Negro races that have been created through ninety years of patient effort by the good people of both races. It has planted hatred and suspicion where there has been heretofore friendship and understanding.

Without regard to the consent of the governed, outside agitators are threatening immediate and revolutionary changes in our public school systems. If done, this is certain to destroy the system of public education in some of the states.

With the gravest concern for the explosive and dangerous condition created by this decision and inflamed by outside meddlers:

We reaffirm our reliance on the Constitution as the fundamental law of the land.

We decry the Supreme Court's encroachments on rights reserved to the states and to the people, contrary to established law and to the Constitution.

We commend the motives of those states which have declared the intention to resist forced integration by any lawful means.

We appeal to the states and people who are not directly affected by these decisions to consider the constitutional principles involved against the time when they too, on issues vital to them, may be the victims of judicial encroachment.

Even though we constitute a minority in the present Congress, we have full faith that a majority of the American people believe in the dual system of government which has enabled us to achieve our greatness and will in time demand that the reserved rights of the states and of the people be made secure against judicial usurpation.

We pledge ourselves to use all lawful means to bring about a reversal of this decision which is contrary to the Constitution and to prevent the use of force in its implementation.

In this trying period, as we all seek to right this wrong, we appeal to our people not to be provoked by the agitators and troublemakers invading our states and to scrupulously refrain from disorder and lawless acts.

Source: Henry Steele Commager, ed., *Documents of American History* (New York: Appleton-Century-Crofts, 1963), 641–643.

DOCUMENT 64: President Johnson Urges Enactment of the Voting Rights Act of 1965

After winning the 1964 election, President Lyndon B. Johnson initiated the Great Society in his annual message to Congress in January 1965. The Great Society called for improvement in life for all Americans. In a March 15, 1965, address to a full Congress, Johnson urged voting rights legislation. Five months later, in August 1965, Congress passed the act, which ensured all Americans the right to vote. This act rejected the case-by-case procedure and authorized the U.S. attorney general to dispatch federal examiners to register voters. The act also suspended literacy tests and other strategies used to deprive citizens of the vote in states and counties. The Voting Rights Act has been chal-

lenged on numerous occasions over the last thirty years. In the following docoment, Johnson urges Congress to pass voting rights legislation.

* * *

The Constitution says that no person shall be kept from voting because of
his race or his color. We have all sworn an oath before God to support and
to defend that Constitution. We must now act in obedience to that oath.

. . .

This bill will strike down restrictions to voting in all elections, federal,
state, and local, which have been used to deny Negroes the right to vote.

This bill will establish a simple, uniform standard which cannot be
used, however ingenious the effort, to flout our Constitution. It will provide for citizens to be registered by officials of the United States government, if the state officials refuse to register them.

. . .

There is no constitutional issue here. The command of the Constitution
is plain. There is no moral issue, It is wrong—deadly wrong—to deny
any of your fellow Americans the right to vote.

There is no issue of states' rights or national rights. There is only the
struggle for human rights.

Source: http://www.historyplace.com/speeches/johnson.htm. See also "Give Us
the Ballot," a 1957 speech of the Reverend Dr. Martin Luther King, Jr. at http://
www.stanford.edu.

DOCUMENT 65: U.S. Commissioner of Education Harold Howe II on the Relationship of the Federal Government to State and Local Education, December 17, 1966

The Great Society altered the role of the federal government in education. State and local education officials voiced concerns about federal intervention. Harold Howe II, the U.S. commissioner of education,
explained the new federal role to the American people.

* * *

The relationship of the federal government to state and local education
authorities is a tender one for three reasons. First and most important is
the nature of the school programs supported by money from Washington. They are not "general aid" programs which provide dollars without
prescription for their use. Instead they represent efforts to achieve specific ends: better education for the children of poverty . . . [and] support

for education leading to employment. In effect, the Congress has voted programs to meet deficiencies in the schools or to enable the schools to make a greater contribution to our national strength or prosperity.

. . .

[School officials'] fears are only partially allayed by declarations from the Congress that no federal control over curriculum, personnel, or administration in local schools is intended or allowed. They think that some aspects of the administration of present programs already reach into these forbidden directions. . . .

A second reason for abrasions lies in Title VI of the Civil Rights Act. This legislation says that federal money can't go where discrimination is practiced. Particularly in the South, where Office of Education policy seeks an end to the dual school system, charges frequently have been made that the schools are being controlled from Washington. . . .

A third source of strain lies in the decision by Congress to authorize and finance a new educational system which local and state educational authorities do not control. Head Start, the Job Corps, large sections of the Neighborhood Youth Corps, and other endeavors . . . have been . . . outside the umbrella of duly constituted local and state educational authorities. . . .

Source: Harold Howe II, "The U.S. Office of Education; Growth and Growing Pains," *Saturday Review*, December 17, 1966.

DOCUMENT 66: A Journalist Reports on the Effects of the 1964 Civil Rights Act, January 12, 1967

Beaufort, South Carolina, is a small town in the South. In 1967 James K. Batten, a writer on the civil rights movement, wrote an article on the results of Title VI of the 1964 Civil Rights Act. Batten described the effects of the civil rights movement on this southern community and public schools.

* * *

Beaufort . . . is on a side road to the coast off busy Route 17. . . . Its well-kept old mansions and live oaks heavy with Spanish moss evoke the mood of another era, when rice, cotton, and slaves made life comfortable for the plantation aristocracy.

[Beaufort, South Carolina] saw little change in its genteel, relaxed brand of white supremacy during the decade following the Supreme Court's school desegregation decision in 1954. But in midsummer of

1964, two months before nine Negro children finally broke the color line in Beaufort County's public schools, Congress passed the Civil Rights Act. Title VI of that law prohibited the use of federal funds to support racially segregated programs. . . .

. . .

. . . This year, Washington will provide . . . 28 per cent of the school budget. A year ago, when it appeared that the Office of Education was about to veto Beaufort's desegregation plan, . . . [the school superintendent] warned . . . that if the federal money were lost, the county would be forced to raise property taxes sharply, close the schools after seven months, or charge $20 a month tuition for the last two months of the school year.

. . .

. . . [P]ublic-school men fear that each increase in desegregation will prompt another group of white parents to send their children to . . . private school[s]. . . .

Source: James K. Batten, "Title VI Disturbs the Moss of Beaufort," *Reporter*, January 12, 1967.

DOCUMENT 67: Press Interview with George Wallace, 1968

Governor George Wallace of Alabama was a leading spokesperson for the southern states' rights cause. He blocked admission of black students into the University of Alabama and led a national movement to campaign for president in 1968 and 1972 on conservative political principles. In the following interview, conducted on September 17, 1968, he responded to questions concerning the authority of the federal government, segregation, and public education.

* * *

Q. We have a Constitution that's served in this country over a great many years, and now we have got lots of new problems and things of that kind. Do you think the Constitution is as good today as it was when it was written or does it need some updating, an amendment or something?

A. The constitution of the country is still just as good a document as it was when written, as far as I'm concerned. It has provisos for amendment process.

Q. Right.

A. And I can think of at least one amendment that ought to be submitted to the people of the country; submitted to the legislatures, rather. And that's the one involving the public school system.

Q. What would that be, Governor?

A. It would be an amendment declaring that absolute control of the public school systems should vest in the states, and all matters involving privileges and immunities and due process of law that arose thereunder, insofar as schools were concerned, would be decided by the state courts. That really was the law, in my judgement, prior to the take-over of the public school system by the Federal courts and the Federal Government. By usurpation of authority, the judges nullified the 10th Amendment.

Q. This would be, in essence, an amendment that would revoke the 1954 [school desegregation] decision of the Court?

A. Well, not necessarily—the 1954 decision was an anti-discrimination decision. I don't know that anybody argues with an anti-discrimination decision. In the long run, of course, what the argument was about was that they knew and we knew that this was not just anti-discrimination and we were correct. It was a matter of forceful take-over, and forced compliance with whatever guidelines are written by the Federal Government. They have jumped from non-discrimination to complete control.

For instance, we had freedom of choice in the public school system in Alabama and Texas and the other states of this region, but the Federal authorities filed a suit in which they said not enough people chose to go to the proper schools.

That showed that they were not truthful when they said they believed in this decision; they really didn't believe in this decision unless it did what they wanted it to do.

And so the free choice proposition of being able to choose to go to any school you want to go to regardless of race didn't work, and bring about those changes that the pseudo-intellectuals, the smart folks, the people that want to handle my child's life and tell me what to do with my child, and what neighborhood for him to go to school wished,—It didn't work. That is, the people didn't choose like they thought they would choose.

And so now they say you must choose for them, and if you don't choose for them, then we are going to choose for them. And so, in Alabama, for instance, they just arbitrarily ordered the closing down of 100 schools, including some new multimillion-dollar high schools—just closed them down.

Q. May I ask you another question, a direct question? Are you a segregationist?

A. Well, what do you mean by a segregationist?

Q. Do you believe in segregation?

A. Well, segregation of the races? In what respect?

Q. Schools and hospitals?

A. In the first place, you are asking me a question about something that never has existed in the history of the country. We have never had what your definition of segregation is, to exist in the South. In fact, we have had more mixing and mingling and togetherness and association there than you have had in New York City, where The New York Times is located, We have worked together, we have sat together, we have ridden together, we have been completely together in the South.

We did have in the school system a separation because the schools in the rural South were the social center. And we did have social separation as you have in New York, and as you have in your family life. And so we just had a common sense social separation—the schools were the social center. But if you mean complete separation of the races, we have never had that and I hope we never will have it.

Q. But do you advocate a return to segregation of the schools?

A. No sir. I do not advocate that.

Q. In Alabama?

A. No, sir. I don't advocate that. I am running for the Presidency of the United States on the platform of turning the control of the public school systems back to the people of the states. And I would say that you would not have a completely segregated system in Alabama.

But, you would have a control of the system that would mean it would never deteriorate to such a status as the Washington school system, and some of the schools in New York City have deteriorated into. God help us if our schools ever get to be a jungle like you have some in New York City, and like you have in Washington, and like you have in Philadelphia—

Q. Well, the reason—

A. They can't even play high school football games before crowds. In Philadelphia they play football games behind locked gates with just the cheerleaders—no spectators, because they had had a race riot at every football game. I think schools should be controlled locally.

Q. The reason I asked the question is that I wondered if you have changed your views?

A. No, sir, I haven't changed my views at all. I said I thought the segregated school system was the best school system in Alabama. It was a system that has peace and tranquility. And after all, there is something to say for peace and tranquility?

Although the theoreticians and the newspapers and others think it is not so important to have a peaceful and tranquil community and a peaceful and tranquil school system. It is a real good school system compared to some they have in some parts of the country. So a segregated system has been the best school system for Alabama, that is correct.

Q. Well, do you think—?

A. I am running for Presidency of the United States, and I want to leave it to the states. And so I would make no recommendation to Alabama.

Q. To the states or to local school boards?

A. Well, to the states, as every local school board is a creature of the state and the states created—all political subdivisions—so leave it to the states. The states have, by enactment of their legislatures, given authority to local school boards to administer school affairs in their particular localities.

The reason local school boards have control of schools in Alabama is because the State of Alabama, the sovereign, granted that power to the local school boards. The local school boards granted no authority to the states. So when you leave it to the states, you are leaving it, in effect, to the local school boards.

Q. Do you think whites and blacks, they just ordinarily want to stab one another?

A. Want to do what?

Q. Want to stab one another.

A. I didn't say that they want to stab one another. I just said in your school systems and parts of the country you have fights and friction and violence every week.

Q. Well, what does that have to do with segregation and integration, now?

A. Forced mixing in the big school systems at an abnormal rate has brought violence in the school systems, that's correct.

Source: Arthur M. Schlesinger, Jr., ed., *History of U.S. Political Parties* (New York: Chelsea House, 1973), 4:3475–3490.

DOCUMENT 68: Reagan Resurrects States' Rights, January 1981

Ronald Reagan was a conservative governor from California who had national ambitions to be president. In 1976, he was defeated by the incumbent, Gerald Ford, as the Republican nominee for president. In 1980, he secured the GOP nomination and ran against President Jimmy Carter. Reagan led an anti–big government campaign and won both the 1980 and 1984 elections. His First Inaugural Address as follows, emphasized his devotion to states' rights and a view of the Constitution that suggested a compact of government created by the states.

* * *

Mr. President (President Carter):

I want our fellow citizens to know how much you did to carry on this tradition. By your gracious cooperation in the transition process, you have shown a watching world that we are a united people pledged to maintaining a political system which guarantees individual liberty to a greater degree than any other, and I thank you and your people for all your help in maintaining the continuity which is the bulwark of our Republic.

The business of our nation goes forward. These United States are confronted with an economic affliction of great proportions. We suffer from the longest and one of the worst sustained inflations in our national history. It distorts our economic decisions, penalizes thrift, and crushes the struggling young and the fixed-income elderly alike. It threatens to shatter the lives of millions of our people.

Idle industries have cast workers into unemployment, causing human misery and personal indignity. Those who do work are denied a fair return for their labor by a tax system which penalizes successful achievement and keeps us from maintaining full productivity.

But great as our tax burden is, it has not kept pace with public spending. For decades, we have piled deficit upon deficit, mortgaging our future and our children's future for the temporary convenience of the present. To continue this long trend is to guarantee tremendous social, cultural, political, and economic upheavals.

You and I, as individuals, can, by borrowing, live beyond our means, but for only a limited period of time. Why, then, should we think that collectively, as a nation, we are not bound by that same limitation?

We must act today in order to preserve tomorrow. And let there be no misunderstanding—we are going to begin to act, beginning today.

The economic ills we suffer have come upon us over several decades. They will not go away in days, week, or months, but they will go away. They will go away because we, as Americans, have the capacity now, as we have had in the past, to do whatever needs to be done to preserve this last and greatest bastion of freedom.

In this present crisis, government is not the solution to our problem.

From time to time, we have been tempted to believe that society has become too complex to be managed by self-rule, that government by an elite group is superior to government for, by, and of the people. But if no one among us is capable of governing himself, then who among us has the capacity to govern someone else? All of us together, in and out of government, must bear the burden. The solutions we seek must be equitable, with no one group singled out to pay a higher price.

We hear much of special interest groups. Our concern must be for a special interest group that has been too long neglected. It knows no sectional boundaries or ethnic and racial divisions, and it crosses political party lines. It is made up of men and women who raise our food, patrol our streets, man our mines and our factories, teach our children, keep our homes, and heal us when we are sick—professionals, industrialists, shopkeepers, clerks, cabbies, and truck drivers. They are, in short, "We the people," this breed called Americans.

Well, this administration's objective will be a healthy, vigorous, growing economy that provides equal opportunity for all Americans, with no barriers born of bigotry or discrimination. Putting America back to work means putting all Americans back to work. Ending inflation means freeing all Americans from the terror of runaway living costs. All must share in the productive work of this "new beginning" and all must share in the bounty of a revived economy. With the idealism and fair play which are the core of our system and our strength, we can have a strong and prosperous America at Peace with itself and the world.

So, as we begin, let us take inventory. We are a nation that has a government—not the other way around. And this makes us special among the nations of the Earth. Our Government has no power except that granted it by the people. It is time to check and reverse the growth of government which shows signs of having grown beyond the consent of the governed.

It is my intention to curb the size and influence of the Federal establishment and to demand recognition of the distinction between the powers granted to the Federal Government and those reserved to the States or to the people. All of us need to be reminded that the Federal Government did not create the States; the States created the Federal Government.

Now, so there will be no misunderstanding, it is not my intention to do away with government. It is, rather, to make it work—work with us, not over us; to stand by our side, not ride on our back. Government can and must provide opportunity, not smother it; foster productivity, not stifle it.

If we look to the answer as to why, for so many years, we achieved so much, prospered as no other people on Earth, it was because here, in this land, we unleashed the energy and individual genius of man to a greater extent than has ever been done before. Freedom and the dignity of the individual have been more available and assured here than in any other place on Earth. The price for this freedom at times has been high, but we have never been unwilling to pay that price.

It is no coincidence that our present troubles parallel and are proportionate to the intervention and intrusion in our lives that result from unnecessary and excessive growth of government. It is time for us to realize that we are too great a nation to limit ourselves to small dreams. We are not, as some would have us believe, doomed to an inevitable decline. I do not believe in a fate that will fall on us no matter what we do. I do believe in a fate that will fall on us if we do nothing. So, with all the creative energy at our command, let us begin an era of national renewal. Let us renew our determination, our courage, and our strength. And let us renew our faith and our hope. . . .

Source: http://www.netstep.net/review/rrlstia.html.

DOCUMENT 69: Contract with America, 1994

On September 24, 1994, over three hundred Republican candidates for the U.S. House of Representatives stood on the steps of the U.S.

Capitol. They pledged to accomplish ten policy objectives within the first one hundred days of the 104th Congress. The 1994 elections swept Republicans into majority status in both the House and the Senate for the first time since Dwight D. Eisenhower was president. The new House Speaker, Newt Gingrich of Georgia, began his legislative plan for fulfilling the Contract with America. Republicans claimed a federal government too large and unresponsive to its constituents had to be pared in size. By cutting back the scope and activities of the national government, they hoped to promote more efficiency. They called on states to assume greater responsibility. Only one of the ten objectives was signed into law within the one hundred days.

* * *

[W]ithin the first hundred days of the 104th Congress, we shall bring to the House Floor the following bills, each to be given full and open debate, each to be given a clear and fair vote, and each to be immediately available this day for public inspection and scrutiny.

The Fiscal Responsibility Act

• A balanced budget/tax limitation amendment and a legislative line-item veto to restore fiscal responsibility to an out-of-control Congress, requiring them to live under the same budget constraints as families and businesses.

The Taking Back Our Streets Act

• An anti-crime package including stronger truth in sentencing, "good faith" exclusionary rule exemptions, effective death penalty provisions, and cuts in social spending from this summer's crime bill to fund prison construction and additional law enforcement to keep people secure in their neighborhoods and kids safe in their schools.

The Personal Responsibility Act

• Discourage illegitimacy and teen pregnancy by prohibiting welfare to minor mothers and denying increased AFDC [Aid to Families with Dependent Children] for additional children while on welfare, cut spending for welfare programs, and enact a tough two-years-and-out provision with work requirements to promote individual responsibility.

The Family Reinforcement Act

- Child support enforcement, tax incentives for adoption, strengthening rights of parents in their children's education, stronger child pornography laws, and an elderly dependent care tax credit to reinforce the central role of families in American society.

The American Dream Restoration Act

- A $500-per-child tax credit, begin repeal of the marriage tax penalty, and creation of American Dream Savings Accounts to provide middle-class tax relief.

The National Security Restoration Act

- No U.S. troops under UN command and restoration of the essential parts of our national security funding to strengthen our national defense and maintain our credibility around the world.

The Senior Citizens Fairness Act

- Raise the Social Security earnings limit, which currently forces seniors out of the workforce, repeal the 1993 tax hikes on Social Security benefits, and provide tax incentives for private long-term care insurance to let older Americans keep more of what they have earned over the years.

The Job Creation and Wage Enhancement Act

- Small business incentives, capital gains cut and indexation, neutral cost recovery, risk assessment/cost-benefit analysis, strengthening of the Regulatory Flexibility Act and unfunded mandate reform to create jobs and raise worker wages.

The Common Sense Legal Reforms Act

- "Loser pays" laws, reasonable limits on punitive damages, and reform of product liability laws to stem the endless tide of litigation.

The Citizen Legislature Act

• A first-ever vote on term limits to replace career politicians with citizen legislators.

Source: Newt Gingrich and Dick Armey, *Contract with America* (New York: Times
Books, 1994), pp. 9–11.

DOCUMENT 70: The Devolution Tortoise and the Centralization Hare: The Slow Process in Down-Sizing Big Government, 1998

John Kincaid, a professor of government and public service at Lafay-
ette College, differentiates devolution from decentralization, deregu-
lation, and delegation. Devolution suggests giving up a function by a
superior government to a subordinate government, in this case to the
states. Because surrender of power cannot occur easily under the U.S.
Constitution, Kincaid asserts that what is referred to as devolution is
really "rebalancing" or "restoration" of powers between the federal
government and the states. The rebalance, he suggests, is more in line
with what the writers of the Constitution had in mind.

* * *

There has been much talk in recent years of devolving powers and
functions from the federal government to the states. Some observers even
proclaim a "devolution revolution," the result of which will be a more
efficient and effective federal government and more robust and responsive states. The generally recognized objectives of devolution include (1)
more efficient provision and production of public services; (2) better
alignment of the costs and benefits of government for a diverse citizenry;
(3) better fits between public goods and their spatial characteristics; (4)
increased competition, experimentation, and innovation in the public
sector; (5) greater responsiveness to citizen preferences; and (6) more
transparent accountability in policymaking.

These are ambitious objectives, although, to date, no consensus on direction is apparent, no plan of execution is in place, and examples of
devolution are scarce. Indeed, there are only two commonly cited examples of devolution: congressional repeal of the national 55-mph speed
limit and welfare reform. . . .

. . .

Forces for Restoring State Powers

The most immediate force propelling discussions of shifting powers back to the states was the 1994 midterm elections, which brought a Republican majority into both house of Congress. The 1994 elections ended more than sixty years of nearly continuous Democratic control of the Congress. . . .

The Republicans' "Contract with America" contained several provisions aimed at curbing federal power and restoring state powers, beginning with mandate reform, which was enacted in 1995 with bipartisan support as the Unfunded Mandates Reform Act (UMRA). The state-friendly provisions of the "Contract with America" reflected long-standing Republican concerns dating back to President Dwight D. Eisenhower. . . .

. . .

President Richard M. Nixon's New Federalism . . . was, despite General Revenue sharing (1972 to 1986), no more successful in stemming the growth of federal power. President Ronald Reagan began his Administration with strong, emphatic support for a New Federalism aimed at shifting substantial power back to the states. . . .

This brief history suggests two hypotheses. First, many of the Republicans elected to the Congress in 1994 arrived with strong commitments to long-frustrated desires to limit federal power, which for some, though not all, also means restoring state powers. This was reinforced by the new Republicans elected from the increasingly Republican South and from the Mountain West—both growing regions historically suspicious of, and often hostile to, the federal government. Second, it is the Congress more often than the White House that alters the balance of power in the federal system. If these conclusions are correct, then some significant restorations of state powers are likely to occur if the Republicans maintain control of the Congress, if the Republicans capture the Presidency in 2000, and if the currently federalism-friendly majority on the U.S. Supreme Court is maintained or increased after 2000.

These prospects are further strengthened by support for rebalancing federal-state power among more members of the Democratic party than was true in the past. In a 1997 statement, for example, the Democratic Leadership Council, with which President Clinton was affiliated, said:

The New Democrat movement has consistently rejected the old-fashioned liberal prejudice against state governments and state officials. . . . Now more than ever, state officials represent the future of our party and our country. State capitals are the battlegrounds where the big challenges of American domestic policy on the eve of the 21st century are being met.

The 1996 Democratic party platform even claimed that "Republicans talked about shifting power back to the states and communities—Democrats are doing it."

This is a far cry from Governor George Wallace standing in the doorway of the University of Alabama in 1963 defying federal authority, but the states have since experienced a remarkable rehabilitation, which has placed them in a much more favorable light. Well into the 1970s, most Americans expressed more trust and confidence in the federal government than in the states. Since then, however, public trust and confidence—to the extent the public has any trust and confidence in any governments—has shifted gradually and substantially from the federal government to the states. . . .

Source: John Kincaid, "The Devolution Tortoise and the Centralization Hare," *New England Economic Review* (May–June 1998): 13–40.

DOCUMENT 71: U.S. Supreme Court Expands States' Rights

On June 23, 1999 the U.S. Supreme Court announced three important decisions concerning states' rights. By 5–4 majorities the U.S. Supreme Court bolstered the cause of states' rights activists. The three decisions most likely brought a balance rather than a grand revolution to the issue of federalism and the role of the states.

Alden v. Maine (1999), represented the court's opinion for the three cases. Sixty-five state probation officers and juvenile caseworkers in Maine sued the state in Federal court for violating the Fair Labor Standards Act. At the core of the debate was the original intent of the framers of the Constitution. Just as important was the meaning of the Eleventh Amendment, which had been adopted in 1798 following *Chisholm v. Georgia* (1793). In that decision the court upheld the right of citizens of one state (South Carolina) to bring a suit against another state (Georgia) in the Supreme Court. The Eleventh Amendment passed five years later and provided that the federal courts had no authority in suits by citizens against a state. Since the passage of the Eleventh Amendment, the Supreme Court narrowed the protection that this amendment provided to the states. In cases appearing before the court during the 1800s and continuing into the 1970s, justices decided that state officials were not protected if they exceeded their authority or held a negligent disregard of state law or individual rights. Supreme Court Justices ruled that the Eleventh Amendment was not a shield for a state official. Moreover, the Eleventh Amendment came under attack when Congress attempted to force states to defend themselves in federal courts under laws enacted under Article I of the Constitution, particularly laws that regulate interstate commerce. Since the 1970s the Supreme Court has been moving in the direction of reviving protections guaranteeing state sovereignty.

What follows is an excerpt from the Supreme Court's decision, *Alden v. Maine.* Justice Anthony M. Kennedy wrote the majority opinion.

* * *

We look first to evidence of the original understanding of the Constitution. Petitioners contend that because the ratification debates and the events surrounding the adoption of the Eleventh Amendment focused on the States' immunity from suit in Federal courts, the historical record gives no instruction as to the founding generation's intent to preserve the states' immunity from suit in their own courts.

We believe, however, that the founders' silence is best explained by the simple fact that no one, not even the Constitution's most ardent opponents, suggested the document might strip the states of the immunity. In light of the overriding concern regarding the states' wartime debts, together with the well-known creativity, foresight, and vivid imagination of the Constitution's opponents, the silence is most instructive. It suggests the sovereign's right to assert immunity from suit in its own courts was a principle so well established that no one conceived it would be altered by the new Constitution [of 1787].

. . .

Relying on custom and practice and, in particular, on the states' immunity from suit in their own courts, they [the framers] contended that no individual could sue a sovereign without its consent. It is true the point was directed toward the power of the Federal judiciary, for that was the only question at issue. The logic of the argument, however, applies with even greater force in the context of a suit prosecuted against a sovereign in its own courts, for in this setting, more than any other, sovereign immunity was long established and unquestioned. . . .

Although the Constitution grants broad powers to Congress, our federalism requires that Congress treat the states in a manner consistent with their status as residuary [delegated] sovereigns and joint participants in the governance of the nation. . . . The principle of sovereign immunity preserved by constitutional design "thus accords the states the respect owed them as members of the federation."

. . .

It is unquestioned that the Federal Government retains its own immunity from suit not only in state tribunals but also in its own courts. In light of our constitutional system recognizing the essential sovereignty of the states, we are reluctant to conclude that the states are not entitled to a reciprocal privilege.

Underlying constitutional form are considerations of great substance. Private suits against nonconsenting states especially suits for money damages may threaten the financial integrity of the states. . . . Congress [does not have] a power and a leverage over the states that is not contemplated by our constitutional design. The potential national power would pose a severe and notorious danger to the states and their resources.

A Congressional power to strip the states of their immunity from private suits in their own courts would pose more subtle risks as well. . . .

When the Federal Government asserts authority over a state's most fundamental political processes, it strikes at the heart of the political accountability so essential to our liberty and republican form of government.

The asserted authority would blur not only the distinct responsibilities of the state and national governments but also the separate duties of the judicial and political branches of the state governments. . . .

Congress cannot abrogate [use their authority to do away with] the states' sovereign immunity in Federal court; were the rule to be different here, the National Government would wield greater power in the state courts than in its own judicial instrumentalities.

. . .

The case [*Alden v. Maine*] at one level concerns the formal structure of federalism, but in a Constitution as resilient as ours form mirrors substance. Congress has vast power but not all power. When Congress legislates in matters affecting the states, it may not treat these sovereign entities as mere prefectures [provinces] or corporations. Congress must accord states the esteem due to them as joint participants in a federal system, one beginning with the premise of sovereignty in both the central Government and the separate states. Congress has ample means to ensure compliance with valid Federal laws, but it must respect the sovereignty of the states.

In apparent attempt to disparage a conclusion with which it disagrees, the dissent attributes our reasoning to natural law. We seek to discover, however, only what the framers and those who ratified the Constitution sought to accomplish when they created a Federal system. . . .

Source: As quoted in "Excerpts from the Court's Decision Broadly Expanding State Sovereignty," *New York Times*, 24 June 1999, sec. A, p. 23.

DOCUMENT 72: Minority Opinion Challenges State Immunity from Law Suit

In *Alden v. Maine* (1999), Justice David H. Souter wrote the minority opinion. Souter states that the natural law conception of sovereign immunity did not indemnify states against prosecution. The natural law conception placing the sovereign above the law was archaic or inapplicable to a republican form of government. Souter refers to the legal arguments surrounding *Chisholm v. Georgia* (1793) to support his position. This case, he argues, made no reference to the Bill of Rights, particularly the Tenth Amendment, which had been ratified two years earlier. Souter, disagreeing with Justice Kennedy, does not perceive the natural right basis of sovereignty as included in the original intent of the framers of the Constitution.

* * *

The Court's principal rationale for today's result, then, turns on history: was the natural law conception of sovereign immunity as inherent in any notion of an independent state widely held in the United States in the period preceding the ratification of 1788 (or the adoption of the Tenth Amendment in 1791)?

The answer is certainly no. There is almost no evidence that the generation of the Framers thought sovereign immunity was fundamental in the sense of being unalterable. Whether one looks at the period before the framing, to the ratification controversies, or to the early republican era, the evidence is the same. . . .

If the natural law conception of sovereign immunity as an inherent characteristic of sovereignty enjoyed by the state had been broadly accepted at the time of the founding, one would expect to find it reflected somewhere in the five opinions delivered by the [John Jay] Court in *Chisholm v. Georgia*. Yet that view did not appear in any of them. And since a bare two years before *Chisholm*, the Bill of Rights had been added to the original Constitution, if the Tenth Amendment had been understood to give Federal constitutional status to state sovereign immunity so as to endue [introduce] it with the equivalent of the natural law conception, one would be certain to find such a development mentioned somewhere in the *Chisholm* writings. In fact, however, not one of the opinions espoused the natural law view, and not one of them so much as mentioned the Tenth Amendment. . . .

. . .

The framers' intentions and expectations count so far as they point to the meaning of the Constitution's text or the fair implications of its structure, but they do not hover over the instrument to veto any application of its principles to a world that the framers could not have anticipated.

If the framers would be surprised to see states subjected to suit in their own courts under the commerce power, they would be astonished by the reach of Congress under the Commerce Clause generally. The proliferation of government, state and Federal, would amaze the framers, and the administrative state with its reams of regulations would leave them rubbing their eyes. . . .

. . .

There is much irony in the Court's profession that it grounds its opinion on a deeply rooted historical tradition of sovereign immunity, when the Court abandons a principle nearly as inveterate [firmly established], and much closer to the hearts of the Framers: that where there is a right, there must be a remedy. . . .

. . .

It will not do for the Court to respond that a remedy was never available where the right in question was against the sovereign. A state is not the sovereign when a Federal claim is pressed against it, and even the English sovereign opened itself to recovery and, unlike Maine, provided the remedy to complement the right. To the Americans of the founding generation it would have been clear (as it was to Chief Justice Marshall) that if the king would do right, the democratically chosen Government of the United States could do no less.

Source: As quoted in "Excerpts from the Court's Decision Broadly Expanding State Sovereignty," *New York Times*, 24 June 1999, sec. A, p. 23.

Part VI

Conclusion

The issue of states' rights and American federalism began in the colonial period. It was articulated in the constitutional period and proved divisive in events leading to the Civil War. Although the Civil War gave shape to the meaning of the Union, it did not end the issue of states' rights and compact theory of government. Just as the compact theory drew the attention of Federalists in the Hartford Convention and later in the speeches of John C. Calhoun, these same thoughts form a foundation for contemporary groups as diverse as the neoconservative and the militant multiculturalists espousing programs that are designed to forward particular interests. It is understandable that there is a countermovement to the strong national politics dating back to Woodrow Wilson's New Freedom and culminating in Lyndon Johnson's Great Society.

Until recent years, the states' rights position was almost exclusively equated with conservative economic beliefs, resistance to increasing civil rights protections, and opposition to social legislation on a national level. In the late twentieth century, renewed interest in governmental autonomy of the states is, in part, a response to the overwhelming nature of national power, especially the welfare state with its enormous bureaucratic quasi-judicial authority. The renewal is also due to serious reflection on the American historical experience of the colonial and Revolutionary periods when consensus beliefs articulated that states could better solve pressing issues and were better in protecting the rights of individuals. The confidence in local control, albeit controversial, preceded a confidence in the national government.

In many ways, local confidence is as old as Puritan and Antifederalist distrust of central authority. One might assume that states' rights began with colonial rights versus the British empire representing a federalist position to counter home rule. During the American Revolution, the Articles of Confederation represented the states' rights position, while the U.S. Constitution established a stronger national government. Thereafter, key individuals provided parallel implementations of the two theories of government. Leaders such as Alexander Hamilton, John Marshall, Henry Clay, Daniel Webster, John Quincy Adams, Abraham Lincoln, Theodore Roosevelt, Woodrow Wilson, Franklin D. Roosevelt, Harry Truman, Lyndon Baines Johnson, Jimmy Carter, and Bill Clinton represent the views of those who favor a stronger national influence regarding the relationship between government and the people. Thomas Jefferson, Andrew Jackson, John C. Calhoun, Jefferson Davis, William Howard Taft, Herbert Hoover, Strom Thurmond, Barry Goldwater, Ronald Reagan, and Pat Buchanan represent those who advocate a closer relationship between the states and the people.

Perhaps James Madison's call for a "practicable sphere" or "middle ground" is still a worthy goal in balancing out the interests of the national and the interests of the particular. Indeed, the documents in this book illuminate the discussion of finding the middle ground in the vital and ongoing debate of the merits of states' rights vis-à-vis American federalism.

Index

Abolitionists, 100, 127, 148
Adams, John, 26, 79
Adams, John Quincy, 224
Addams, Jane, 163
Affirmative action, 178
African Americans, xviii, xxiii, 99, 135, 139, 140, 141, 174, 176, 177, 178, 185, 203; citizenship, 100, 139, 140, 141; civil rights, 164, 173; migration; 142; southern suffragists, 162; voting, 144, 148, 151, 162
Age of reason. *See* Enlightenment
Agrippa. *See* James Winthrop
Albany Plan of Union, 19, 20, 21–23
Alien and Sedition Acts, xvii, 72, 79, 81, 84, 85, 98
Amendments, xxii; First, xxii, 72, 81, 82, 179; Fourth through Eighth, xxii–xxiii; Fifth, 69, 75, 91, 92, 93, 125; Ninth, xxiii; Tenth, xix, xx, xxiii, 68, 69, 70–72, 75, 82, 83, 96, 106, 193, 209, 221; Eleventh, 88, 218–219; Thirteenth, 141; Fourteenth, xxiii, 69, 75, 91, 141, 151, 155, 179, 200, 201, 203, 204; Fifteenth, 141, 163; Seventeenth, 47; Nineteenth, 143, 144, 148, 162, 163, 164, 165
American Creed, 174
American Equal Rights Association, 148

American Revolution, xv, xviii, xxii, 1, 5, 6, 9, 86, 129, 219, 220
Annapolis convention, 5–6
Anthony, Susan B., 143, 148, 163
Antifederalists, xvi, xvii, xxiii, 7, 8, 64–66, 67, 75, 96, 97, 98, 114, 160, 223; differences with Federalists, 8; general government, 8; republicanism, 8
Anti-Slavery Society, 148
Anti-Suffragists, 163
Apportionment, 44, 47, 48, 49, 76, 179
Aristotle, xxii, xxv. *See* "Mixed government" theory
Articles of Confederation, xiv, xvi, xxi, xxiii, 2, 4, 5, 6, 9, 31, 35, 43, 47–48, 58, 60, 70, 96, 119, 129, 224; Article II, 35, 70–71
Atlanta Cotton States and International Exposition, 139, 149

Bailyn, Bernard, xv
Bakke, Allan, 178. *See also* Supreme Court of the United States, *Regents of Univesity of California v. Bakke*
Banning, Lance, 10; Tenth *Federalist*, 10; Fifty-first *Federalist*, 10; "practicable sphere," 10
Barron v. Baltimore. *See* Supreme Court of the United States

Beard, Charles A., 9, 10, 58; economic interpretation of the Tenth *Federalist*, 9–10, 58
Beecher, Lyman, 148
Benson, Ezra Taft, 175
Bill of Rights, xiv, xvii, xxi, xxii, xxiii, 12, 67, 68, 69, 71, 73, 74–79, 91, 221; limitation to national government, 91; negative rights, 75; as proposed by James Madison, 7 4–79; rejection by Congress of Madison's extension to states, 75
Black, Hugo L., 180
"Black Power," 177
Bourbons, 142
Brant, Irving, 10
British empire, 2, 21, 23, 24, 223; American Revolution, 2
Brown, Olympia, 148
Bryan, William Jennings, 146
Buchanan, James, 125
Buchanan, Pat, 224
Burke, Thomas, 35
Byrd, Harry, 203
Byrnes, James F., 176, 177, 197, 198

Calhoun, John C., xvii, xviii, xxiii, 32, 72, 81, 95, 96, 97, 98, 99, 100, 101, 104, 105, 106, 107, 114, 115, 118, 123, 223–224; Supreme Court, 106, 107; Tenth Amendment, 106
Carmichael, Stokely, 178
Carter, Jimmy, 180, 211, 224
Chase, Salmon P., 145
Citizenship, xxi, xxiii, xxiv, 3, 4, 5, 7, 49, 51, 53, 54, 75, 100, 123–125, 148, 151, 187, 189, 201; African Americans, 100, 139, 140, 141; *Dred Scott* decision, 123–125; dual, xx, 31, 53, 72, 92; gradualism, xxiii, 141, 149–151, 155, 185, 190, 200; "grandfather" clause, 152; immigration, 197; local prejudices, 97, 153–154, military service, 76, 89; virtue, 3, 5, 7, 27, 30, 59, 95, 96; voting, 154
Civil rights, 140, 142, 151, 174, 175, 177, 181, 182, 183, 185, 186, 187, 188, 189, 190, 194, 195, 196, 197, 198

Civil Rights Acts: of 1957, 174, 177; of 1960, 177; of 1964, 174, 177, 207, 208; of 1968, 174
Civil Rights Amendments, 141, 142
Civil society, 9, 61, 95, 109, 111, 158
Civil War, xviii, xxii, 91, 95, 96, 99, 100, 126, 141, 144, 145, 146, 166, 223
Clark, Kenneth, 200
Clay, Henry, 224
Clinton, William Jefferson, 217, 224
Colonial period, xvi, 219
Commerce, 2, 3, 4, 10, 18, 24, 25, 31, 33, 34, 39, 41, 47–48, 49, 61, 84, 118–119, 120, 145–147, 150–151, 158, 160, 161, 166, 168, 174, 180, 192, 219
Committee on Government Contract Compliance, 176
Common good. *See* Public good
Compact, 12, 40, 68, 72, 86, 97, 102, 104, 120, 127, 129, 130, 134, 144, 175, 179, 213; compact theory, 72, 81–82, 84–85, 99, 100, 105, 130–132, 180, 181, 182, 223
Compromise of 1850, 121, 123
Concurrent majority, xviii, 116–117
Confederate States of America, xix
Confederation system, xix, 106
Connecticut Compromise, 7
Constitution of the United States, xiii, xiv, xv, xvi, xvii, xix, xxi, xxii, xxiii, 1, 2, 4, 5, 6, 7, 14, 31, 37, 43, 67, 73, 75, 80, 84, 96, 99, 100, 101, 102, 109, 112, 113, 118, 119, 124, 126, 127–132, 133, 145, 147, 157, 172, 184, 187, 188, 192, 193, 195, 199, 205, 206, 208, 218, 219, 220, 221, 222; Article I, 221; Article IV, 130, 133, 145; Daniel Webster, 103, enumerated (delegated) powers, xix, 82, 125, 126; equal protection, 141, 155; fugitive slave law, 96; general welfare clause, 71, 127; implied (undelegated) powers, 8; Madison's opposition to structural changes, 71, 75–79; "necessary and proper" clause, xx, 70, 71, 126, 145; Preamble, xxi, xxii; presidency, 126,

133; ratification, 7; supremacy clause, xx, 70

Constitutional governments, xxi, 12, 157

Contract with America, 213–216, 217

Coolidge, Calvin, 165, 166

Cooperative federalism. *See* Federalism

Croly, Herbert, 161

Dahl, Robert, 10

Davis, Jefferson, 224

Declaration of Independence, xxi, xxii, xxiii, 2, 3, 5, 31–34, 96, 100, 122, 129, 130, 132, 151, 186

Declaration of Rights. *See* Bill of Rights

Declaration of Sentiments, 148

Democratic party, 146, 149, 160, 174, 182, 184, 191, 194, 195, 217

Democratic-Republican party, 79, 160

Depression, Great, 141, 142, 167–168, 169, 174

Desegregation. *See* Race relations

"Devolution Revolution," 180–181, 216–218

Dewey, Thomas E., 195

Diamond-Dahl interpretation of Tenth *Federalist*, 10

Diamond, Martin, 10

Dickinson, John, 24, 35, 43, 46, 47; proportional representation, 46; states electing U.S. Senators, 46

Dirksen, Everett McKinley, 175, 177

Distribution of power, 9

Dixiecrats. *See* States' rights, States' rights party

Dred Scott v. Sandford. See Supreme Court of the United States

Dual citizenship. *See* Citizenship

Dual federalism. *See* Federalism

Du Bois, William Edward Burghardt, 141, 151

Due process of law, 69, 83, 84; state as protector, 81–86

Dulles, John Foster, 175

Eisenhower, Dwight D., 175, 178, 196, 198, 214, 217; Federalism, 175–176; "hidden-hand leadership," 175, 177, 196

Eleventh Amendment. *See* Amendments, Eleventh

Emancipation Proclamation, 135–137, 151

"Enlightened statesmen," 10, 67

Enlightenment, xxii, 68

"Equal protection of the laws." *See* Amendments, Fourteenth

"Extended republic," 6, 7, 9, 38, 43, 59, 64, 65

Fair Employment Practices Committee, 182, 183, 187, 188

Fair Labor Standards Act, 218

Farrand, Max, 46

Faubus, Orval, 177

Federal government, xviii, 174, 178, 181, 187, 189, 195, 199, 208, 209, 213, 214, 216, 218, 219; as creation of states, 213

Federal system, xiv, xix, xx, xxiii, 2, 3, 178; characterstics, xix–xx; distribution of power, xx, xxi

Federalism, xiii, xiv, xv, xix, xx, xxi, xxii, xxiv, 7, 12, 14, 16–17, 18, 23, 26, 46, 59, 95, 96, 99, 107, 117, 119, 141, 154, 160, 165–166, 167, 168, 169–171, 175–176, 180, 181, 194, 198, 199, 213, 218–219, 223–224; cooperative, xx, xxiv, xxv n.15; defined, xix; devolution, 216–218; dual, xx, xxiv, xxv n.15, 157, 205; "happy combination," xxiv; reconstruction implications, 141

Federalist, The, 157; Number 9, 12 n.13; Number 10, xxiii, 9–11, 100 n.3; Number 14, 12 n.13, 64; Number 15, 133; Number 22, 100 n.3; Number 39, 12 n.13, 64, 100 n.3; Number 51, xiv, xv, 10, 58–59, 100 n.3; Number 78, 100, n.3

Federalist party, 72, 79, 89, 98, 114, 159, 160

Federalists, xxiii, 7, 8, 9, 160, 223–224; differences with antifederalists, 8

Fifth amendment. *See* Amendments, Fifth

Foedus, xix, 12

Force Bill, 105
Ford, Gerald, 211
Fort Hill Address, 104–105
Fourteenth amendment. *See* Amendments, Fourteenth
Franklin, Benjamin, 19
Freedom of press. *See* Amendments, First
Freedom of religion. *See* Amendments, First
Freedom of speech. *See* Amendments, First
Fundamental (or Higher) law, xxiii, 31, 96, 100
Fundamental Orders of Connecticut, 13–16

Garrison, William Lloyd, 148
General courts, 15, 16, 17, 18
General government, xvi, xvii, xviii, xix, 14, 16, 18, 21, 23, 24, 26, 43, 47, 53, 54, 68, 73, 79, 80, 84, 93, 104, 105; "not expressly delegated powers," 35, 36; not unlimited submission, 80
General welfare clause. *See* Constitution of the United States
General will, xvi
Gingrich, Newt, 214
Goldwater, Barry, 224
Gordon, Kate, 143, 162
Government, empowered, xiv, xv; federal, 69, 92; local, xvi, xviii, xix
Gradualism, Policy of. *See* Citizenship
"Grandfather" clause. *See* Citizenship
Grayson, William, 71
Great Society, xviii, 174, 178, 180, 205, 206, 213
Griffing, Josephine Sophia White, 148

Hamilton, Alexander, 7, 9, 10, 71, 79, 145, 155, 224
Happiness in government, 26, 27, 32, 65, 66, 76
"Happy combination," xiii, xxiv, 63
Hartford Convention, 81, 89–91, 98, 223
Hayne, Robert Y., 98, 101

Hooker, Isabella Beecher, 148
Hoover, Herbert, 167, 169, 224
Howe, Harold II, 206
Howe, Julia Ward, 143
Human rights. *See* Civil rights

Individual rights, xiii, xiv, xv, xviii, xx, xxi, xxii, xxiii, xxiv, 4, 6, 7, 9, 38, 41–43, 60, 61, 62, 64, 68, 69, 72, 73, 75, 85, 97, 98, 100, 190; relationship to state and national governments, 69; reserved powers, 72
Interposition. *See* State interposition
Iroquois Confederation, xxv n.17; bicameralism, xxv n.17; Great Binding Law, xxv n.17; tricameralism, xxv n.17; unicameralism, xxv n.17

Jackson, Andrew, 98, 105, 107, 159, 194, 224
Japanese-Americans, 187, 189
Jay, John, 9, 221
Jefferson, Thomas, xvii, xxi, 1, 2, 31, 72, 79, 81, 104, 159, 162, 194, 224; Kentucky Resolutions, 81–86, 97
Jim Crow laws. *See* Race relations
Johnson, Lyndon Baines, xviii, 174, 175, 177, 178, 180, 205, 206, 223, 224

Kansas-Nebraska Act, 121, 123
Kearney, Belle, 144
Kennedy, Anthony M., 219, 221
Kennedy, John F., 177
Kentucky Resolutions, xvii, 72, 81–86, 97, 98, 104
Keynes, John Maynard, 178
King, Martin Luther, Jr., 177, 178, 206

Laissez-faire policy, 146
Lee, Richard Henry, 37
Legislative tyranny, 6; Madison and, 6
Liberalism, 146; negative, 146; positive, 146, 160, 161, 169
Liberty, 14, 17, 18, 24, 43, 59, 60, 68, 69, 73, 75, 78, 101, 104, 121, 154, 168, 174, 195, 211

Life, liberty, and property (pursuit of happiness), 32, 69, 76, 125, 126, 133
Limited government, xiv, xv, xxiii, 9, 35, 69, 86, 92, 159
Lincoln, Abraham, 109, 132, 135, 145, 155, 156, 224
Little Rock, Arkansas, Central High School, 177
Lockean liberalism, 5
Logan, Adella Hunt, 144
Lutz, Donald S., xvi, 12
Lynchings. *See* Race relations

Madison, James, xiii, xxi, xxiii, xxiv, 1, 2, 3, 6, 7, 9, 10, 11, 37, 43, 50, 51–53, 58, 59, 60, 64, 67, 68, 69, 71, 72, 74–79, 81, 91, 159, 224; on Articles of Confederation, 38; Bill of Rights, 74, 75; citizenship, 3, 60; compares Virginia Plan and New Jersey Plan, 50–53; economic problems, 3; enlightened statesmen, 61; extended republic, 6, 7; federal negative (or veto power), 6, 7, 38, 44, 45, 50; federalism, xiii, xiv; *Federalist* Number 10, xxiii, 9–11, 58–64; *Federalist* Number 51, xiv, xv, xxiii, 58–59; government, 6; "happy combination," xiii, xxiv; injustice of governments, 41; legislative tyranny, 6, 78; limited government, xxiii; majority rule, xxiii, 38; minority rights, xxiii; "practicable sphere," xxiii, 220; republican government, 2, 3; reserved powers, 71–72, 78; state encroachment on rights, 75, 77, 78, 79; Tenth Amendment, 71; "Vices of the Political System," 37–43; Virginia Plan, 43; Virginia Resolution, 72; virtue, 3, 59–60
Majority rule, xvi, xvii, xxiii, 3, 4, 8, 9, 14, 38, 68, 72, 132; John C. Calhoun on, 98
Majoritarian tyranny (injustices), 4, 38, 41, 50, 60, 63, 97, 154
Marshall, John, 69–70, 87, 91, 145, 222, 224; Marshall court, 87, 91
Marshall, Thurgood, 200

Martin v. Hunter's Lessee. See Supreme Court of the United States
Mason, George, 73
Massachusetts model of government, 26
"Massive Resistance." *See* Race relations
Mayflower Compact, 12–13, 14
Mercantilism, 2, 61, 120
Mexican War, 114; cession, 118
Minority rights, xxiii, 4, 9, 68, 132
Missouri Compromise, 117, 123
"Mixed government" theory, xxii, xxv; British system, xxii; French system, xxii; Iroquois Confederation, xxv n.17
Montesquieu, Charles baron de, 8, 64
Murphy, Edgar Gardner, 151
Myrdal, Gunnar, xxiii, 173; *An American Dilemma*, xxiii, 173

National Association for the Advancement of Colored People (NAACP), 141, 173, 176, 200
National government, xiv, xv, xviii, xix, xx, xxiii, 1, 6, 7, 10, 46, 50, 67, 69, 71, 73, 75, 158, 160, 166–167, 169, 180, 190, 200, 220; encroachment on individual rights, 75, 205; encroachment on states' rights, 193, 198, 203, 205; in violation of compact, 97
National supremacy, 87–88, 159
National Suffrage Association, 148
National Woman Suffrage Association, 143, 144
National Woman's party, 144
"Necessary and proper" clause, xx, 70, 71
Negative rights, 75
New Deal, xviii, xx, 142, 178, 180
New Federalism, xviii, 180, 181, 217
New Freedom, xviii, 161, 223
New Jersey Plan, 7, 47, 50–53
New Nationalism, 146
Niagara Movement, 141
Ninth Amendment. *See* Amendments, Ninth

Nixon, Richard M., xviii, 180, 217
Northwest Ordinance, 14, 54–58, 116–117
Nullification, theory of, xviii, 72, 81, 87, 96, 97, 98, 105, 106, 107, 112, 130

O'Connor, Sandra Day, 72

Paterson, William, 47, 50, 52
Penn, William, 19
Phillips, Wendell, 143
Poll tax, 182, 188
Popular sovereignty, xvii, xxiv, 9, 72, 75, 96, 99, 100, 101, 102, 121
Populism. See Reform movements
Powell, Adam Clayton, 176
"Practicable sphere," xxiii, 10, 11, 38, 59
Pritchett, C. Herman, xxi
Private rights. See Individual rights
Progressives and Progressive period. See Reform movements
Public good, xiii, 5, 6, 7, 9, 10, 15, 24, 32, 41, 59, 61
Publius, 9, 100 n.3, 133

Race relations, 99, 123, 141, 155, 156, 178, 179, 182, 187, 188, 191; desegregation, xx, 196, 198, 200; Jim Crow laws, 142, 149, 162; lynchings, 140, 142, 174; racism, 99, 142, 179, 188; reverse discrimination, 178; segregation, xx, 173, 182, 188, 195, 202, 203, 208, 209, 210, 211; Social Darwinism, 140; Southern Manifesto, 203; White Citizens' Councils, 203. See also Citizenship
Radical Republicans, 141, 144
Randolph, Edmund, 7, 43, 50, 52
Reagan, Ronald, xviii, 180, 211, 224
Reconstruction period, 139, 141, 196; views of, 144–145
Reform movements: populism, 142; progressive period, 142, 161; Seneca Falls, 142, 148
Representative government, 9, 27, 28, 32, 33, 38
Republican experiment, 1, 3, 4, 5, 64,

157. See also Republican government, virtues
Republican government xiv, xvi, 2, 3, 6, 8, 27, 41–42, 45, 58, 62–64, 78, 85, 211, 221; characteristics of, 8; virtues, 3
Republican party, 100, 145, 157, 159, 160, 165, 182, 191, 195, 214, 217, 218
Republicanism, 5, 7, 8, 9, 37, 40, 51, 59, 64–65; representative government, 5; virtuous citizenry, 5, 27
Reserved powers, 71–72, 75, 78, 81, 83, 96, 117. See also Amendments, Tenth
Rittenhouse, David, 86–87
Roosevelt, Franklin D., xviii, 142, 169, 174, 178, 180, 224
Roosevelt, Theodore, 146, 155, 157, 224
Root, Elihu, 157
Rousseau, Jean Jacques, xvi; Rousseauean "general will," xvi
Rule of law, 9, 109, 110

Schapsmeier, Edward L. and Frederick H., 175
Secession, xviii, 72, 89, 91, 98, 126, 127–132, 145, 182; Mississippi resolutions, 127–128; response of Daniel Webster, 112–114; South Carolina declarations, 128–131; Virginia ordinance, 131–132
Sedition Act, 72, 79, 83
Segregation. See Race relations
Seneca Falls, 142, 148
"Separate but equal," 141, 201. See Supreme Court of the United States, Plessy v. Ferguson
Seward, William H., xxiii, 31, 95, 96, 100, 118, 121, 122, 137
Shays, Daniel, 1
Shays's Rebellion, 1
Sherman, Roger, 43, 46
Slavery, 51, 54, 58, 70, 83, 99, 110–111, 112, 116, 118–121, 122, 123, 126, 127–132, 133, 134, 135
Social contract, xxiii

Social Darwinism, 140; Huntington, Ellsworth, 140; Ratzel, Friedrich, 140; Semple, Ellen, 140; Spencer, Herbert, 140

Social rights. *See* Civil rights

Souter, David H., 221

South Carolina's Exposition and Protest, 97, 99, 104

Southern Christian Leadership Conference (SCLC), 177

Southern Manifesto. *See* Race relations

Southern States Woman Suffrage Conference, 144, 162

Special interests, 10, 60–61; Tenth *Federalist*, 10, 60–61

"Square Deal," 146

Stanton, Elizabeth Cady, 143, 147, 148, 163

State constitutions, xiv, 96, 152

State governments, xiv, xv, xvi, xviii, xix, xxiii, 5, 6, 7, 33, 34, 46–47, 69, 73, 75, 77, 81, 96, 180; and Bill of Rights, 75; encroachment on rights, 75, 77, 78, 79; power to act, 81

State interposition, 81, 87, 97, 203; Webster's opposition to, 101–103

States' rights, xvi, xvii, xviii, xxi, 3, 10, 54, 56–58, 58, 81, 85, 86, 92, 96, 97, 98, 100, 105, 123, 132, 159, 162, 180, 181, 182, 183, 191, 193, 194, 213, 218, 223, 224; definition of, xvi; doctrine, xvi, 104; parochialism, 97; platform, 193; principles, 194; suffragists, xviii, 162; Tenth Amendment, 70–72; States' rights party, 174, 182, 191, 193

State sovereignty, 35, 36, 85, 127–132, 144; and immunity, 219, 221, 222. *See also* Amendments, Eleventh

Stevens, Thaddeus, 145

Stevenson, Adlai, 176

Stone, Lucy, 143

Story, Joseph, 145

Student Nonviolent Coordinating Committee (SNCC), 177, 178

Suffrage. *See* Citizenship

Suffragists. *See* Women's rights

Sumner, Charles, 145

Supremacy clause, and Constitution of the United States, xx, 70; Fundamental Orders of Connecticut, 14

Supreme Court of the United States, xx, 69, 81, 99, 123, 134, 141, 199, 200, 203, 204, 207, 209, 217, 218; *Alden v. Maine* (1999), 180, 218, 219–220; *Baker v. Carr* (1962), 179; *Barron v. Baltimore* (1833), 69, 75, 91–93; *Brown v. Board of Education of Topeka, Kansas* (1954), 142, 174, 175, 178, 179, 196; *Chisholm v. Georgia* (1793), 218, 221; *Colegrove v. Green* (1946), 179; *Dartmouth College v. Woodward* (1818), 145; *Dred Scott v. Sandford* (1857), 99, 100, 123–125; *Engle v. Vitale* (1962), 179; *Garcia v. San Antonio Metropolitan Transit Authority* (1985), 180; judicial power (review), 84, 105; *Martin v. Hunter's Lessee* (1816), 88, 89; *Plessy v. Ferguson* (1896), 141, 149, 179, 200, 201, 202, 204; *Printz v. United States* (1997), 180; reconstruction, 141; *Regents of the University of California v. Bakke* (1978), 178; *Reynolds v. Sims* (1964), 179; *Seminole Tribe of Florida v. Florida* (1996), 180; *Texas v. White* (1869), 145; *United States v. Lopez* (1995), 180; *United States v. Peters* (1809), 86–89; *Younger v. Harris* (1971), 180

Taft, William Howard, 224

Taney, Roger B., 99, 100, 123

Tariff issue, 101, 105

Taylor, John, 97

Tenth Amendment. *See* Amendments, Tenth

Thurmond, Strom, 175, 182, 190, 191, 193, 224

Trial by jury. *See* Due process

Truman, Harry S, 173, 174, 176, 177, 181, 185, 190, 193, 195, 224

Union, nature of, 12 n.13, 19, 21, 31, 34, 39, 40, 44, 47, 50–52, 59–60, 64, 72, 74, 81, 87, 95, 96, 99, 104,

106, 108, 109, 111, 112, 113, 114–
117, 121, 124, 125–126, 127–132, 144,
145, 151, 156, 157, 158, 159, 180,
181, 183, 223; as creation of citizens,
98, 101–104; as creation of states,
72, 97–99, 100, 105, 115; equality of
states, 55, 57, 58, 105; Hugo Black
on, 180; Lincoln on, 132, 133–135;
as "mystic chords of memory," 133,
135; as "sacred knot," 12 n.13, 133
Unitary system, xix
U.S. Commission on Civil Rights, 174,
181, 187, 193

Veto, 6, 7, 29, 38, 44, 45, 50–51, 119;
federal, 51; state, 97–98, 105
Vinson, Fred, 199
Virginia Plan, 43–45, 46, 50–53
Virginia Resolutions, 72, 81, 97, 98,
104, 105
Virtual representation, 26
Voting. See Citizenship
Voting Rights Act of 1965, 174, 205–
206

Wallace, George, 178, 208, 218
War of 1812. See Hartford Convention

Warren, Earl, 178, 179, 199, 200
Washington, Booker T., xxiii, 139, 140,
141, 149, 151; Tuskegee Institute,
141, 151
Webster, Daniel, 98, 101, 112, 224
Wheeler, Marjorie Spruill, 143
Whig opposition tradition, 3, 4, 26
White Citizens' Councils. See Race re-
lations
Wilson, James, 37, 53; on dual citizen-
ship, 53–54
Wilson, Woodrow, xviii, 146, 159, 160,
194, 223, 224
Winthrop, James, 8, 64
Winthrop, John, 17, 18
Woman Suffrage Association, 148
Women's rights, 70, 141; activists,
xviii, xxiii; southern activists, xviii;
suffrage, 147, 148, 164; suffragists,
143, 162
Wood, Gordon S., xvii, 5, 10; on
Tenth Federalist, 10
World War I, 141, 142, 143, 146, 163
World War II, 141, 174
Wright, Fielding, 181

Zuckert, Michael P., 7

About the Editors

FREDERICK D. DRAKE is Assistant Professor of History and Director of Undergraduate Programs in History and Social Science Education at Illinois State University.

LYNN R. NELSON is Associate Professor of Social Studies Education and Director of the James F. Ackerman Center for Democratic Citizenship at Purdue University.